ENGAGEMENTS WITH HYBRIDITY IN LITERATURE

Engagements with Hybridity in Literature: An Introduction is a textbook especially for undergraduate and graduate students of literature. It discusses the different dimensions of the notion of hybridity in theory and practice, introducing the use and relevance of the concept in literary studies. As a structured and up-to-date source for both instructors and learners, it provides a fascinating selection of materials and approaches.

The book examines the concept of hybridity, offers a historical overview of the term and its critique, and draws upon the key ideas, trends, and voices in the field. It critically engages with the theoretical, intellectual, and literary discussions of the concept from the time of colonialism to the postmodern era and beyond. The book enables students to develop critical thinking through engaging them in case studies addressing a diverse selection of literary texts from various genres and cultures that open up new perspectives and opportunities for analysis.

Each chapter offers a specific theoretical background and close readings of hybridity in literary texts. To improve the students' analytical skills and knowledge of hybridity, each chapter includes relevant tasks, questions, and additional reference materials.

Joel Kuortti is Head of Department and Professor of English at the University of Turku, Finland.

Jopi Nyman is Professor of English at the University of Eastern Finland, Joensuu Campus, Finland.

Mehdi Ghasemi is Senior Researcher at the University of Tampere, Finland, and Adjunct Professor of English at the University of Turku, Finland.

ENGAGEMENTS WITH HYBRIDITY IN LITERATURE

An Introduction

Joel Kuortti, Jopi Nyman, and Mehdi Ghasemi

NEW YORK AND LONDON

Designed cover image: Getty

First published 2024
by Routledge
605 Third Avenue, New York, NY 10158

and by Routledge
4 Park Square, Milton Park, Abingdon, Oxon, OX14 4RN

Routledge is an imprint of the Taylor & Francis Group, an informa business

© 2024 Joel Kuortti, Jopi Nyman, and Mehdi Ghasemi

ISBN: 978-1-032-21711-6 (hbk)
ISBN: 978-1-032-21710-9 (pbk)
ISBN: 978-1-003-26967-0 (ebk)

DOI: 10.4324/9781003269670

Typeset in Galliard
by Deanta Global Publishing Services, Chennai

CONTENTS

ACKNOWLEDGEMENTS

The authors wish to thank the four peer reviewers for their positive feedback. Their constructive comments helped us improve the manuscript. Additionally, the authors would like to acknowledge with gratitude the instructors and learners who use the book as a textbook for their courses. Furthermore, we extend our appreciation to the editors at Routledge for their assistance in completing the volume.

Joel Kuortti is grateful to Tabish Khair for his continuous encouragement and generosity in granting permission to publish his poem. He also thanks the School of Languages and Translation Studies at the University of Turku for support while writing the book.

Jopi Nyman acknowledges the support of the University of Eastern Finland and the grant by the Association of Finnish Nonfiction Writers (Suomen Tietokirjailijat ry) for this particular book project. He also thanks Dr John A. Stotesbury for his insightful comments on the draft chapters and expert language revisions.

Mehdi Ghasemi acknowledges the grant by the Association of Finnish Nonfiction Writers (Suomen Tietokirjailijat ry) for this particular book project.

The poem "Unhybrid" by Tabish Khair appears by the kind permission of the author.

INTRODUCTION

Theorizing Hybridity and How to Put It into Critical Practice

Joel Kuortti

Hybridity

In literary, cultural, and social studies, *hybridity* is a buzzword that became fashionable in the 1980s and 1990s. The purpose of our book, *Engagements with Hybridity in Literature: An Introduction*, is to discuss the several ways hybridity has been applied especially in literary studies, but referring also to studies of interconnected fields, such as music.

First, we provide a historical overview of the term in its various guises from biology to linguistics and to cultural and literary studies. We discuss its significance in the world today and the reasons for specifically engaging with the concept of hybridity within the present landscape and amidst transforming discourses, survey the most up-to-date approaches to hybridity, and introduce the essential thinkers and provide tools to apply critically their work. We also explore how hybridity functions to challenge and transform some of the routine patterns and cliché practices in various disciplines, and elucidate the historical, literary, and cultural contexts surrounding the study of hybridity. We address the *continuing relevance of hybridity* and explain in clear terms how we are critically engaging with particular cultural, artistic, and literary works to illustrate how the employment of hybridity opens up new possibilities for interpreting and offers alternative perspectives for reading literary and artistic works. In each chapter, we offer several text passages as exercises for further study and pose some questions for consideration to direct students' (and teachers') attention to particular areas that manifest hybridity to demonstrate how hybridity is present in literature and culture critical practice and spark further reading

DOI: 10.4324/9781003269670-1

and research. These sections encourage students to apply theories of hybridity to critical analyses of literary and cultural texts. Moreover, at the end of each chapter, we suggest relevant Further Readings, including a list of literary works, lending themselves to the study of hybridity from perspectives examined in each particular chapter. Then, each chapter closes with a full bibliography.

In addition, in this introduction, we orient the instructors and learners to the architecture of the textbook. We offer a general overview of some key theories related to hybridity, such as those by Sara Ahmed, Gloria Anzaldúa, Mikhail Bakhtin, Homi K. Bhabha, Edward Kamau Brathwaite, Néstor García Canclini, Paul Gilroy, Édouard Glissant, Stuart Hall, Françoise Lionnet, Chandra Talpade Mohanty, Mary Louise Pratt, Edward W. Said, and Gayatri Chakravorty Spivak.

Before engaging with the modern, contemporary definitions, interpretations, and applications of the term, it is in place to have a look into the history of the term. It dates back to classical antiquity, and its route continues from the Renaissance and Enlightenment eras to Modernity.

Etymology and History of 'Hybrid' and Hybridity

Already the ancient Romans used the term *hybrid*, although the exact origin of the word is uncertain. Sometimes its etymology is derived from the Greek word ὕβρις (húbris), 'insolence,' but for example the classics scholar Minton Warren (1884) contests this view. In the most justifiable, established explanation, then, the origins are in the Latin term *hybrida* that stands for a progeny of a male wild boar and a female domestic sow. In Early Modern English sources, this definition is used for example in Edward Topsell's (1607, 697) bestiary *The Historie of Foure-footed Beastes* where he discusses the mixed-breed swine: "the pigs so begotten, are cald *Hybridae*, that is, by way of contumely, bastards." In an earlier source, *The Dictionary of Syr Thomas Eliot Knyght* (Eliot 1538), the use is already expanded to mixed-breed dogs so that "hybrida, is a dogge, ingendred betwyxte a hounde and a mastyue, called a [...] mongrell." How common the use of the term hybrid has been in the English context remains unclear but it is evident that it has been used in the context of interspecies mixing, pejoratively or not.

Already ancient Latin sources on hybridity extended the word to denote humans. Among these, one can mention Horace's ([1856] 1895, 144–45; 1926, 91) *Satire* from the first century BCE where he refers to "hybrida [...] Persius" (*mongrel Persius*) (I.VII, 1–3), mocking the mixed ancestry of his contemporary satirist Persius. In his book *The History of the World* (first century CE), then, Pliny, the Elder ([77] 1634, I.8.79) comments that "natos antiqui hybridas vocabant ceu semiferos" (*the offspring of such unions in old days were called 'hybrids,' meaning half-wild*), again comment-ing on miscegenation: "For so was *C. Antonius,* colleague with *Cicero* in the Consulship, nicknamed." Thus, when 'hybrid' was in later centuries taken up for scholarly (and popular) use, it had both the biological and the metaphorical roots, burdened with pejorative overtones.

With European Enlightenment, scientific explanations of the world began to take root over religious and spiritual ones. Within this discourse, hybridity is one term that was used in relation to what was to be known as human 'evolution.' The eighteenth-century transformists studied the vari-ation between species and challenged the predominant Christian religious creationist views. Since 1742, the eminent taxologist Carl Linnaeus' (1760) studies on hybridization had shown that hybrid forms could, indeed, breed. This new observation threatened the previously held, and widely shared, conviction that the infertility of hybrids was "a mechanism of divine provi-dence for keeping the chain of being in order" (Jenkins 2015, 135). The existence of fertile hybrids challenged the chastity of existence – designed by the Creator – by letting pure, discrete elements to be violated through mixing.

In his *Histoire Naturelle,* Comte de Buffon, George Louis Leclerc (1766/1884, 469–504), formulated a theory of "transformation pro-gressive des espèces," *progressive transformation of species.* Together with Buffon's theory, the German zoologist Johann Friedrich Blumenbach's (1775, 5–19) ideas on procreation and hybridization were influential in generating a theory of *monogeneism,* referring to a common origin of all human 'races' that had since the beginning of the world, due to hybridi-zation, degenerated in varying degrees. In this way, the 'enlightened' European ideas gave birth to biological, (pseudo)scientific racism. This is a timely reminder that all scholarship is not beyond criticism but needs to be taken with a pinch of salt.

In opposition to the monogenists, the anatomist Paul Broca, in his work *Recherches sur l'hybridité animale en général, et sur l'hybridité humaine en particulie*r (1860) endorsed *polygenism,* multiple origins of the humans. Although Broca was an abolitionist and at least superficially regarded the annihilation of native peoples by colonial powers as objectionable, his the-ory, too, can be seen as racist as it categorizes different hybrids produced by racial mixing from infertile to beneficial. Such racist mindset darkened also 'colonial benevolence' and turned the potential humanitarian aspirations into predatory self-interest, succumbing the 'lesser races' paternalistically under the supremacy of 'pure' European colonizers.

The racist attitudes developed in many places into policies, like the laws against intermarriage in the United States, or the Apartheid legislation in South Africa. Promoted in terms of sanctions against amalgamation, or *miscegenation*, these policies were strictly against hybridization of ethnicities, vouching instead for 'racial purity,' a notion that carries no factual grounds, but owes much to the Christian interpretation of the 'natural' order of things. Miscegenation is a term coined by journalists David G. Croly and George Wakeman. In their anonymously published pamphlet, *Theory of the Blending of the Races, Applied to the American White Man and Negro* (1864), they allegedly promoted racial mixing. However, it became evident that the work was a hoax aimed at discrediting President Abraham Lincoln, the Republicans, and the abolitionists before the 1864 presidential election.

Mythical and Real Hybrids

In the art and literature of ancient cultures, we encounter portrayals of numerous hybrid creatures. These may be either non-human or human–animal hybrids, composed of two or more species (called *chimeras*). There are several types of religious, moral, and social taboos against zoophilia (attraction to animals) and bestiality (sex between human and non-human animals). Prohibitions have not, however, hindered people from creating ideas about such conjunctions.

All over the globe, various forms of composite deities, or 'unnatural monstrosity,' have populated the pantheons; creatures such as the Egyptian *Horus* (human–falcon) and the *Sphinx* (woman–lion–serpent–eagle), the Greek *Minotaur* (human–bull) and the *Centaur* (human–horse), the Hindu *Kurma* (human–tortoise), the Inuit *Sedna* (woman–fish), the Japanese *Nure-onna* (woman–snake), the Mesoamerican *Quetzalcoatl* (snake–eagle–mongoose), the Persian *Manticore* (human–lion), and the Scottish *Glaistig* (woman–goat). Liane Posthumus (2011, 1) comments on the human–animal hybrids as follows:

> Hybrid monsters, those that combine human and animal elements into a single form, add an interesting angle to the topic of mythological monster figures: these creatures combine the familiar and the foreign, the Self and the Other, into a single complex being.

But why are they so common? After all: "These supernatural figures are so widespread – so contagious – that they cry out for a cognitive explanation" (Maiden 2021).

In cognitive sciences, the popularity of hybrid creatures in religo-mythological contexts has been approached through the idea of 'counterintuitive concepts,' such as hybrid creatures. According to Biblical scholar Brett Maiden (2021), "[m]any experimental studies have shown that such counterintuitive concepts are cognitively optimal and more likely to stick around in human minds – to become what we refer to as 'culture.'" In this approach, cognitive aptitude is combined with the study of archaeological material and so, "by combining ancient iconographic evidence with modern cognitive theories," we have one way of interpreting the allure of hybrids (ibid.).

Later on, in literature and popular culture, this attraction has been preserved, giving rise to fictional hybrids, imaginary in another sense than religo-mythological iconography. There are *cyborgs* ranging from the Tin Woodman in L. Frank Baum's *The Wonderful Wizard of Oz* (1900) or the Shrike in Dan Simmons' *Hyperion*-series (1989–1997) to human-like creatures like the Golem of Jewish Talmud or Ava (played by Alicia Vikander) in the film *Ex machina* (2014); there are vampires, werewolves, harpies, and mermaids. The list is as endless and varied as imagination itself.

Beside mythological and imaginary hybrids, there are actual, real-life hybrids. The origins of the term hybrid are, as we have seen, in biology, in the interbreed of a male wild boar and a female domestic sow. Selective crossbreeding (breeding within a species) is common with livestock, sheep, chicken, dogs, and other animals (as well as with vegetables and other plants). Breeding interspecies hybrids, then, is much more uncommon, although 'hybrid vigour' of interbreeding, "a phenomenon that describes the survival and performance superiority of a hybrid offspring over the average of both its genetically distinct parents" (Baranwal et al. 2012, 6309), was contemplated already by Charles Darwin that the best qualities of both breeds could be transferred into the new breed. Examples of interbreeding are the infertile *mule* (of male donkey and female horse) and the *hinny* (of female donkey and male horse), or the *beefalo* (earlier called also *cattlelo*), a fertile hybrid of domesticated male bull and female American bison (Hedrick 2009, 413).

Hybrid animals are also begotten naturally, although these cases are rare. They are met likewise in forest fowls – for example, male Eurasian black grouse and female capercaillie ('rakkelhane' in Norwegian; Kleven et al. 2020, 34) [while crosses between male capercaillie and female black grouse are very rare, or nonexistent; Appleton 2014]) – and bears, such as polar bear and grizzly bear ('grolar'/'grizzlar' bear; Pongracz et al. 2017). One rare hybridization was documented in 1985 between bottle-nose dolphin (*Tursiops truncatus*) and male false killer whale (*Pseudorca crassidens*), which generated a veritable hybrid *wholphin* (Chen et al. 2017, 288). In captivity (in zoos and such), such as of big cats *liger* (male lion, female tiger) and *tigon* (male lion, female lion) have been begotten, although neither their natural habitats nor their species-specific behaviour would not usually enable natural interbreeding (Guynup 2003, 8). As environmental journalist Sharon Guynup (2003, 11) rightly asks, "how exactly do you define a species?" – when hybrids challenge the order of species established by the traditional Linnaean taxonomy.

These examples from mythology and biology demonstrate the capacity of the hybrid to persistently unsettle strict categories between species, the domain from where the whole idea of hybridity stems from. How, then, have we ended up with hybridity as a term in literary and cultural studies? In the following, we outline key theories related to hybridity in literary and cultural studies. In the separate chapters, then, we engage with discussing the concept in racial, cultural, political, geographical, textual, religious, and ideological types of hybridity.

Key Theories Related to Hybridity: Creolization, Syncretism, and Transculturation

Before hybridity was introduced into popular theoretical discussion, there were other terms used to explain cultural mixing. The three most prominent ones are *creolization*, *syncretism*, and *transculturation*. *Creolization* is an old concept – dating back to the era of European colonial expansion – that has variously been used to describe linguistic and ethnic mixing. It has a strong provenance in Caribbean studies (Ashcroft et al. 1989), and the poet and critic Edward Kamau Brathwaite (2005, 296) defines creolization as "the single most important factor in the development of Jamaican society […] – a 'new' construct, made up of newcomers to the landscape and cultural strangers each to the other; one group dominant, the other legally and subordinately slaves."

Emphasizing the African element in Jamaica, Brathwaite recognizes a "creative friction" (Brathwaite 2005, 101), an ambivalence in creolization that did not, could not contain the process: "African influence remained, even if increasingly submerged, as an important element in the process of creolization. European adaptations or imitations could never be wholehearted or complete" (Brathwaite 2005, 231). Brathwaite's (2005, 310) "idea of creolization is based on the notion of an historically affected sociocultural continuum" where influences flow and are interconnected in a new context. Already in 1970, another Caribbean poet Derek Walcott – the first Caribbean winner of Nobel Prize for literature if we do not take into account the Guadalupe-born French writer Saint-John Perse, i.e., Alexis Leger – anticipated the emergence of the discourse of hybridity in his introduction to his collection of plays, *Dream on Monkey Mountain, and Other Plays*. Self-ironically Walcott (1970, 10) wrote about the African revivalist movement in the Caribbean that what is needed is [...] the faith of using the old names anew, so that mongrel as I am, something prickles in me when I see the word Ashanti as with the word Warwickshire, both separately intimating my grandfathers' roots, both baptising this neither proud nor ashamed bastard, this hybrid, this West Indian.

He uses the idiom "mulatto of style" for such a 'bastard hybrid' as himself: "The traitor. The assimilator" (Walcott 1970, 9). For him, writers would not argue with their Muse for writing in their chosen style. Walcott's position resonates with the African American civil rights activist W.E.B. Du Bois's (1903, 2) concept of "double consciousness":

It is a peculiar sensation, this double consciousness [...]. One ever feels his twoness, an American, a Negro; two souls, two thoughts, two unreconciled strivings; two warring ideals in one dark body, whose dogged strength alone keeps it from being torn asunder.

The hybrid construction of identity can take many forms, neither of which is less problematic when one is troubled with a "sense of always looking at one's self through the eyes of others, of measuring one's soul by the tape of a world that looks on in amused contempt and pity" (Du Bois's 1903, 2). In the poet and literary critic Édouard Glissant's (1981, 28) works the idea of creolization is put in terms of Relation, a metamorphosis that takes place when people are transplanted or transferred into new environments and change through exchange. It is based on a rhizomatic understanding of identity as interconnected and spread out in a relationship with the Other (Glissant 1990, 23). Such a Relation exceeds mere métissage, a synthesis between two elements, and produces instead multiple, limitless, and unpredictable results, which distinguish creolization from simple hybrids: "C'est processus, et non pas fixité" ("It is a process, not a fixity") (Glissant 1990, 46; 64). For Glissant (1981, 28), this is one of the best kept secrets of creolization. As we can see also here, the terminological genealogies have long and winding routes, looking at the same phenomena from various perspectives.

Another older term – with a somewhat uncertain etymology but in use at least since the Middle Ages – especially about fusions of religions but also cultures is *syncretism*, "coexistence of elements of diverse origin interacting ambiguously" (Pye 1971, 92; see also Leopold and Jensen, eds. 2014 [2004]). Such fusion creates ambiguity as it challenges orthodoxy and authenticity of particular religions but has nevertheless been a constant feature in the way religions have developed in contact with each other. In anthropologist Charles Stewart's (1999, 41) words, "syncretism describes the process by which cultures constitute themselves at any given point in time." Considering struggles over boundaries in ethnic politics and multiculturalism, Stewart (1999, 53) concludes that cultures "can be viewed as a contest over cultural mixture: how much should be allowed/required, and at what sociopolitical level?" This remains a crucial question relating to syncretism.

The third early concept was introduced by the anthropologist Fernando Ortiz (1995, 98) who, in his 1940 study of sugar and tobacco in Cuba, coined the notion of *transculturation* ('transculturación') to capture the economic, social, and historical contrast – or counterpoint – between these two products. Ortiz suggests the new term to replace *acculturation* in order to better understand "the extremely complex transmutations of culture" in Cuba (Ortiz 1995, 98). The concept indicates layered multidirectionality of cultural influences that concern sugar and tobacco. Their contrapuntal differences are present on all levels: cultivation, manufacturing, marketing. This contrapuntality is, then, "reflected in the history of the Cuban nation from its very ethnological formation to its social structure, its political fortunes, and its international relations" (Ortiz 1995, 5). For Ortiz, tobacco and sugar are the veneer that marks the indigenous and colonial transcultural hybrid composition of 'cubanidad.' Also the literary and cultural critic Edward Said (1984, 186) applies the idea of contrapuntality in relation to exile:

> Most people are principally aware of one culture, one setting, one home; exiles are aware of at least two, and this plurality of vision gives rise to an awareness of simultaneous dimensions, an awareness that – to borrow a phrase from music – is contrapuntal.

Said's musical metaphor, counterpoint, refers "to the musical art of combining two or more simultaneous and independent lines, [...] is associated with specific historical developments in [Western] music" and "connotes theoretical rigor and a systematic method of compositional instruction" (Lachman 2014, 62–63).

Hybridity in Literary and Cultural Studies

In the context of modern literary and cultural studies, the first key theorist to explicitly emphasize the significance of hybridity (гибридности, *gibridnosti*) is the formalist literary theorist Mikhail Bakhtin. Although his major works were originally written in the 1920s to 1940s, they gained recognition posthumously in the 1970s and 1980s. In his studies of literature, especially of Fyodor Dostoyevsky, Bakhtin considered the inherent polyphony of language that is particularly noticeable in literature. In a formalist manner, Bakhtin distinguishes two forms of hybridity – organic and intentional. For Bakhtin (1981, 358), "unintentional, unconscious hybridization is one of the most important modes in the historical life and evolution of all languages." While the hegemonic *centripetal* structures of philosophy, state, and church have upheld the idea of a monologic "unitary language" (Bakhtin 1981, 270–271), the *centrifugal* forces of heteroglossia (разноречие; *raznoreçie*) maintain "the uninterrupted processes of decentralization and disunification" (Bakhtin 1981, 272).

Bakhtin's work is undoubtedly the source through which hybridity gained contemporary theoretical popularity, but he is not, nevertheless, the origin of the idea. The word 'hybridity' had been introduced into the Russian language in 1896 when botanist Andrei Beketov published the first Russian textbook *Geography of Plants* (*География растений*). He notes that "the only exact criterion for establishing the species is the experiment on crossbreeds [помесями, *pomesyami*] (hybridization) [гибридизация, *gibridizaçia*]" (Beketov 1896, 12). The idea of crossbreeding became attractive in the 1910s and 1920s also to artists who created avant-garde forms like montage and collage, fostering cultural acceptance of mixing. In "Discourse in the Novel," where Bakhtin (1981, 268) develops the ideas of dialogism, polyphony, and hybridity, he refers to the philologist Viktor Vinogradov's work *On Artistic Prose* (1930). In the chapter on rhetoric and poetics, Vinogradov (1930, 104) discusses "the living literary reality" of "the hybrid formations" (гибридных-образований; *gibridnykh obrazovaniy*) of genres. Without going deeper into the genealogy, this demonstrates the revolving and evolving characteristics of ideas that the concept of hybridity itself represents.

Together with Bakhtin, the other key theorist in developing the concept of hybridity in literary and cultural studies is cultural theorist Homi K. Bhabha. Bhabha's argumentation is not simple and straightforward in its complex deconstructive ethos, but his main ideas about hybridization – a process rather than a product – are both significant and influential. In 1983, Bhabha still speaks of the ambivalent "fear/desire of miscegenation" when referring to racial mixing (Bhabha 1983, 22), but soon abandons the term for hybridity. As his concept of hybridization as a process is itself fluid, it escapes precise definition. It is conceived as a liminal, interstitial, in-between space – metaphorically a stairwell – that both separates and connects. He sees that "the precondition for the articulation of cultural difference" is the Third Space of Enunciation that has "a colonial or postcolonial provenance" (Bhabha 1989, 131). The colonial condition, always ambivalent, is revealed as inauthentic through mimicry that it prompts in the colonized. The desire to become like the colonizer by miming does never fully represent that which is imitated but transpires as ironic slippage, "*a subject of difference that is almost the same, but not quite*" (Bhabha 1984, 126, emphasis in original) – "*Almost the same, but not white*" (Bhabha 1984, 130, emphasis in original).

In his 1985 article "Signs Taken for Wonders: Questions of Ambivalence and Authority under a Tree outside Delhi, May 1817," Bhabha (1985a, 150) elaborates his novel idea about the "traumatic scenario of colonial difference." Following the psychiatrist and philosopher Franz Fanon's revolutionary ideas, he argues that the relationship and difference between the colonizer and the colonized are ambivalent. The framework he works in is French poststructuralism – i.e., Jacques Derrida, Michel Foucault, Jacques Lacan – as he discusses the "*différance* produced within the act of enunciation" (ibid.). For Bhabha, such enunciation occurs in a hybrid place that eludes polarization and enables communication. He calls this place specifically a "Third Space of Enunciation" that destroys "hierarchical claims to the inherited originality or 'purity' of cultures" and "may open the way to conceptualizing an *inter*national culture, based not on exoticism or multiculturalism of the *diversity* of cultures, but on the inscription and articulation of culture's *hybridity*" (Bhabha 1989, 130). In this configuration, no culture is pure, original, and unified. While the colonial subjects engage in mimicry, they also contest colonial domination and deconstruct essentialist identities as well as the perceived binary opposition of the colonizer and colonized. It is this ambivalent, liminal space and the incessant process that produce hybridity in culture.

A comprehensive explication of theories around hybridity is beyond the scope of this book, if it were even possible within a single work. This is due to the fact that in critical discourse, the issues of cultural contact and influence have over time been approached using a very wide variety of concepts. In diverse fields and contexts, critics have discussed cultural contacts and used such varying terms as acculturation, amalgamation, ambiguity, ambivalence, appropriation, articulation, assimilation, bastardization, blending, border-crossing, bricolage, code-switching, collage, contact zone, cosmopolitanism, creolization, cyborg, dialogism, diaspora, diversity, double/dual consciousness, fusion, globalization, heteroglossia, hypertextuality, in-betweenness, interdependence, liminality, magical realism, mélange, mestizaje/métissage, mimicry, miscegenation, mixing, mongrelization, montage, mulatto, multiculturalism, multiplicity, palimpsest, passing, pastiche, patchwork, pluralism, polyphony, the rhizome, sly civility, spatio-temporality, syncretism, third space, transculturation, transformation, and transnationalism (see Friedman 2008, 22–24 for a more extensive list). Our focus is particularly on hybridity, but we will also discuss its connections to the most relevant of these other terms, often interchangeable, parallel, or overlapping. In line with Joel Kuortti and Jopi Nyman (2007, 2), we emphasize that in literary and cultural criticism, hybridity "implies a markedly unbalanced relationship" and by no means just any imaginable "mixing of cultural materials, backgrounds, or identities."

Further Developments of Hybridity

In their attempts to overcome perceived problems with particular concepts concerning hybridity-related issues, critics have both criticized these concepts and tried to develop them further. Spivak (2003, 164; emphasis added) argues that the "*invocation* of [...] 'hybridity' serv[es] to obliterate the irreducible hybridity of language!" (see Coda for more on such criticism). For example, parallel concepts to transculturation have been developed especially in border studies that consider the interconnectedness of cultures on border areas, like in such works as the Chicana poet and theorist Gloria Anzaldúa's autobiographical work *Borderlands/La Frontera* (1987) and literary scholar Mary Louise Pratt's study *Imperial Eyes: Travel Writing and Transculturation* (1992). Anzaldúa (1987, 77) challenges the idea of racial purity and sets against it a "mixture of races" that, "rather than resulting in an inferior being, provides hybrid progeny, a mutable, more malleable species with a rich gene pool. From this racial, ideological, cultural, and biological cross pollinization, an 'alien' consciousness is presently in the making – a new *mestiza* consciousness, *una conciencia de mujer*. It is a consciousness of the Borderlands." Drawing on her own heritage and experiences, and connecting them with the people of *la frontera*, Anzaldúa (1987, 3; 2) declares that "the U.S.–Mexican border *es una herida abierta*," on open wound "running down the length of my body." Borders are unnatural and create a division between 'us' and 'them,' and the borderland is a place of ambivalence and unrest, a place where a new consciousness is developing. Another related development is the notion of *contact zones* introduced by Pratt (2003, 4). For her, the contact zones indicate "social spaces where disparate cultures meet, clash, and grapple with each other, often in highly asymmetrical relations of domination and subordination" (Pratt 2003, 4). These spaces are not only such where cultures meet, but furthermore, they provide ways "how subordinated or marginal groups select and invent from materials transmitted to them by a dominant or metropolitan culture" (Pratt 2003, 6). Such inventive and selective agency is common in transcultural contexts, as we have seen in the preceding discussion.

Also the scholar of francophone literature Françoise Lionnet adopts a view of active agency in her study of cultural appropriation, multiculturalism and contemporary postcolonial francophone women writers. Referring to cultural anthropologist Renato Rosaldo (1988, 87), Lionnet (1992–1993,

100–101) discusses 'border zones' of culture as "areas on the periphery of stable metropolitan cultural discourses" where "there is an incessant and playful heteroglossia, a bilingual speech or hybrid language that is a site of creative resistance to the dominant conceptual paradigms." Like Rosaldo in relation to ethnographic preconceptions of culture, Lionnet pays attention to the "creative practices" at the borders of cultures that too easily become invisible in the shadow of dominant discourses. Furthermore, Said (1994, 331; 332; 334) considers the monopolizing, homogenizing, and colonizing relationship between culture and imperialism and suggests instead a transgressive "nomadic practice" that has "a genuine potential for an emergent non-coercive culture." In Bhabha's (1985b, 77–78) deconstructive reading of John Stuart Mill's liberal universalism, such non-coercive native resistance would be "sly civility" – "the native refusal to satisfy the colonizer's narrative demand." The ambivalent attitude towards the colonizer's civilizing mission simultaneously outwardly complies 'civilly' with it while 'slyly' subverts its authority. In Lionnet's and Shu-mei Shih's (2005, 5) introduction to *Minor Transnationalism*, this is expressed as follows: "The transnational, on the contrary, can be conceived as a space of exchange and participation wherever processes of hybridization occur and where it is still possible for cultures to be produced and performed without necessary mediation by the center." Lionnet (2018, 7) argues that by focusing on the creolizing method, it is possible to find "unpredictable connections" with local dialects or traditions and "put an end to the rigid dichotomy between the metropolitan and the postcolonial." In a similar way to Ortiz's, Lionnet looks at the global interconnectedness of sugar and fish in artistic works from the francophone Mascarene Archipelago to critique the structural violence embedded in the production and trade of these commodities. Glissant (1981, 36), then, sees creolization as a two-fold method of resistance – *un détour et un retour*, a tactical detour and a return, where the diversion requires a return – not a return to a primordial unchanging origin but precisely to the "point d'intrication," the moment of entanglement.

Within the varied discourses of diversity, there are also voices that challenge the established ideas discussed above. The intersectionalist feminist scholar Sara Ahmed has discussed hybridity especially in terms of inclusive critical diversity: diversity of gender, sexuality, and race. Ahmed (1999, 88) describes "hybridization as the very temporality of passing through and between identity itself without origin or arrival," thwarting any idea of differentiation between dimensions of identity. Ahmed (2009, 203) is aware of the risk that the discourse of diversity could suggest, that it might imply "the possibility of a pure racial identity." Considering diversity in the context of educational institutions, especially universities, Ahmed (2012, 53) recognizes ways in which diversity has been used as a façade to give an impression of inclusivity and equality: "Diversity can […] function as a containment strategy." Furthermore: "To privilege difference against totality is to keep the opposition in place. Valuing difference and heterogeneity through a critique of totality works to reify difference by assuming it can exist as a pure, undifferentiated category" (Ahmed 2009, 48). Such containment and reification essentialize and fetishize difference, be it gender, sexuality, ethnicity, or race. Universalism is not pitted against individualism, but difference entails an ethical relationship, encountering "others *as* other" (Ahmed 2000, 138; emphasis original).

A similar type of critique of essentialism can be found in the work of the feminist cultural critic Gayatri Chakravorty Spivak. Spivak (1995a, 197; 1995b, xxv) has criticized the ways in which 'Third World' literature and people have been understood and interpreted within "hegemonic notions of a hybrid global culture" and suggested instead to supplement it "with the experience of an impossible global justice." Such 'impossible' justice on the global scale can, in Spivak's (1995b, xxv) terms, only be "glimpsed through remote and secret encounters with singular figures." Contesting "diagnostic theories of mimicry or hybridist triumphalism as an end in itself" (Spivak 1999, 403), Spivak's (1999, 384) effort of ethical singularity is to connect with the subaltern in a "relationship of singularity and responsibility and accountability" where responses are reciprocal and which "can be called a secret encounter."

Chandra Talpade Mohanty (1984, 333), a postcolonial and transnational feminist theorist, is another scholar who has a critical approach to the 'production' and 'colonization' of the 'Third World' woman "as a singular monolithic subject in some recent (Western) feminist texts," leading "to the construction of a […] reductive and homogeneous notion of […] 'Third World Difference'" (1984, 335). Like Ahmed and Spivak, Mohanty (1984, 345) pays attention to historical specificity and "careful, politically focused, local analyses," because "the postmodern critique of essentialist notions of identity" has generated, among other things, "discourses of diversity and pluralism grounded in an apolitical, often individualized identity politics" (Mohanty 1995, 69). Thus, Ahmed, Spivak, and Mohanty recognize the heterogeneity of the racialized, gendered Other in contrast to the structural domination under colonization and its "suppression – often violent – of the heterogeneity of the subject(s) in question" (Mohanty 1984, 333).

In his evaluation of youth cultures, especially in relation to racism, cultural studies scholar Paul Gilroy (1993, 6) considers them as "essentially hybrid social and political forms" that challenge "the logic of racial national and ethnic essentialism," making "the crudity of racisms seem obviously and irrevocably absurd." In Gilroy's (1993, 7–8) view, it was the punk music movement that, at least in Britain, ended the neo-fascist skinhead cultural era and that "African diaspora culture" can produce

> a webbed account of culture and identity that transcends the boundaries of nationality, puts essentialist ideas of race into question and focuses on the flows, the inbetween and the interculture [that] is actively demanded by the fractal forms that the culture takes.

Gilroy (1993, 9) uses hip hop as a concrete example of this in-between cultural form of such 'dis-organic' cultural formations as dance, graffiti, language, and style that "warranted the desire to borrow and steal from everywhere, to cannibalise the everyday." The heterogeneity and hybridity of culture is not, thus, a feature of 'high' culture' or, indeed, any given form of culture.

Already in 1990, the Argentinian cultural theorist Néstor García Canclini, particularly interested in the dynamics of hybridization, published a critical book on hybridity, *Culturas Híbridas: Estrategias para entrar y salir de la Modernidad* (*Hybrid Cultures: Strategies for Entering and Leaving Modernity*). In the book, García Canclini (1995, xxvii) contests the infertile biologism of the term and notes "the productivity and innovative power of many cross-cultural mixtures." It is an influential book that has shown the way for much of research in border studies, migration, transnationalism, and transculturalism. It is especially noteworthy here that the book widened the discourse on hybridity, dominated by Anglo-American research, effectively to Latin America and the Spanish-speaking world. In a later interview, García Canclini explains that the critical reception of his book helped him understand that "by interpreting social processes with the category of hybridity, we run the risk of covering up contradictions," and, instead of covering up, or reconciling different and unequal things as fusion, "we must also consider what is left out, other processes of contradiction and of conflict" (Montezemolo 2009, 740).

García Canclini's approach to hybridity questions identitarian essentialism. Another scholar who has outstandingly investigated identity in relation to hybridity is the Jamaican cultural theorist Stuart Hall. Hybridity describes the situation of cultural contact, especially recognizable in interculturality and globalization. Hall (1995, 206; emphases original) notes that diasporic people "belong to more than one world, speak more than one language (literally and metaphorically); inhabit more than one identity, have more than one home"; they "have learned to negotiate and translate *between* cultures and […], because they are irrevocably the product of several interlocking histories and cultures, have learned to live with, and indeed speak from, *difference*." Hall's words serve as a concluding remark on the development of the theories around hybridity. Hybridity is not a destination but a path, a route between cultures, identities, and histories, always different, always ambiguous.

As we can see from the theoretical overview, the development of hybridity theories in literary and cultural studies has taken many turns when a given approach has been perceived to be too universalizing, essentialist, culturally biased, unhistorical, or otherwise suspect. When we look back at the various theoretical approaches to the phenomena concerning cultural contact outlined in the preceding sections, we can conclude that despite their variance, they share a critical stance towards the idea of monoculturalism and aspire for ethical interpretations. Most commonly, they understand cultural contact and mixing as a process rather than a product – hybridization rather than the hybrid, transculturation rather than the transcultural – a space rather than a place, a continuum rather than a station, although the individual studies are concerned with particular contexts. The use of the concept of hybridity has also been criticized for its perceived Anglo-American bias. As we can see from the sources here, this is not necessarily the case, as the ideas have been developed in many cultural and linguistic contexts. What is true, however, is that the English-language academia and publications feature strongly in the discourse around hybridity. With all the caveats and reservations, we think that it is nevertheless crucial to continue the discussion. The millennia-long concerns about mixing – hybridity – remain ever relevant.

The Structure of the Book

To conclude this introduction, we briefly orient the instructors and learners to the architecture of the volume. As a comprehensive textbook, *Engagements with Hybridity in Literature: An Introduction* forms an effective source for both instruction and self-directed learning, enhancing the students' engagement and performance. Since choosing study materials is demanding for teachers, and teacher-generated or collected materials from different sources might neither match with the learners' competence levels nor constitute a consistent texture, we expect that this textbook would facilitate teachers and encourage them to use our textbook in their courses where hybridity is a relevant issue. Moreover, the book enables students to develop critical thinking through engaging them in case studies on several literary works. The book would also function as a resource for researchers.

As our textbook aims to improve the students' analytical skills, each chapter includes relevant tasks, questions, and additional reference materials. The tasks and questions engage the learners to study the texts through hybridity and improve their capability for independent and critical study and analysis. In addition, the book includes a *glossary of terms* regarding hybridity and related concepts in different contexts. In the general list of references, further information is provided on works about hybridity. To manifest the presence and forms of hybridity in literary texts, we choose texts from different genres, eras, and contexts for our case studies and the exercises. Furthermore, to make the book useful and appealing to international readers, the texts are selected from both native and non-native writers of English.

Engagements with Hybridity in Literature: An Introduction approaches hybridity in the wider contexts of four main themes. While the individual chapters are thematically and conceptually intertwined, they are structured so that they may also be read autonomously. In Chapter 1, "Hybridity, Boundaries, and Borders," we consider how hybridity can question literary, cultural, and ideological phenomena that have commonly been presented as clear-cut and allegedly pure, with established boundaries. In reviewing debates concerning geopolitical, linguistic, cultural, national, bodily, and generic borders, this chapter shows that such crossings resist monological views and nationalisms by generating new, different formations of hybridity, such as transgender, human–animal, human–machine/cyborg, and as mixed languages and mixed identities, and the way they are represented culturally.

In Chapter 2, "Race, Ethnicity, Migration, and Hybridity," then, we focus on debates concerning hybridity as challenging fixed racialized categories of race, ethnicity, and immigration, rooted in discourses of colonialism where hybridity has been understood in a negative manner in racist discourses. The chapter starts with a discussion of the debate concerning the ideologies of purity and hybridity, continues by addressing hybridity as a means to challenge diverse essentialisms and nationalisms, and, by explaining the role of migration and diaspora, extends to reflections on debates concerning hybridity and cultural appropriation.

Chapter 3, "Hybridity in Postcolonial Literary Contexts," discusses various aspects of hybridity, its effects on emerging cultures, and how it relates to postcolonial literature. Hybridity, one of the thematic axes of the discourse of postcolonial cultures, is an operational articulation of ambiguity and changeability, showing the dynamics of opposition and resistance to the dominant colonial hegemony, offering a break with duality and opposition. From this creative field grows the discourse of postcolonial literature as a hybrid that goes beyond inert and monolithic identities.

Chapter 4, "Echoes of Hybridity in Postmodern Literature," examines the notion of hybridity in relation to postmodern literature. As an antithesis to essentialism and fixity, it shows how the plural, relative, and fragmented hybrids that abound in postmodern literature question hegemony, mono-logic forces, and metanarratives. The chapter introduces in theory and prac-tice several hybrid postmodern techniques to describe how mixed forms within postmodern literature function.

Finally, in "Coda: Critique of Hybridity – Whither Hybridity?" we con-sider the various types of criticism and the future relevance of hybridity and related concepts in literary and cultural studies. The Coda draws upon the main critiques, paradoxes, and objections to hybridity from the perspectives of different disciplines and discusses a number of factors that hinder or deter hybridity and raise consequent cross-cultural clashes, which maintain binary thinking intact within nations. It shows how anti-hybridity senti-ments result in disintegration and formation of societies within societies and towns within towns. Additionally, "post-ethnicity" and "post-hybrid-ity," along with possible future development of the theories of hybridity, in the study of literature are discussed.

Further Reading

Guignery, Vanessa, Catherine Pesso-Miquel, and François Specq, eds. 2011. *Hybridity: Forms and Figures in Literature and the Visual Arts*. Newcastle: Cambridge Scholars Publishing.

Kalra, Virinder S., Raminder Kaur, and John Hutnyk. 2005. *Diaspora and Hybridity*. London: Sage.

Pultz Moslund, Sten. 2010. *Migration Literature and Hybridity: The Different Speeds of Transcultural Change*. New York: Palgrave Macmillan.

Werbner, Pnina, and Tariq Modood, eds. 1997. *Debating Cultural Hybridity: Multi-cultural Identities and the Politics of Anti-racism*. London: Zed.

Young, Robert J.C. 1995. *Colonial Desire: Hybridity in Theory, Culture, and Race*. London: Routledge.

References

Ahmed, Sara. 1999. "'She'll Wake up One of These Days and Find She's Turned into a Nigger': Passing through Hybridity." *Theory, Culture & Society*, vol. 16, no. 2, pp. 87–106. https://doi.org/10.1177/02632769922050566

Ahmed, Sara. 2000. *Strange Encounters: Embodied Others in Post-coloniality*. London: Routledge.

Ahmed, Sara. 2009 [originally published 1998]. *Differences that Matter: Feminist Theory and Postmodernism*. Cambridge: Cambridge University Press.

Ahmed, Sara. 2012. *On Being Included: Racism and Diversity in Institutional Life*. Durham: Duke University Press.

Anzaldúa, Gloria. 1987. *Borderlands/La Frontera*. San Francisco: Aunt Lute Books.

Appleton, Dave. 2014. "Eurasian Capercaillie x Black Grouse." *Birdhybrids Blog* (May 30, 2014). http://birdhybrids.blogspot.com/2014/05/eurasian -capercaillie-x-black-grouse.html

Ashcroft, Bill, Gareth Griffiths, and Helen Tiffin. 2002 [originally published 1989]. *The Empire Writes back: Theory and Practice in Post-colonial Literatures*. 2nd ed. London: Routledge.

Bakhtin, Mikhail. 1981 [originally published 1934–1935]. "Discourse in the Novel." In *The Dialogic Imagination: Four Essays* by Mikhail Bakhtin, edited by Michael Holquist, 259–422. Translated by Caryl Emerson and Michael Holquist. Austin: University of Texas Press. ["Слово в романе," in Bakhtin, *Вопросы литературы и эстетики: исследования разныхлет* (Problems of literature and esthetics: Research over the years). Москва: Художественная литература, 1975, 72–233.]

Baranwal, Vinay Kumar, Venugopal Mikkilineni, Usha Barwale Zehr, Akhilesh K. Tyagi, and Sanjay Kapoor. 2012. "Heterosis: Emerging Ideas about Hybrid Vigour." *Journal of Experimental Botany*, vol. 63, no. 18, pp. 6309–6314. https://doi.org/10.1093/jxb/errs321931

Beketov, Andrei Nikolaevich. 1896. *География растений: очерк учения о распространении и распределении растительности на земной поверхности: С особым прибавлением о Европейской России* (*Geography of Plants: An Outline of the Doctrine of the Distribution and Distribution of Vegetation on the Earth's Surface: With a Special Addition about European Russia*). St. Petersburg: V. Demakov.

Bhabha, Homi K. 1983. "The Other Question: Homi K. Bhabha Reconsiders the Stereotype and Colonial Discourse." *Screen*, vol. 24, no. 6, pp. 18–36. https://doi.org/10.1093/screen/24.6.18

Bhabha, Homi K. 1984. "Of Mimicry and Man: The Ambivalence of Colonial Discourse." *October*, no. 28 (Discipleship: A Special Issue on Psychoanalysis), pp. 125–133. http://www.jstor.org/stable/778467.

Bhabha, Homi K. 1985a. "Signs Taken for Wonders: Questions of Ambivalence and Authority under a Tree outside Delhi, May 1817." *Critical Inquiry*, vol. 12, no. 1 ("Race," Writing and Difference), pp. 144–165. https://doi.org/10.1086/448325.

Bhabha, Homi K. 1985b. "Sly Civility." *October*, no. 34, pp. 71–80. https://www.jstor.org/stable/778489.

Bhabha, Homi K. 1989. "The Commitment to Theory." In *Questions of Third Cinema*, edited by J. Pines and P. Willemen, 111–132. London: British Film Institute.

Blumenbach, Johann Friedrich. 1775. *De generis humani varietate nativa*. Illustris facultatis medicinae consensu pro gradu doctoris medicinae disputavit die XVI septembris MDCCLXXV Ioann. Frider. Blumenbach Gothanus. Göttingen: F.A. Rosenbusch.

Brathwaite, Edward Kamau. 2005 [originally published 1971]. *The Development of Creole Society in Jamaica 1770–1820*. Kingston, Jamaica: Ian Randle.

Broca, Paul. 1860. *Recherches sur l'hybridité animale en général, et sur l'hybridité humaine en particulier*. Paris: J. Claye. [In English: *On the Phenomena of Hybridity in the Genus Homo*. Translated by C. Carter Blake. London: Published for the Anthropological Society by Longman, Green, Longman, & Roberts, 1864.]

Chen, Jie, Mi Luo, Shengnan Li, Min Tao, Xiaolan Ye, Wei Duan, Chun Zhang, Qinbo Qin, Jun Xiao, and Shaojun Liu. 2017. "A Comparative Study of Distant

Hybridization in Plants and Animals." *Science China: Life Sciences*, vol. 61, no. 3, pp. 285–309. https://doi.org/10.1007/s11427-017-9094-2

Croly, David G., and George Wakeman. 1864. *Theory of the Blending of the Races, Applied to the American White Man and Negro*. New York: H. Dexter, Hamilton & Co. https://www.lincolncollection.org/collection/creator-author/item/?cs =H&creator=Howell%2C+E.+C.&item=91738

Du Bois, W.E.B. 1903. *The Souls of Black Folk*. Chicago: A.C. McClurg & Co.

Elyot, Thomas. 1538. *The Dictionary of Syr Thomas Eliot Knyght*. London: Thomæ Bertheleti.

Friedman, Susan Stanford. 2008. "One Hand Clapping: Colonialism, Postcolonialism, and the Spatio/Temporal Boundaries of Modernism." In *Translocal Modernisms: International Perspectives*, edited by Irene Ramalho Santos and António Sousa Ribeiro, 11–40. Bern: Peter Lang.

García Canclini, Néstor. 2005 [originally published 1995]. *Hybrid Cultures: Strategies for Entering and Leaving Modernity*. Translated by Christopher L. Chiappari and Silvia L. López. Minneapolis: University of Minnesota Press. [*Culturas Híbridas: Estrategias para entrar y salir de la Modernidad*, 1990.]

Gilroy, Paul. 1993. "Between Afro-centrism and Euro-centrism: Youth Culture and the Problem of Hybridity." *Young*, vol. 1, no. 2, pp. 2–12. https://doi.org /10.1177/110330889300100201

Glissant, Édouard. 1981. "Le retour et le détour." In *Le discours antillais*, by Édouard Glissant, 28–37. Paris: Éditions du Seuil.

Glissant, Édouard. 1990. *Poétique de la relation*. Poétique III. Coll. 'Blanche'. Paris: Gallimard.

Guynup, Sharon. 2003. "The Mating Game: Ligers, Zorses, Wholphins, and Other Hybrid Animals Raise a Beastly Science Question: What Is a Species?" *Science World*, vol. 59, no. 8, pp. 8–12.

Hall, Stuart. 1995. "New Cultures for Old." In *A Place in the World? Places, Cultures and Globalization*, edited by Doreen Massey and Pat Jess, 175–214. Milton Keynes: Open University Press.

Hedrick, Philip W. 2009. "Conservation Genetics and North American Bison (*Bison bison*)." *Journal of Heredity*, vol. 100, no. 4, pp. 411–20. https://doi.org /10.1093/jhered/esp024

Horace. 1895 [originally published 1856]. *Satira* I.VII. In *The Works of Horace, with English Notes* by A.J. Macleane, 144–145. Revised twentieth edition by Reginald H. Chase. Boston: Allyn & Bacon. https://www.gutenberg.org/files /46938/46938-h/46938-h.htm#SATIRA_I_VII_poem

Jenkins, William Hugh Wright. 2015. "New Perspectives on Edinburgh Lamarckians and Other Transformist Thinkers: Evolutionary Debates in the Athens of the North, 1790–1844." PhD Diss., University of Edinburgh. https://era.ed.ac.uk/handle/1842/19523

Kleven, Oddmund, Henrik Brøseth, Kyrre Jonassen, and Hans Christian Pedersen. 2020. "Backcrossing of a Capercaillie × Black Grouse Hybrid Male in the Wild Revealed with Molecular Markers." *European Journal of Wildlife Research*, no. 66, art. 35, pp. 1–4. https://doi.org/10.1007/s10344-020 -01377-y

Kuortti, Joel, and Jopi Nyman. 2007. "Introduction: Hybridity Today." In *Reconstructing Hybridity: Post-colonial Studies in Transition*, edited by Joel Kuortti and Jopi Nyman, 1–18. Amsterdam: Rodopi.

Lachman, Kathryn. 2014. *Borrowed Forms: The Music and Ethics of Transnational Fiction*. New edition. Liverpool: Liverpool University Press.

Leclerc de Buffon, George Louis. 1884 [originally published 1766]. "De la dégénération des animaux." In *Œuvres complètes de Buffon, tome IV: Histoire naturelle des animaux*, edited by Jean-Louis de Lanessan, 469–504. Paris: A. Le Vasseur.

Leopold, Anita Maria, and Jeppe Sinding Jensen, eds. 2014 [originally published 2004]. *Syncretism in Religion: A Reader*. London: Routledge.

Linnaeus, Carl. 1760. *Disquisitio de sexu plantarum*. Manuscript. Petropoli. https://linnean-online.org/144162/#?s=0&cv=0

Lionnet, Françoise. 1992–1993. "'Logiques métisses': Cultural Appropriation and Postcolonial Representations." *College Literature*, vol. 19/20, no. 3/1 (Teaching Postcolonial and Commonwealth Literatures), pp. 100–120. http://www.jstor.org/stable/25111992

Lionnet, Françoise. 2018. "Sugar and Fish: Islands of Labor, Bodies of Violence." In *Hybrid Genres/L'Hybridité des genres*, edited by Jeanne Garane, 4–23. Leiden: Brill Rodopi. https://doi.org/10.1163/9789004361065_003

Lionnet, Françoise, and Shu-mei Shih, eds. 2005. "Introduction: Thinking through the Minor, Transnationally." In *Minor Transnationalism*, edited by Françoise Lionnet and Shu-mei Shih, 1–23. Durham: Duke University Press. https://doi.org/10.1215/9780822386643-001

Maiden, Brett. 2021. "Cognitive Science and the Ancient Near Eastern Religious Imagination." *Friends of ASOR* (The American Society of Overseas Research), vol. 9, no. 8, online. https://www.asor.org/anetoday/2021/08/cognitive-science-religious-imagination

Mohanty, Chandra Talpade. 1984. "Under Western Eyes: Feminist Scholarship and Colonial Discourses." *Boundary 2*, no. 12/13, pp. 333–358. https://doi.org/10.2307/302821. [Revised and extended version in *Feminist Review*, no. 30 (1988), pp. 61–88.]

Mohanty, Chandra Talpade. 1995. "Feminist Encounters: Locating the Politics of Experience." In *Social Postmodernism: Beyond Identity Politics*, edited by Linda Nicholson and Steven Seidman, 68–86. Cambridge: Cambridge University Press. https://doi.org/10.1017/CBO9780511520792.004

Montezemolo, Fiamma. 2009. "Tijuana: Hybridity and beyond: A Conversation with Néstor García Canclini." Translated by John Pluecker. *Third Text*, vol. 23, no. 6, pp. 733–750. https://doi.org/10.1080/09528820903371156

Ortiz, Fernando. 1995 [originally published 1940]. *Cuban Counterpoint: Tobacco and Sugar*. Translated by Harriet de Onís. Durham, NC: Duke University Press. [1st English ed. New York: Alfred A. Knopf, 1947; original *Contrapunteo Cubano del tabaco y el azúcar*. Habana: Jesus Montero, 1940.]

Pliny, the Elder. 1634. *The History of the World, Commonly Called the Naturall Historie of C. Plinius Secundus (Naturalis historia)*. Translated by Philemon Holland. London: A. Islip. https://doi.org/10.5962/bhl.title.66548

Pongracz, Jodie D., David Paetkau, Marsha Branigan, and Evan Richardson. 2017. "Recent Hybridization between a Polar Bear and Grizzly Bears in the Canadian Arctic." *Arctic*, vol. 70, no. 2, pp. 151–60. https://doi.org/10.14430/arctic4643

Posthumus, Liane. 2011. "Hybrid Monsters in the Classical World: The Nature and Function of Hybrid Monsters in Greek Mythology, Literature and Art." MPhil Thesis. Master of Philosophy in Ancient Cultures, University of Stellenbosch. http://hdl.handle.net/10019.1/6865

Pratt, Mary Louise. 2003 [originally published 1992]. *Imperial Eyes: Travel Writing and Transculturation*. London: Routledge.

Pye, Michael. 1971. "Syncretism and Ambiguity." *Numen*, vol. 18, no. 2, pp. 83–93. https://www.jstor.org/stable/3269648

Rosaldo, Renato. 1988. "Ideology, Place, and People without Culture." *Cultural Anthropology*, vol. 3, no. 1, pp. 77–87. https://www.jstor.org/stable/656310

Said, Edward W. 1984. "Reflections on Exile." *Granta*, no. 13, pp. 157–172. [Also in *Reflections on Exile and Other Essays*, by Edward Said, 173–186. Cambridge, MA: Harvard University Press, 2000.]

Said, Edward W. 1994 [originally published 1993]. *Culture and Imperialism*. New York: Vintage.

Spivak, Gayatri Chakravorty. 1995a. "Afterword." In *Imaginary Maps: Three Stories*, by Mahasweta Devi, 197–205. London: Routledge.

Spivak, Gayatri Chakravorty. 1995b. "Translator's Preface." In *Imaginary Maps: Three Stories*, by Mahasweta Devi, xxiii–xxix. London: Routledge.

Spivak, Gayatri Chakravorty. 1999. *A Critique of Postcolonial Reason: Toward a History of the Vanishing Present*. Cambridge: Harvard University Press.

Spivak, Gayatri Chakravorty. 2003 [originally published 1999]. "Literature." In *A Critique of Postcolonial Reason: Toward a History of the Vanishing Present*, by Gayatri Chakravorty Spivak, 112–197. New York: Harvard University Press.

Stewart, Charles. 1999. "Syncretism and Its Synonyms: Reflections on Cultural Mixture." *Diacritics*, vol. 29, no. 3, pp. 40–62. https://www.jstor.org/stable/1566236

Topsell, Edward. 1607. *The historie of foure-footed beastes: Describing the true and liuely figure of euery Beast, with a discourse of their seuerall names, conditions, kindes, vertues (both naturall and medicinall), countries of their breed, their loue and hate to mankinde, and the wonderfull worke of God in their creation, preseruation, and destruction*. London: William Iaggard. http://name.umdl.umich.edu/A13820.0001.001

Vinogradov, Viktor Vladimirovich. 1930. "Риторика и поэтика" (Ritorika i poetika). In *О художественной прозе* (O khudozhestvennoĭ proze; On artistic prose), by Viktor Vinogradov, 74–105. Moscow & Leningrad: Gosudarstvennoe izdatel'stvo. http://detective.gumer.info/etc/vvinogradov.pdf

Walcott, Derek. 1970. "What the Twilight Says: An Overture." Introduction to *Dream on Monkey Mountain and Other Plays*, by Derek Walcott, 1–40. New York: Farrar, Straus, and Giroux.

Warren, Minton. 1884. "On the Etymology of Hybrid (Lat. Hybrida)." *The American Journal of Philology*, vol. 5, no. 4, pp. 501–502. https://www.jstor.org/stable/287370

1

HYBRIDITY

Crossing Boundaries and Borders

Jopi Nyman

Introduction

This chapter argues that hybridity has the potential to question literary, cultural, and ideological phenomena that have commonly been presented as clear-cut and allegedly pure, with established boundaries, by dividing them into categories in order to problematize such conceptions. The examination of hybridity in terms of deconstructing boundaries and borders is discussed as a means of transforming cultural codes and formulating new forms of collective politics and economics. As the ability to move across geopolitical, linguistic, cultural, bodily, and generic borders creates new transcultural forms, this chapter shows how they appear as hybrids, such as transgender, human–animal, human–machine/cyborg, and as mixed languages and mixed identities.

In contrast to negative views of hybridity that understand it as a way of breaching naturalized categories (see Young 1995), border-crossings generate a sense of hybridity with the potential for transforming cultural codes and formulating new forms of collective politics. By examining the emergence of fluid and transforming identities in the context of deconstructing boundaries and borders of various kinds, this chapter reveals how border-crossings generate new national and cultural identities and communities. Although the commonplace idea of the border centres upon geopolitical and territorial borders, borders are also social, cultural, and symbolic, and crossing them is a way to challenge fixed ideas and borders. Borders are not natural but rather "contingent social and cultural productions" and "instruments of power" that "determine and often also substantiate our

DOI: 10.4324/9781003269670-2

perception of the world" (Fellner 2020, 8). The following sections address diverse borders (geopolitical, linguistic, generic, and cultural) and the impact of border-crossing. Following a discussion of the relevant debates, the chapter will close with a reading of border-crossing hybridity in Louise Erdrich's Native American novel *Tracks* (1989).

Crossing Geopolitical Borders

Territorial borders are often represented by means of a focus on their hard characteristics, which suggests that such borders are maintained and patrolled in order to keep people apart from each other. This is often referred to as b/ordering, a term suggesting that borders are both means of limiting and ordering. Originally coined to analyze the management of space and mobility in geopolitical contexts where the borders of the nation-state function remain closed (van Houtum, Kramsch, and Zierhofer 2005, 2; van Houtum 2021), the term can be extended to another kind of borders whose crossing challenges established national and social orders in a similar way. However, contemporary border studies suggest that borders are more than mere lines of division separating "us" from "them" or "self" from "the other." Rather, they have a double function as "barriers and bridges" (Wilson and Donnan 2012, 3): they are also porous and cross-able, not absolute. Allowing for contacts and interchange, they function as sites of hybridity generating new positions of identity. Mireille Rosello and Stephen F. Wolfe (2017, 12–13) suggest that the border is a site where narratives imagine and negotiate otherness, problematizing orderings and binary polarizations and generating opportunities for bottom-up agency. In this sense, borders contribute to the formation of hybridity rather than preventing it.

It should also be noted that borders are not only national or political: the concept is similarly valid in the context of ethnic and racial, social, cultural, symbolic, and linguistic borders separating people from each other. A world without such borders dictated by the state or nation is often referred to as "cosmopolitan," a term that has traditionally been defined in contrast to nationalism and regarded as promoting equality (see Kymlicka 2001, 204). Conventionally, the border has been thought to guarantee the maintenance of allegedly national and cultural purity; alternatively, it can be transgressed and crossed, generating transnational and hybrid con-figurations and identities. Borders are markers of liminality and danger, and as indicators of security and transgression, they show the limits of our knowledge and experience and mark the unknown as Other. What cross-ing the border or the experience of living in the borderlands between two cultures, such as between the United States and Mexico, leads to is a sense of heightened awareness of being a member of more than one hermetically sealed national culture, ethnic group, or linguistic community – in other words, of transculturality. In her analysis of early modern travel writing in the Americas discussing colonial conquest, Mary Louise Pratt (1992, 7) describes such locations of cultural encounters and mutual influence as "contact zones" where the meeting of cultures leads to mutual interaction as both cultures impact on each other. Borders, in other words, are sites of encounter and transformation. In the view of the border theorist Chiara Brambilla (2015, 22), borders are not lines but extended spaces, borderscapes, sites of constant interaction where cultural encounters lead to alternative affiliations and identities, that is, to hybridity. So, borders are not merely territorial but shifting, generating different geopolitical, linguistic, and cultural hybridities peculiar to the borderlands and their specific identities.

In contemporary social and cultural theory, border-crossings and hybrid identities are primarily associated with contemporary changes involving crossing national borders. Yet such contacts have much longer histories as seen in the global histories of exploration, trade, and travel. This is evidenced in the mappings of diverse colonial histories and encounters provided in the work of such writers exploring global mobilities as the Zanzibar-born Nobel laureate Abdulrazak Gurnah and the Indian novelist Amitav Ghosh. While Ghosh's *The Glass Palace* (2002) addresses histories of migrant Indian labourers dispersed in South-East Asia, Gurnah's *By the Sea* (2001) brings together Euro-African encounters as well as histories of contacts between East Africa and Asia, linking colonial pasts with today's refugee situations and processes of migration. Such fiction shows that hybridization does not follow any predicted pattern, for example, from West to East, or centre to periphery. Rather, the cross-cultural fertilization shows that different mobilities of people, ideas, and cultures create different kinds of hybridities in different parts of the world that are linked with each other.

Border-Crossings across Cultures

What characterizes today's global processes is the pace with which culture and the media cross national borders, taking ideas and values from one place to another. The sociologist Arjun Appadurai (1996, 33–37) has suggested that such border-crossing cultural interchange involves five different flows of people, objects, and ideas moving from one culture and nation to another: ethnoscapes, mediascapes, technoscapes, financescapes, and ideoscapes. Mediascapes, for instance, involve not only the presence and consumption of, for example, American television series and cinema all over world but also the ways such texts are hybridized and cross-fertilized in different local contexts. Examples may include, for example, *Bride and Prejudice* (2004), Gurinder Chadha's cinematic Bollywood adaptation of Jane Austen's classic novel, or the several remakes of the Nordic Noir television series *The Bridge* (2012) set on the Danish/Swedish border, in which the discovery of a dead person leads to a cross-cultural crime investigation. The adaptations of the series locate the events in different border locations such as the US/Mexico, Britain/France, Germany/Austria, Russia/Estonia, and Malaysia/Singapore, each with its own peculiarities (SBS 2019).

Such local adaptations or appropriations are signs of the hybridity produced by cultural border-crossings, and in postcolonial contexts, they are often critical of the colonial or Western form they are rewriting. Examples of such cultural mixing can be found in any genre, including localized versions of US rap music in European culture, literary and dramatic appropriations of Shakespeare in the Arab countries and Southern Africa, and Asian British comedy. In literature, one way to examine the hybridization process is evident in the mixing of genres and extensive use of intertextuality. This can be seen, for instance, in the phenomenon of fanfiction where fans rewrite their favourite works according to their own values and ideas, or in the case of the US novelist Seth Grahame-Smith's reworking of Jane Austen's famous novel into the hybrid novel *Pride and Prejudice and Zombies* (2009), mentioning Austen as a co-author (Ghasemi 2022). At another level, hybridization involves literary history, as may be seen in the critique and reconstruction of national canons that in many Western countries have tended to reflect nationalist concerns as national and cultural identity may be equated with the official national language.

In addition to demanding the recognition of the literatures of long-established national and ethnic minorities previously undervalued in nationalist contexts, the increased mobility of recent decades has generated new forms of writing by border-crossers that challenge established literary norms and nationalist claims. While in some countries such as Britain and Canada, writing by minorities is recognized through inclusion into the national canon, in other national contexts ideologies and institutions oppose such challenges and promote strategies of containment and separation. For instance, in France, there is a tendency to undervalue the significance of multilingualism and multiculturalism and prefer fixed national canons and self-understandings, rather than aiming to revise and change them (see Sievers and Vlasta 2018, eds; Reeck 2020). Frequently, such texts are also undervalued aesthetically and seen primarily as social documentation of migration.

As the above discussion shows, cultural hybridity challenges the insistence on borders and their maintenance characterizing the allegedly sealed and monocultural nation-state resting on shared values and practices. This is an effect of globalization, a term that describes the way in which mobility and encounters at the global level cross borders and, in so doing, restructure international relations, increase the movement of capital, labour, and consumer goods, recast the role of the nation-state, and generate cultural transformations. According to the sociologist Anthony Giddens (1990, 64), it is a part of the general process of modernity and refers to "the intensification of worldwide social relations which link distant localities in such a way that local happenings are shaped by events occurring many miles away and vice versa." As a result, people inhabiting different parts of the world are connected through the global economy and are affected by the decisions of transnational companies and organizations in different ways (Giddens 1990, 64–65).

While global historians have distinguished between the different phases of the phenomenon, starting as a premodern Eurasian process promoted by political empires in the Middle Ages and involving European expansion into other spaces since the early modern period based on political and economic interests (Held et al. 1999, 415–424), the depth and speed of globalization have created today's "historically unique" epoch when "patterns of globalization, unlike earlier periods, are no longer associated with, or reliant on, the expansionary logic or coercive institutions of empire" (Held et al. 1999, 425). In discourses involving simplification and often adopted by proponents of populist movements appealing to the alleged purity of their traditions, globalization is seen as a synonym for such ideologies as Americanization and McDonaldization, whose alleged aim is to abolish national differences and generate uniformity all over the world. In an analysis of debates concerning the nation–hybridization nexus, Jan Nederveen Pieterse (2009, 44) suggests that three distinct positions can be found: cultural differentialism, cultural convergence, and cultural hybridization. According to Nederveen Pieterse (2009), the first position sees cultures as incommensurable and their values as clashing, as suggested in the historian Samuel Huntington's polarizing "clash of civilization" thesis (Nederveen Pieterse 2009, 44–50), and the second one emphasizes increasing cultural homogenization, as proposed in the sociologist George Ritzer's McDonaldization theory predicting uniformity (Nederveen Pieterse 2009, 51–54). For Nederveen Pieterse (2009, 55), the third perspective of cultural mixing challenges older perspectives:

> Hybridization is an antidote to the cultural differentialism of racial and nationalist doctrines because it takes as its point of departure precisely those experiences that have been banished, marginalized, tabooed in cultural differentialism. It subverts nationalism because it privileges

border-crossing. It subverts identity politics such as ethnic and other claims to purity and authenticity because it starts out from the fuzziness of boundaries.

In the context of this statement, it can be said that current understandings of globalization and literature pay attention to the ways in which increased mobility generates hybrid identifications. Critics recognize the long historical process of globalization as a means of generating cultural interaction (see Gunn 2001; Jay 2001), but also pay attention to the increased formation and speed with which globalization hybridizes culture and generates multicultural sites of interaction today. In literature, this can be seen in texts that explore, for instance, urban spaces and their transformation into sites of global encounters. Contemporary representations of Western metropolises such as New York, London, and Paris frequently underline the role of hybridity, often from the perspective of the migrant looking for a new start at the end of the journey. For instance, John McLeod's *Postcolonial London: Rewriting the Metropolis* (2004, 28–34) scrutinizes histories of migration and the transforming cityscape since the 1950s, as shown in texts as diverse as Sam Selvon's migrant novel *The Lonely Londoners* (1956) and Lord Kitchener's (Aldwyn Roberts) London-focused calypso music). In McLeod's (2004, 12) reading, the metropolis emerges as a site of hybridity, a "vexed space of inter-cultural exchange." Yet these responses, he claims, are historical and changing, including both optimistic belief in the transforming city with hybrid inhabitants as in Zadie Smith's *White Teeth* (2000), and more reserved responses in texts by black British writers such as Bernardine Evaristo, David Dabydeen, and Fred D'Aguiar that locate new "alternative spatial practices that resituate, remap and transform London" (2004, 188). Suman Gupta (2009, 38–39) sees such sites as "global cities" that, like New York in Don DeLillo's novel *Cosmopolis* (2003), are home to diverse and heterogeneous migrant and mobile populations interacting in a shared space.

Such spaces of hybridity are the results of migrant border-crossings, as we will address in more detail in the following chapter, but the crossing itself may be problematic and dangerous, taking the crosser into what Homi K. Bhabha (1994, 37–39) terms a space of in-betweenness, neither here nor there, that always leaves a mark on the crosser as it leads to a new self-definition that hybridizes their experience. In Bhabha's (1994, 37) view, the formation of hybridity means crossing into an interstitial space of meaning where former nationalist or colonialist identities resolve as the Third Space "constitutes the discursive conditions of enunciation that ensure that the meanings and symbols of culture have no primordial unity or fixity." This means that the experience of the border and its crossing – or that of living in the borderlands – generates a particular perspective and involves transformation of identity, which is also seen in Johan Schimanski and Stephen F. Wolfe's (2007, 18) view of the hybrid border subject as being aware of and inhabiting "a repeated narrative of failed or success-ful border-crossings" and "dwell[ing] in the larger historical narratives of border formation." As Debra Castillo (2007, 115–116) writes, the identity generated by the border-crossing is shaped in ways that may be traumatic or nostalgic but attaches itself affectively to familiar objects from the past that give an impetus to narratives. In stories of border-crossing, such items from the past may include photographs, music, and food, among others, that as carriers of minority identity challenge national identity. A good example of this is *The Settler's Cookbook: A Memoir of Love, Migration and Food* (2010), by the British journalist and cultural critic Yasmin Alibhai-Brown, a mix of recipes and memories telling the story of her family's forced migration to the United Kingdom in the early 1970s from Uganda. Aiming at telling the history of a community, the text locates the culinary dishes that it discusses within a larger historical frame and comments on their meaning to uncover the diverse cultural heritage of Asians in East Africa and shows how their relocation to Britain leads to new culinary hybridities:

> But too much of it [British food] was bland and tepid. So began a whole new adventure. Victoria sponges were lifted with lime juice or saffron; shortbread was pepped up with grainy cardamom seeds; grated cheese was added to kebab mixtures; roast chickens were stuffed with pista-chios, figs, almonds, green papayas, spicy eggs or spicy mashed potatoes. [...] Strange but true: England gave us an exciting new food emporium to pick and choose from.
>
> *(Alibhai-Brown 2010, 167)*

In other words, border-crossings involve experiences of displacement and trauma, showing how borders serve as wounds (Anzaldúa 1987), but bor-der-crossings may also lead to new hybridities challenging established and fixed identities. Another significant example of such border-crossings often addressed in hybrid texts concerns religion and the hybridization of different beliefs and practices. While often referred to as syncretism (see P. Johnson 2017), in texts telling of cultural border-crossings, religion emerges as a construct that combines practices and ideas associated with different faiths. Well-known examples include the cases of vodun (i.e., voodoo) and sante-ría, associated with the Caribbean in particular, and combining Christian and Afro-Cuban beliefs, but borderlands generate other appropriations of religion. One example of such religious hybridity is the Mexican cult of the

Virgen de Guadalupe, which combines Catholic ideas with other modes of religious practice (see Schemien 2013).

Crossing Linguistic Borders

Border-crossings also involve the crossing of borders of language, which may take place in different forms and contexts, including the co-presence of different languages within a nation-state, encounters between the colonizer's language and those of the colonized, and use of untranslated words, expressions, and code-switching in cultural texts. What these indicate is that language and linguistic identities contribute to hybridity in significant ways and, in so doing, challenge attempts at normativity and the dominance of a standard language through a hybridizing discourse. A particularly significant theorist of linguistic hybridity is the Soviet scholar Mikhail Bakhtin (1981, 293; 294), in whose view language marks hybridity rather than purity, as it is situated "on the borderline between oneself and the other" and is "populated [...] with the intentions of others." According to Bakhtin (1981, 304), this makes any utterance a "double-accented, double-styled hybrid construction" that combines two different languages, views, or ideologies in one expression. For Bakhtin (1981, 276), language is always dialogic, involving a relationship between the self and the other that may change the meaning of any expression, which he describes as follows:

> [A] word enters a dialogically agitated and tense environment of alien words, evaluations and accents, is woven into their complex interrelationships, merges with some, recoils from others, intersects with yet a third group: and all this may in an essential manner shape the word, may leave a trace in all its semantic layers, may complicate its expression and influence its entire stylistic profile.

Bakhtin's (1981) theory of linguistic hybridity and the concept of heteroglossia can be used to describe the co-presence of different and often competing languages at societal level or at the level of a particular artistic work such as a novel. In Bakhtin's (1984, 6) view, the novel is polyphonic, containing "a plurality of independent and unmerged voices and consciousnesses" that are "in dialogue with each other." While Bakhtin (1981, 272) refers explicitly to divisions within the speakers of a group when he writes about "languages that are socio-ideological: languages of social groups, 'professional' and 'generic' languages, languages of generations and so forth," the same holds for ethnic and linguistic minorities within a nation-state and reveals how the minority-language literature has challenged prevalent ideas of national unity in many countries and may lead to hybridization of the national canon (see Sievers and Vlasta, eds. 2018).

The Bakhtinian theory of multiple, competitive meanings and language as an interface between different parties clarifies how the language of postcolonial literatures is a means to challenge and appropriate, and use to one's own purpose, colonial languages associated with the imperial centre through writing. Such appropriations are frequent in postcolonial, migrant, and minority literatures, where the standard language can be critiqued in various ways. With particular reference to the role of the colonizer's language in the colonized world, history, however, shows instances of both appropriation and also strong resistance, especially in the context of decolonization. While key African postcolonial writers such as Nigerian Chinua Achebe have chosen to write in English, indicating that such a strategy is acceptable, others such as Kenyan Ngũgĩ wa Thiong'o see the use of English as a political choice and have rejected English and European languages altogether in favour of the language of their community (see Talib 2002, 90–103). In other contexts, such as the Caribbean, intellectuals have sought to present alternative models of identity when a non-standard, hybridized form language may connect the people and show resistance to standard English and the cultural power of the once imperial centre controlling the alleged peripheries. A particular case in point is the Barbadian poet Edward Kamau Brathwaite's (1984, 6) notion of nation language, "the kind of English spoken by the people who were brought to the Caribbean, not the official English now, but the language of slaves and labourers, the servants who were brought in."

In their now classic work *Empire Writes Back: Theory and Practice in Post-Colonial Literatures*, Ashcroft, Griffiths, and Tiffin describe linguistic strategies used by postcolonial writing. In their view, such texts respond critically to the culture of the colonizer by using the means of appropriation, "the process by which the language is taken and made to 'bear the burden' of one's own cultural experience" (Ashcroft, Griffiths, and Tiffin 1989, 38) by "bring[ing it] under the influence of a vernacular tongue" (1989, 39). This indicates that the language is hybridized at two levels, both as a code (grammar, lexis) and as a strategic tool, whereby it challenges the monological perspective of the colonizer. Ashcroft, Griffiths, and Tiffin (1989, 45–47) also use the concept of abrogation, indicating that postcolonial language users may refuse to use the standard language and hence replace it with, for example, code-switching and vernacular forms to show their difference from the standard. Hybridization of language involves a variety of strategies such as those identified by Ashcroft, Griffiths, and Tiffin (1989, 59–77), including glossing (parenthetical explanation of borrowed words), untranslated expressions, interlanguage (including neologisms), syntactic fusion, and code-switching, strategies that inscribe cultural difference in the text (Ashcroft 2009, 177). In some cases, as in black British, Caribbean, and African American writing, the language used may be highlighted in the text by the use of phonetic markers. For example, Linton Kwesi Johnson's dub poem "Inglan Is a Bitch" (1980) uses Jamaican English in a way that defamiliarizes the text for the reader/listener but also shows how migration-induced language variation is part of life in the metropolis in a way that reflects the speaker's non-standard pronunciation to show the plurality of linguistic codes, as well as the relevance of Jamaican English as an aesthetic strategy signifying difference and black identity.

Further illustrations of such strategies include, for example, Raja Rao's classic Indian novel *Kanthapura* (1938) talking about life in a provincial village. In his famous foreword, Rao reflects on the problem of writing in the language of the colonizer and claims that the language of Indian writers is an expression of their bilingualism, a linguistic code that combines English and Indian languages (see Boehmer 1995, 136; Talib 2002, 94). In addition to incorporating elements from English and Kannada and the respective cultures, Rao's novel foregrounds linguistic hybridity through its use of untranslated expressions to show how the Gandhist movement affects one of its characters, Doré, refusing Western clothing and choosing the traditional wear to show his affiliation with the nationalist movement, when earlier

> he had city-ways, read city-books, and even called himself a Gandhi-man. Some two years ago, when he had come back from Poona, he had given up his boots and hat and suit and taken to dhoti and khati, and it was said that he had even given up his city habit of smoking.
>
> *(Rao 1967, 5)*

To assist the reader with the special vocabulary, the novel, in the manner of many postcolonial works, includes a glossary.

Another example is the phenomenon of code-switching, "alternating use of two (or more) languages" (Montes-Alcalá 2012, 68), which could also be seen as an indicator of multi- or plurilingualism. It is, however, more than a mere linguistic marker as it underlines the hybrid constitution of the community portrayed. A good illustration of this is ChicanX writing, often emerging from the borderlands between Mexico and the United States but also extending to metropolitan spaces, creating what can be called linguistic borderscapes. While the most widely known text in this respect is Gloria Anzaldúa's *Borderlands/La Fronter: The New Mestiza* (1987), which imagines a hybrid, queer, and multilingual subject rooted in a multicultural world, the phenomenon is a regular element in the works of many ChicanX writers, especially those writing about the Mexican–US borderlands. As Cecilia Montes-Alcalá (2012, 85) suggests, it conveys the linguistic practices of the group and serves as a stylistic means to address the realities of a bilingual community. The following exchange of dialogue comes from the short story "Compadre" (1986) by the New Mexico writer Denise Chávez. It shows how the characters change with ease from one language to another in the same conversation at the dinner table, indicating a heteroglossic context with linguistic and cultural hybridity:

> "Rocío! Rocío! Are you there?"
> "Prende la luz, Dora, está muy oscuro en la sala."
> "Mother!"
> "Come and eat some tortillas."
> "Llévale una tortilla, Arcy, por favor."
> "Sí, Mamá."
> "You want tortilla?"
> "Thank you."
>
> *(Chávez 1986, 160)*

Such strategies are means to cross linguistic borders and highlight cultural differences, either within the text or between the reader of the text and the world it describes. Similar strategies of border-crossing writing can be found in many other heteroglossic spaces of everyday cultural encounters and hybridity, as in the multiethnic and multicultural space of Gibraltar by the writer M.G. Sanchez whose texts may switch between English, Spanish, and Llanito, a form of Spanish spoken by Gibraltarians. Spaces of plurilingual hybridity also include such entities as the internet where linguistic mixes and choices of linguistic code challenge conventional monolingualisms, as in the case of the mixed style and language(s) of web-based fan fiction writing (Leppänen 2012).

Linguistic borderscapes such as the global metropolises Los Angeles and London reveal how metropolitan spaces emerge as multilingual spaces offering new positions for hybrid linguistic identity, but they also offer locations of belonging for border-crossing migrant communities, challenging nationalisms. This is aptly captured in the essay "Art in America con acento" where the ChicanX poet Cherríe Moraga (1995, 220) reflects on linguistic, national, and cultural identity: "I am an American writer in the original sense of the word, an Américan *con acento*." Such statements hybridize national, not only linguistic, identities and reveal a preference for dialogism. They also show how the presence of different languages and dialects may be a political statement and not only an aesthetic strategy.

Crossing Genre Borders

The hybridization of language is also linked with the hybridization of literary forms and genres. Owing to cultural interchange, literatures are influenced by each other, leading to either appropriation of genres from other traditions, genre mixing, or the formation of new genres. Here we can notice at least three different ways in which genre hybridity can be approached: cultural border-crossings, aesthetic border-crossings, and the formation of new genres.

To start with, the crossing of genre borders can be seen in the way the culturally specific and folkloristic background crosses into a new genre. As a sign of this, many postcolonial texts show textual hybridity in the form of fairy tales, legends, myths, and oral stories that are reworked and given new meanings. An example of this is the play *Death and the King's Horseman* (1975) by the Nigerian playwright Wole Soyinka, which includes various Yoruba proverbs but also works Yoruba cosmology into the play through the mythical stories of Ógún and Esu: together with the Western theories of tragedy such as that of Friedrich Nietzsche, they contribute to the formation of a hybrid genre, as Ato Quayson (2021, 125–131) has shown. Precolonial proverbs and oral stories figure more generally in postcolonial and indigenous writing such as Achebe's *Things Fall Apart* (1956), Witi Ihimaera's *Whale Rider* (1987), and Leslie Marmon Silko's *Ceremony* (1977). Contemporary Native American literatures, for instance, frequently use the figure of the trickster, often in the form of the inventive and resourceful coyote, a supernatural hero and a symbol of cultural survival known in the oral storytelling tradition, as a counter-discursive strategy that brings hybridity to the text. With particular reference to the Native Canadian author Thomas King's novel *Green Grass, Running Water* (1993), Arnold E. Davidson, Priscilla Walton, and Jennifer Andrews (2003, 54) suggest that the function of the Coyote is to challenge Euro American master-narratives such as that of Christianity through alternative stories and memories as well as expressing protest and offering entertainment. Other famous trickster figures include the West African/Caribbean Anansi the Spider and the African American Brer Rabbit, who also represent the inventiveness of their respective communities. In the view of Claudia Sadowski-Smith (2008, 9), the trickster figure plays an important role as a trope in border fiction: capable of crossing boundaries, they mark "the dissolution of boundaries and a state of transition and change." Tricksters, then, belong to the Third Space and resist fixed meanings.

The aesthetics of genre hybridization also involves the formation of such well-knowing postmodernist forms as the metafictional detective novel (e.g., Umberto Eco's *The Name of the Rose* [1980] and Paul Auster's

New York Trilogy [1985–1986]) and the development of the graphic novel to address such questions as the Holocaust as in Art Spiegelman's *Maus* (1991). In addition to such mixes of high and popular culture, scholars of border-crossings in literature have suggested that particular genres are often adapted to address situations involving boundaries and their disappearance. Sadowski-Smith (2008, 9–10) notes that one such form is magical realism, sometimes liberatory, sometimes nostalgic, while Rocío Davis (2001, 17) has argued that the short-story composite – a collection of interlinked short stories – favoured by many ethnic writers is capable of representing "plurality, multiplicity, polyphony, and fragmentation." Genre hybrids, however, signify cultural change and an attempt to challenge conventional modes of expression.

As a result, several new literary genres have been analyzed that often appropriate and rejuvenate more traditional genres. Such forms include the black British Bildungsroman (Stein 2004), the postcolonial picaresque (Elze 2017), and the forms identified by Sarah Ilott (2015), including the British Muslim Bildungsroman, the subcultural urban novel, and multicultural British comedy, as well as such forms as fanfiction (Leppänen 2012). The importance of registering the emergence of such forms can be approached from a perspective that links genre hybridization with change in cultural identity. Mark Stein (2004, 22–31) argues that the contemporary coming-of-age-novels written by black British authors challenge the conventions of the traditional novel of formation (Bildung), usually written from the perspective of the white male, as they are novels of transformation, involving the second-generation migrant's process of locating one's own voice and the redefinition of Britishness. Here Diran Adebayo's *Some Kind of Black* (1996) serves as a good example, as its title already indicates a journey towards a non-normative identity that hybridizes Britishness. Further, Ilott (2015) remarks that the changing socio-cultural setting needs "new modes of narration" (3) that may challenge fragmentation by "de- and re-narrating Britishness" (4). In other words, genre hybridization is linked with shifts in identity perceptions, and the process is ongoing as well as historical (see Ilott 2015).

Crossing Cultural Borders

Crossings of Gender/Sexuality/Queer

Such hybrid identities also include crossing cultural borders such as those of gender and sexuality. With reference to gender and its hybridization, the issue at stake concerns the transgression of the boundaries of established gender norms, practices, and conventions in ways that show how gender is culturally constructed and fluid, performed rather than innate. As literary and cultural texts produced in diverse historical and cultural contexts show, gender is constantly negotiated and reconstructed, often in ways that challenge dominant ideas and underline the performed character of gender (see Butler 1990). Such questioning of gender identity can be noticed in narratives addressing femininity and masculinity and also in transgender narratives, as will be shown in the following.

A good starting point for the discussion concerns the emergence of the figure of the New Woman in the early twentieth century. The controversial figure of the New Woman that has challenged societal norms through her activity and political demands and is often associated with the suffragette movement is also an example of gender hybridity, displayed in "her short haircut and practical dress," as Ann Heilmann and Margaret Beetham (2012, 1) claim. Challenging gender norms with her androgynous or mannish appearance and with the call for sexual autonomy, the New Woman contradicts the period's understanding of ideal femininity. No longer markers of Victorian purity and women's limited political opportunities, the New Woman's hybridity indicates cultural change and the fin-de-siècle gender crisis. Among others, Lyn Pykett (1995, 16–18) emphasizes that the public emergence in the period of the figure of the New Woman and those of the decadent and the homosexual, especially following the case of Oscar Wilde, reveals the extent of the crisis. Early twentieth-century British writers ranging from Virginia Woolf and E.M. Forster to D.H. Lawrence provide diverse and ambiguous representations of the figure that challenge established definitions of gender. To represent them, as Pykett (1995, 20) writes, is only possible "within a discourse of sexual difference in which particular human characteristics and forms of behaviour were gender marked, but in which the gender terms were contradictory, unstable, and fiercely contested." While the New Woman with her demands was often understood as a threat to the desired and unified national and cultural identity, the so-called national purity, Heilmann and Beetham (2012, 4) stress that a cross-national examination of the phenomenon in different national contexts, such as Germany, the United States, and Hungary, shows how the newness of the New Woman challenges established views of women and gender: "New Women defended themselves by protesting that they brought together the best of the national character with the modern in a new and hybrid identity." Such an interweaving of the traditional and the modern is indicative of what gender studies scholars define as "hybrid femininity" that may "fuse [...] practices from traditional models of gender complementarity and more recent models of women's empowerment" (Ispa-Landa and Oliver 2020, 895).

Like femininity, masculinity can be hybridized to cope with, and critique, established and hegemonic gender definitions at least at the surface level. A recent definition of the concept is based on Tristan Bridges and C.J. Pascoe's (2014, 246) work on the hybridization of masculinity that shows how many men, often in position of privilege, construct their identity by incorporating selected elements that are usually "associated with marginalized and subordinated masculinities and femininities." Through the inclusion of "gay," "black," and "feminine" identity markers (Bridges and Pascoe 2014), performances of hybrid masculinity critique the hegemonic, normative masculinity to some extent but also show how such subordinated identity positions may be appropriated for personal benefit since they may distance men from what hegemonic masculinity represents. The notion has been applied by scholars, and Harri Salovaara (2022), for example, places it in the context of mountain-climbing narratives to address the mountain athlete Timothy Olson's mixing of "hard/daring" and "soft/caring" masculinities to form an apparently ecologically valid hybrid version of masculinity. In his analysis of Olson's social media texts, Salovaara (2022, 8) underlines how the hard-bodied athlete and mountain runner links masculinity with ecofeminist concerns by promoting a vision of nature as a site of healing and rejuvenation. While Olson's performance appears problematic, Salovaara (2022, 13) joins Bridges and Pascoe's (2014, 256) claim that hybrid masculinities have "incredible potential for change" and may also prove useful in promoting environmentally aware masculinities.

Another example of hybrid masculinity as a means to negotiate the borderlands of gender, race, and sexuality can be found in the works of the novelist and filmmaker Hanif Kureishi such as the film *My Beautiful Launderette* (dir. Stephen Frears, 1988) and the novels *The Buddha of Suburbia* (1990) and *The Black Album* (1995). While the protagonists of these texts are examples of what Elahe Haschemi Yekani (2011, 156) defines as "male flexibility," the works reveal the role that gender and sexuality play in the formation of hybridity by critiquing established norms and practices to produce an effect that is different from that described by Bridges and Pascoe (2014). While the relationship between the Pakistani Omar and the English skinhead Johnny in *My Beautiful Launderette* can be read as a means of decentring heterosexual hegemonic masculinity, it also emphasizes doubleness and blurs existing binary oppositions (e.g., straight/gay, British/Pakistani, brown/white, migrant/host, tradition/modern) by making them ambivalent. The film explores the thematic by using particular narrative conventions, as Radhika Mohanram (1995) has shown. As the scene that is set at the opening of their business, the launderette, shows, all identities are both dependent on and also embedded in each other, and none can be centred as the acts of the film's two couples mirror each other,

Omar and Johnny making love in the backroom and Omar's Uncle Nasser and his white mistress Rachel dancing in the front room (Mohanram 1995). *The Buddha of Suburbia* is similarly ambivalent, but the sexual identity of its main character Karim is, as Yekani (2011, 165) suggests, both hybrid and queer, as can be seen in his sexual experimentation involving relationships with both men and women. Finally, *The Black Album* shows how its protagonist Shahid, an apparent representation of strong masculinity, is concretely feminized by his partner Deedee in a sex scene where their gender roles are reversed when she applies make-up to him. While the scene is ambiguous in many ways, as Claire Chambers (2019, 50), among others, points out, the text shows how Shahid displays Yekani's (2011, 156) "male flexibility." Yekani (2011, 179) suggests that the following passage in Kureishi's novel contradicts established gendered and ethnicized roles and leads to a more flexible identity. As Kureishi (2000, 117) writes:

She hummed and fussed over him, reddening his lips, darkening his eyelashes, applying blusher, pushing a pencil under his eye. [...] It troubled him; he felt he were losing himself. What was she seeing? She knew what she wanted; he let her take over; it was a relief. For now she refused him a mirror, but he liked the feel of his new female face. He could be demure, flirtatious, teasing, a star, a burden went, a certain responsibility had been removed. He didn't have to take the lead.

In addition to the potentiality of the hybridization of femininity and masculinity, transgression of these concepts can be traced in approaching the queer as a hybrid, as already indicated in the case of Kureishi, and also in the case of transgender identities. The queer is often understood to resist and challenge binary and normative positions such as the distinction between hetero- and homosexuality. As theorists such as Judith Butler (1990) have argued, identity is performative and constructed by complying with already existing cultural scripts and performing them. Through such action, Butler (1990, 136) argues, identities come into existence and are noted in diverse "acts, gestures, enactments" making the performance "*a stylized repetition of acts*" (1990, 140; emphasis original). What is important here in terms of queer theory is that one is not bound to repeat the pre-existing cultural values and norms, but it is possible to question and critique them by citing the script slightly differently, by introducing some sense of difference in the performance, that is, by queering the original. This idea of performing with a difference is for Butler (1990, 137) evident in the idea of drag and the way it challenges normative models of gender identity. In Bhabha's (1994, 86; emphasis original) hybridity theory, a similar effect of ambivalence and of undermining the power of the original script such as colonial discourse is achieved through colonial mimicry where the postcolonial produces a version of the colonial, one "*that is almost the same, but not quite.*" Such performances involve, in Bhabha's (1994, 86) view, "slippage, [...] excess, [... and] difference" and threaten the status of "'normalized' knowledges and disciplinary powers," as shown, for example, in Harry/Harriet, the protagonist of Michele Cliff's novel *No Telephone to Heaven* (1987). Another example of the possibilities of hybrid imagination is *Full-Metal Indigiqueer* (2018), an experimental poetry collection by the Native Canadian writer Joshua Whitehead, where the poet combines the vocabularies of different fields, including technology, popular culture, and posthumanism, to address the hybrid formation of queer indigenous subjectivity (Tatonetti 2020, 391–392).

The notion of queer hybridity, as discussed by Mikko Tuhkanen (2009), proposes a way of linking queer studies and postcolonial studies through the work of Gloria Anzaldúa. Tuhkanen (2009, 97; emphasis original) claims that Anzaldúa's figure of the new mestiza is a site of border-crossing, a future-oriented marker of becoming, an inhabitant of "a universe [...] hybridized through *queer bodies.*" To quote Tuhkanen (2009, 99): "In this ontology, 'the queer of me' – which the new mestiza consciousness de-abjects, de-disavows – is the elusive potential for actualised, possibly politicised connectedness across and between discrete bodies and identities." Whilst the realization of such cross-cultural connections makes hybridity visible and through empowering those often rejecting their queerness, it also links, for instance, queer and minority writing with each other (see Tuhkanen 2009, 108–109). In literature, we can trace queer bodies in texts dealing with both postcolonial and transgender issues. Well-known examples of this include Jeffrey Eugenides's novel *Middlesex* (2002) and Michele Cliff's *No Telephone to Heaven* (1987). While Eugenides's novel focuses on the hermaphrodite Cal/Callie Stephanides, a third-generation Greek American, and their sexual hybridity, linking search of identity with the migration narrative and family history, Cliff's novel approaches the issue through the queer protagonist Harry/Harriet, who does not accept ready-made scripts but performs their identity differently, as proposed by Butler (1990).

In a similar vein, the novel *Trumpet* (1998), by the black Scottish writer Jackie Kay, tells the story of the jazz musician Joss Moody, who lives his life as a man though born female (Josephine). Mark Stein (2008, 258) underlines Joss's performative production of identity in the novel and suggests that "it is not based on the materiality of his physical body but on his ability to project a male-gendered person to his family, friends, colleagues, and to himself" and promotes "a view of identity that transcends the material body and relies upon performance and enunciation." Performativity is emphatically present in Kay's novel, both in Joss's profession as a musical artist and in his gender performance; playing jazz liberates him from material body as well as the pressures of society: "All his self collapses – his idiosyncrasies, his personality, his ego, his sexuality, even his memory. All of it falls away like layers of skin unwrapping. He unwraps himself with his trumpet" (Kay 1998, 21). As in the work of Cliff, transgender identity shows the potential of queering and hybridizing for challenging discourses and institutions associated with power and hierarchies. Such positions are, however, precarious, which is part of the concept of hybridity. Rather than involving celebration and individual choice, Bhabha's Third Space is the location of the reconstruction of identity, a process that may be violent and may shatter formerly uniform ideologies and views of identity.

Crossing across Species

The question of border-crossing between different species and resultant hybridity has played a significant role in the history of the concept where it has taken different forms. The exhibition "On Hybrid Creatures: Sculpture in Modernism" at the Hamburger Kunsthalle (2021–2022), for example, focused on post-World War II European sculpture and its interest in altered humanity. Triggered by events such as the Holocaust and the atom bomb, such art expresses and problematizes the conventional portrayal of humanity by creating works of art where metamorphosis plays a key role and "human body parts converge into amorphous, ambiguous forms or are supplemented with limbs deriving from animals and plants" (Hamburger Kunsthalle 2022). Based on violations against humanity leading to mutated and radiated bodies, the attempt to construct new material configurations of the human is a further link in the long chain of transgression of species borders known since Antiquity.

Ancient mythology, for instance, is known for several beasts that combine different species, human and non-human, with each other. Examples of such hybrids include, among others, the sphinx, the hippocampus, a cross between a horse and a fish or a serpent, the bull-headed Minotaur slain by Theseus in Crete, satyrs, and centaurs. Often taking the form of the monster and threatening humans, they mark the Other and the potential dissolution of boundaries between the human and the non-human. In her study of hybrid monsters in ancient Greek culture, Liane Posthumus (2011, ii) suggests that the transgression of taxonomies as seen in the half-human centaur and monsters at large, a blend of "the familiar and foreign, the Self and the Other," is a way of challenging what is considered ideal in Ancient Greece, In her discussion of Theseus's defeat of the Minotaur, Posthumus (2011, ii) claims that such narratives are of ritual importance and reveal processes of cultural transformation required in renewing society. In colonialist thinking, hybridity equals mongrelization and miscegenation, and, unsurprisingly, early modern literary and cartographical discourses imagined non-Europeans as non-human creatures, as cynocephali, savage hybrid creatures resembling humans but with the head of a dog (see Hulme 1992, 21; Mackenthun 1996, 54–56). In the context of early modern Europe, such monsters are signs of Otherness and construct the hybrid as a threat but also as something that challenges its cultural and racial hierarchies.

Similarly, the world of superheroes such as Batman, Spiderman, and Wolverine tells of their more-than-human qualities and special characteristics that are rooted in discourse of race and Victorian thinking but transgress such limitations. Chris Gavaler (2018) traces the origins of superhero hybridity back to the early twentieth century and the discourse of eugenics. Gavaler (2018, 59–61) writes that as the threatening Other is associated with degeneration and emerges in the modern city in the form of the non-human, the hero is similarly involved in hybridity and crosses the species border to be successful in defeating the Other. Gavaler (2018) associates the threat posed by the non-human Other with the popularity of the trope of duality promoted in texts such as Robert Louis Stevenson's *Strange Case of Dr. Jekyll and Mr. Hyde* (1886) and H.G. Wells's *The Island of Dr. Moreau* (1896). In an essay on Batman, Andreas Reichstein (1998) draws attention to the similarities between the superhero and Dr. Jekyll. Reichstein (1998, 346) underlines their dual identity, consisting of one by day and something else by night, and points to a process of species transgression where the human adopts qualities associated with the non-human and "blur[s] the line between man and beast. He is the Bat-Man, a mixture of man and beast, of good and evil." Such a character escapes the limitations of animalism and uses non-human powers as a means to manage the world, showing how hybridity becomes a form of empowerment.

In the contemporary world, similar hybridities challenging established taxonomies and categories include those between humans and machines, defined by Donna Haraway (2016) as "cyborgs," cybernetic organisms, known to many through such humaniform examples as the androids of Philip K. Dick's novel *Do Android's Dream of Electric Sheep?* (1968) or its film version *Blade Runner* (dir. Ridley Scott, 1982). Haraway (2016, 5–6) defines such creatures as follows: "A cyborg is a cybernetic organism, a hybrid of machine and organism, a creature of social reality as well as a creature of fiction. Social reality is lived social relations, our most important political construction, a world-changing fiction." Haraway's wide-ranging work on hybridity extends from feminist study of technology and science to human–animal studies. While the notion of the cyborg is easily associated with robots and droids such as R2-D2 and C-3PO in *Star Wars*, in

Haraway's thinking the concept is more general and aims to characterize the transformation of subjectivity in the contemporary world where
human–machine hybridity serves as an example of such fusion. Haraway
(2016, 9; 7) claims that nature and culture have been redefined and become
mutually constitutive to the extent that "one can no longer be the resource
for appropriation or incorporation by the other" and that "we are all chimeras, theorized and fabricated hybrids of machine and organism – in short,
cyborgs." Haraway (2016, 8–13) underlines the significance of three issues
in redefining subjectivity: (i) the dissolution of the human–animal, (ii)
the dissolution of the machine–organism distinction in the era of autono-
mous machines, and (iii) the problematization of the physical–nonphysical
boundary leading to invisible, miniaturized machines through the micro-
chip. The aim in deconstructing such dualisms is a political act that paves
the way for "a cyborg world" where "people are not afraid of their joint kin-
ship with animals and machines, not afraid of permanently partial identities
and contradictory standpoints" (Haraway 2016, 15).

In her other work, Haraway has addressed ways in which encounters
between different species transform both participants – both humans
and non-humans – and argued for interdependence between, for example, humans and bacteria. By making the boundary between humans and
non-humans fuzzy, Haraway is involved in the posthuman theorization of
cultural mixing. Haraway's work has been particularly important in developing thinking about humans and companion species as sites of hybridity
and joint identity formation. What Haraway's (2008, 19; emphasis original)
view of human–non-human interaction emphasizes is that such activities
lead to new identifications, joint moments of "becoming with," or "messy"
and fuzzy categories of identity:

> To knot companion and species together in encounter, in regard and
> respect, is to enter the world of becoming with, where *who and what are*
> is precisely what is at stake. [...] Species interdependence is the name of
> the worlding game on earth, and that game must be one of response and
> respect. That is the play of companion species learning to pay attention.
> [...] I am who I become with companion species, who and which make
> a mess out of categories in the making of kin and kind.

Following Haraway's idea of joint becomings, or the hybridization of
human and non-human through their shared activity, literary animal
studies have addressed the interconnectedness between the various species. Susan McHugh (2011, 2) suggests that animals are not mere "supple-
ments to human subjects" but contribute to the "shaping" of humans. In
addition to the emotional role that companion animals play as significant

others, such as the dog in Virginia Woolf's *Flush* (1936) or the cat in Ernest Hemingway's "Cat in the Rain" (1925), scholars have examined the strong human–animal bond in contexts where the two species are involved in joint action, such as narratives involving humans and horses. McHugh's (2011) reading of the genre of girl–horse stories shows how cross-species intimacy as represented in such texts as Enid Bagnold's 1935 novel *National Velvet, or The Slaughterer's Daughter* and its 1963 film version with Elizabeth Taylor, telling the story of a girl jockey, works towards a new vision of female agency and desire in a world of a sport dominated by men.

The entity formed by the horse and its rider is often referred to as dyadic, even as a centaur (Game 2001), which indicates their jointness and shared agency. In such examples of "becoming with," the human and the non-human form a shared material actor where the different parts cannot be separated from each other. Examples of this can be found in the novels *Horse Heaven* (2000) by the US novelist Jane Smiley and *Foal's Bread* (2011) by the Australian writer Gillian Mears (see Nyman 2019). Mears's novel is a particularly good example of the extent of intertwined identity. Set in mid-twentieth century rural Australia, the novel replaces the conventional emphasis on human mastery over non-human animals with a narrative based on the entanglement of humans, animals, and their shared natural world. In the novel, the main characters' interaction with their horses is rooted in their "sense of balance," which allows them to jump successfully without "bridle and saddle" or "reins" (Mears 2012, 22; 33). The idea of balance, in other words, is more than a marker of physical expertise as it marks the human–horse relationship as one where the material body serves as a means of communication rather than as a language. It describes young Noah's first act of show-jumping: "It seemed it was just she and the horse, finding the way to best reach that jump" (Mears 2012, 23). Such representations of species-crossings leading to joint action are also indicative of what ecocritics such as Pieter Vermeulen (2017, 186) see as an expression of entanglement characterizing the Anthropocene, where "[h]uman life in the Anthropocene discovers that what is believed to be its human history has now to be remembered differently – as always already entangled with non-human life."

The problematization of the different identities of humans and non-humans is in fact something that non-Western literatures such as Native American – as we will show later – and indigenous writing recognize: humans can metamorphose into animals, and vice versa. The idea of shape-shifting and metamorphosis has often been used as a topos in postcolonial writing to address the multiple heritage and attachments of such identities, which are rooted in several cultures and folkloric traditions, as seen, for instance, in the work of the Guyanese writer Pauline Melville (e.g., *Shape-Shifter*

[1990]). An example of metamorphosis and the interchangeability of the human and the animal can be found in the US author Rafi Zabor's post-modernist novel *The Bear Comes Home* (1999 [1998]) telling of a bear who is a talented saxophone player with misshapen, human-like paws. In Zabor's (1999, 22) novel, the liminal world of jazz musicians is where the boundary between the human and the non-human may be negotiated, as both inhabit Bhabha's (1994) Third Space, where new hybrid identities emerge:

> He [the Bear] was led instantaneously to consider, now that he was on stand with the demonstrably bearlike McCall and the smaller but equally ursine Blythe, whether there was some deep, even fundamental connection between his own species and that of the jazz musician in general. Bird had taken on some bearish qualities when he put on weight and years. Mingus was a grizzly. Jaki Byeard. Jack the Bear. But Ellington was a tiger, everybody knew that, elegant too, to the tips of his claws and his velvet voice.

Hybrid environmentalist texts such as Margaret Atwood's *Oryx and Crake* (2003) address a world where genetic engineering has created new hybrid species such as pigoons, wolvogs, and crakers, some more dangerous than others (Sanderson 2013). In Atwood's more recent comic book *Angel Catbird* (2016), the cast of characters includes humans whose genetic inheritance is mixed with that of non-human species such as cats and rats, and they often are capable of shape-shifting (Kenyeres 2021).

In a similar vein, science fiction narratives also often delve into hybridity, showing how human bodies interact with other material bodies, radiation, or microbes, generating mixed identities and bodies. The hybrid figure of the mutant will serve as a good example here, shown in narratives ranging from Marvel Comics such as *X-Men* and films such as *Mad Max: Fury Road* (2015) to New Weird narratives by Jeff VanderMeer, Paolo Bacigalupi, and China Miéville. In the latter genre, the function of the mutant figure is, in the view of the posthumanist critic Kaisa Kortekallio (2020a, 2020b), to problematize human-centred thinking, and works by Bacigalupi and VanderMeer provide moments of transformation that problematize the mutant figure's non-human status, with the effect that the conventionally prioritized naturalness of the human body disappears and uncertainty increases. As Kortekallio (2020b, 71) suggests, VanderMeer's *Annihilation* (2014, 194) closes with its scientist-protagonist entering further into Area X, where she will attain full non-humanness:

> Will I melt into this landscape, or look up from a stand of reeds or the waters of the canal to see some other explorer staring down in disbelief? Will I be aware that anything is wrong or out of place?).

To sum up, the concept of hybridity involves border-crossings and reconstruction of identity in ways that are unpredictable and may involve transgression and change. Such crossings extend from geopolitical and linguistic borders to those of gender and species. The following section provides further examples of hybridity in literature and of ways of approaching the thematic.

Textual Analysis: Louise Erdrich, Tracks

The contemporary US novelist Louise Erdrich has a German American and Ojibwe (Anishinaabe) background and explores the formation of Native American identities in her highly acclaimed works. *Tracks* (1988) is the third in a series of four novels narrating the lives of several interrelated families living on a fictional reservation in North Dakota. While the author's background can be seen as a sign of hybridity, the concept is relevant for discussing the novel's form and thematics at large. In this novel looking back at early twentieth-century events, the stories of the Nanapush and Pillager families allow Erdrich to address the cultural, economic, and environmental consequences of colonialism and imagine hybridity as a means of coming to terms with it. The following analysis aims at highlighting how Erdrich's novel engages with hybridity and border-crossings in several ways, revealing that hybridity is both productive and disruptive, as John Hutnyk (2005, 81) has suggested.

Border-crossings of various kinds are central to the hybridity of Erdrich's novel, including its form. First, rather than a self-contained novel, it is a part of a tetralogy with recurring characters and events spanning several generations in a shared setting. Instead of being a single story focusing on an individual, *Tracks* consists of several stories that are related to each other and cross into other texts, forming a large canvas or tapestry. In so doing, it reflects an emphasis on community and relationality, aspects central to Erdrich's vision of identity as "transpersonal" (Smith 1997, 74). When examined from the perspective of hybridity theory, such a narrative strategy exemplifies Bakhtin's idea of polyphony, of several voices that hybridize the text and provide different versions of the events as well as problematizing the idea of a single truth in the narrative. In doing so, they reveal the multiplicity of perspectives and the possibility of contradictory and alternative stories. In *Tracks*, polyphony can be seen in the use of two alternating first-person narrators. Gerry Nanapush's chapters, addressed to her granddaughter, Fleur's daughter Lulu, aim at telling the mother's story to the daughter, who has been absent for several years. In contrast, the chapters narrated by Pauline Puyat, an Ojibwe woman disliked in her community, who becomes a devout Catholic nun, provide a different version of the events and characters from a perspective that emphasizes her views. The use of multi-perspectival narrative strategies problematizes Western conceptions of individualism and reveals more communal forms of storytelling.

Through the act of storytelling, understood by Nanapush as necessary and providing depth in life, as well as through the inclusion of oral stories and Ojibwe cultural practices from love potions to dreamcatchers, the novel hybridizes Western and Native traditions and becomes a contact zone. Passages such as the following one link the text with the Ojibwe world view but also serve as markers of hybrid polyphony in the contemporary novel where "the Manitous all through the woods spoke through Fleur, loose, arguing. I recognized them. Turtle's quavering scratch, the Eagle's high shriek, Loon's crazy bitterness, Otter, the howl of Wolf, Bear's low rasp" (Erdrich 1989, 59). In this universe, human and non-human are equal actors. Hybridity is further evident in the discourse of the novel through the use of linguistic hybridity. While *Tracks* is not a realist novel aiming at an exact representation of language and dialect, and is conducted mainly in English, it includes Ojibwe words, concepts, and folklore. It presents the indigenous collective self-identification (Anishinabe) as early as on its first page. Further, it includes stories such as that of the lake monster Misshepeshu, references to mythical creatures such as *odjibs*, and descriptions of shamanistic practices rooted in the Ojibwe world view, which hybridize the text and resist attempts to read it as a conventional monocultural novel. The different worlds are equally present through the linguistic elements, terms, and references that relate to a non-Western world view.

Furthermore, the text addresses cultural hybridity by showing how cultural practices cross-fertilize and fuse into each other. An example of this is when the discourse of gambling is used to describe the Ojibwe heaven, where gamblers throw dice and play cards but also gamble with objects such as deer knuckles and small bones (Erdrich 1989, 160). As a hybrid text, *Tracks* introduces and negotiates cultural differences in the text, showing both familiar and unfamiliar features, using English to narrate a world where Ojibwe is the norm. Occasionally both languages are present in the text, not merely as translations but to indicate the difference between the way they imagine the world and how they emplace people in it, which reveals that *Tracks* is a plurilingual text that both uses non-English words and translates them for the reader: "Our son, Thomas, also named Asainekanipawit, Standing in a Stone, was there too. [...] Ombaashi, He Is Lifted By Wind, raised his hands, running past, exalted, almost flying" (Erdrich 1989, 220).

As a part of its attempt to relate a holistic idea of the world, the novel portrays a universe where humans and animals are interconnected and the borders between different species crossed, suggesting shape-shifting. In addition to portraying a world where different spirits take the form of non-human animals and are communicated with, the humans of the novel take on animal-like features, blurring the alleged boundary between the species. In the case of Fleur, her braids are described as resembling "the tails of animals," she has only four toes, is "half-tamed," and grins like a wolf (Erdrich 1989, 18; 23). Further, her husband Eli kills a moose and straps the pieces of meat to his body so that, frozen, it "stood on its own in pieces, a moose transformed into the mold of Eli" (Erdrich 1989, 104), making human and non-human bodies similar. One of the characters, Fleur's cousin Moses, chooses to become "half animal" and live "in a den" with his cats (Erdrich 1989, 35), but he is not alone in this hybridity. Human and animal identities are, then, interchangeable and form another layer of hybridity that challenges a further Western binary, one that separates humans from animals.

At a general level, the hybridity of the novel does not aim at a peaceful mixture of Native and American cultures, nor is it a simplistic celebration of hybridity. In *Tracks*, hybridity is a means of challenging naturalized categorizations and alleged purities, such as a dominant sense of Americanness. As Sabine Mabardi (2000, 6) puts it, "hybridity is a threat to colonial and cultural authority; it subverts the concept of pure origin or identity of the dominant authority through the ambivalence created by denial, unsettling, repetition, and displacement." In addition to the textual ambivalences addressed above, Erdrich's (1989, 9) novel is concerned with challenging the dominant authority through a critique of borders created by US colonialism in order to impose its power over Native culture by drawing lines and marking the landscape "with [...] strings and yellow flags," anticipating a loss of shared spaces. As Nanapush describes the diverse effects of borders and encroaching colonialism:

> Before the boundaries were set, before the sickness scattered the clans like gambling sticks, an old man never had to live alone and cook for himself, never had to braid his own hair, or listen to his silence. An old man had some relatives, got a chance to pass his name on.
>
> *(Erdrich 1989, 32)*

In other words, the world inhabited by Erdrich's Native Americans is not a romanticized space of an allegedly pure Native culture. Rather, it is one scarred by racism and colonialist practices, including rampant diseases such as tuberculosis killing a great number of Ojibwe, and the effects of the General Allotment Act of 1887 leading to the loss of land for those Native Americans unable to pay taxes or mortgage for their land (Padget 2001, 37–42). In *Tracks*, the representation of the impending loss of land takes the form of a map where borders play a key role: "[W]e examined the lines and circles of the homesteads paid up [...]. They were colored green. The lands that were gone out of the tribe [...] were painted a pale and rotten pink. Those in question, a sharper yellow" (Erdrich 1989, 173).

Unable to identify with the dominant culture, but also faced with the loss of land and traditions, the novel's Native Americans occupy a marginal and liminal space that equals Bhabha's (1994) space of in-betweenness, a space where their identity is reconstructed so that it is not quite the same. As a sign of this, the novel shows the potential of homelessness and in-betweenness through the character of Fleur Pillager who, rather than sub-mitting to any form of power, gendered or nationed, returns to live in the reservation but away from the other, close to the Lake Matchimanito, in "a lonely place full of the ghosts of the drowned and those whose death took them unaware" (Erdrich 1989, 35), allegedly able to control the lake and its spirits. This space, beyond those of the villagers and the colonizes, affords her a unique position that combines nature and culture, land and water, life and death, secular and the sacred, where she can reconstruct her own hybrid identity.

This Third Space, both familiar and unfamiliar, resembles what Sigmund Freud (1998) has called the uncanny, *das Unheimliche*: in Erdrich's novel, the cultural memory and mythology of the Ojibwe chal-lenge the values of mainstream America in rationality and established his-torical narratives. This is where the novel's hybridity emerges as disruptive when the ethnic tradition challenges the authority of a simplified and allegedly unified American identity. In terms of the narrative, the novel's non-Western vocabularies and histories create ambivalence in the text. For example, the novel's opening chapter shows how the dead continue to affect those who are alive and may transform the latter into supernatural creatures:

> Their names grew within us, swelled to the brink of our lips, forced our eyes open in the middle of the night. We were filled with the water of the drowned, cold and back, airless water that lapped against the seal of our tongues or leaked slowly from the corners of our eyes. Within us, like ice shards, their names bobbed and shifted. Then the slivers of ice began to collect and cover us. We became so heavy, weighted down with the lead gray frost, that we could not move. Our hands lay on the table like cloudy blocks. [...] We had gone half windigo.
>
> *(Erdrich 1989, 6)*

Although the figure of the windigo can be seen as a mere allusion to an evil character in Native American folklore, in Erdrich's novel, the reference also indicates a more general cultural process that the Ojibwe have undergone as a result of US colonialism: the idea of "going half windigo" – or half mad – indicates that their cultural identity is no longer the same but transformed through the violent experiences of the Third Space. Similarly, the episode where Pauline witnesses Fleur's rape, unable to help her, transforms Pauline into a hybrid, but one dominated by negative characteristics since she is described as a "merciful scavenger," who is "dangerously meek and mild" (Erdrich 1989, 69). For Pauline, hybridity is disruptive and leads to her close identification with mutilation, self-torment, and death, the latter seen in her involvement in preparing funerals within the community: "I handled the dead until the cold feel of their skin was a comfort, [...] [I] passed death on" (Erdrich 1989, 69). In her case, hybridity is disruptive for her and her community, while in other cases such as Nanapush's it is empowering: his education with the Jesuits has provided him with a command of English and with white customs, enabling him to work for his community.

In his ability to juggle between cultures, Nanapush resists the binarisms associated with colonialist thinking and its fixed, essentialist identity categories such as us vs. them, culture vs. nature, modernity vs. tradition, Christian vs. heathen, and human vs. animal (see, e.g., Ashcroft, Griffiths, and Tiffin 2000, 18–20). In *Tracks*, a particularly strong representation of such polarities is attached to the Catholic Christianity that Pauline, denying her ethnic origins, converts to, only to create for herself a hybrid version of it, combining shamanistic and Catholic practices (McCafferty 1997). For her, religion provides a platform that allows her to see the Ojibwe as heathen Others, as "them," who need to be "name[d] and baptize[d]" (Erdrich 1989, 140–141). The act of renaming plays a key role as a colonialist practice as it signifies assimilation and loss of identity, shown in the way in which the Ojibwe Pauline becomes a nun and adopts the name Leopolda to signify her new status. In contrast, the value of the name Nanapush – a name that echoes that of the Ojibwe folk hero Nanabozho – is for him such that it cannot be uttered in vain as it links him to the cultural tradition and the trickster hero: "Nanapush. That's what you will be called. Because it's got to do with trickery and living in the bush. Because it's got to do with something a girl can't resist. The first Nanapush stole fire. You will steal hearts" (Erdrich 1989, 33). Nanapush, like many other tricksters, is fond of women, food, and humour and enjoys life, thus contrasting with Pauline and her association with death.

The trickster heroes of US ethnic literatures often indicate "political resistance and creative expression" (Smith 1997, 10). Through their successful challenging of established borders and categories, tricksters speak for both cultural and personal survival that has appealed to ethnic women writers in particular (Smith 1997, 2). However, Erdrich's use of the trickster figure as a cultural saviour is more than a nod towards the tradition since it can be examined in the context of cultural contacts and hybridity. From this perspective, the role of Nanapush as a trickster is different from that of Fleur Pillager. While Nanapush is able to move in two human worlds, both white and native as a cultural interpreter, Fleur links the human and spiritual worlds, seeing mysterious dreams and feeling the presence of the supernatural:

> Fleur stalked to the door, turned away several times, sat in the deep yellow lights of the translucent windows, and sang words I hadn't heard before, chilling and cold as the dead, restless and sharp as the wind of the month when the trees crack.

> *(Erdrich 1989, 171)*

Nanapush's interculturality is not restricted to his education at Saint John's. Erdrich's novel mentions how he communicates fluently in English and that he has served as an interpreter for the government until his dismissal for instructing the Ojibwe negotiator not to sign the Beauchamp Treaty of 1867 (Erdrich 1989, 100). Through the special knowledge of the Other and its ways, Nanapush resists the colonizer's appeals to introduce authoritarianism, revealing the power of disruption embedded in hybridity and seeking opportunities for survival, locating them only in accepting the role of a "tribal chairman" and using the colonizer's written culture as a tool with which to the defend his nation, a "tribe of file cabinets and triplicates," by locating a "loophole" allowing for the reunification of the family (Erdrich 1989, 225). His special task of passing on cultural knowledge is linked with the power that storytelling, stories, and words have in the novel in disrupting established narratives.

As a narrator, Nanapush tells a hybrid history of cultural encounters by introducing native perspectives. In doing so, he voices forgotten and silenced narratives of communal and family history and passes them on to those who have forgotten or never learnt them in the manner of Fleur's daughter Lulu, taken away to a residential school. The encounter with the community and the past may make the anger vanish and return life, even to those who have been close to death. This shows that the intercultural trickster may disrupt the workings of colonialism and discover alternative hybrid narratives in what Mary Magoulick (2018, 98) calls the "liminal place of cultural cross-pollination" that Erdrich's tricksters inhabit. Through hybridity, homogeneous perceptions of identity and history are challenged and found deficient, and alternative worlds introduced.

Further Reading

Anzaldúa, Gloria. 1987. *Borderlands/La Frontera: The New Mestiza*. San Francisco: Spinsters/Aunt Lute.

Bakhtin, M.M. 1981. *The Dialogic Imagination: Four Essays*, edited by Michael Holquist. Translated by Caryl Emerson and Michael Holquist. Austin: University of Texas Press.

Brambilla, Chiara. 2015. "Exploring the Critical Potential of the Borderscapes Concept." *Geopolitics*, vol. 20, no. 1, pp. 14–34. doi: https://doi.org/10.1080/14650045.2014.884561

Haraway, Donna. 2008. *When Species Meet*. Minneapolis: University of Minnesota Press.

Sadowski-Smith, Claudia. 2008. *Border Fictions: Globalization, Empire, and Writing at the Boundaries of the United States*. Charlottesville: University of Virginia Press.

Further Exercises

Brian Chikwava, Harare North *(2010)*

The unnamed Zimbabwean narrator of Chikwava's novel enters the UK posing as a persecuted asylum seeker but turns out to have been a member of the violent state-supported youth militia. Rather than an ideal migrant, he is manipulative and is merely interested in making easy money in London (i.e., Harare North). Narrated in a misleadingly simplistic language mixing different Englishes and expressions from Southern African languages, the novel is a satire of migration and the asylum-seeking process. Read the following passage. How does it portray the main character?

> No one bother to give me proper tips before I come to England. So on arriving at Gatwick airport I disappoint them immigration people when I step forward to hand my passport to gum-chewing man sitting behind desk, I mouth the magic word – asylum – and flash toothy grin of friendly African native. They detain me.
>
> Whatever they reasons for detaining me, them immigration people let me go after eight days. I don't grudge them because they is only doing they graft. But my relatives, they show worryful attitude: I have to wait another two days for my cousin's wife to come and fetch me.
>
> The story I tell them immigration people is tighter than thief's anus. Me I tell them I have been harass by them boys in dark glasses because I am youth member of the opposition party. This is not trying to shame our government in any way, but if you don't spin them smooth jazz numbers then immigration people is never going to give you chance to even sniff first step into Queens land.
>
> *(Chikwava 2010, 4)*

Bharati Mukherjee, Jasmine *(1991)*

The novel *Jasmine* by the South Asian American novelist Bharati Mukherjee has become a significant text in narrating global mobilities and the hybridization of identity. It tells the immigration story of a young Indian girl who goes through several identity transformations on her way from Hasnapur, India, to Florida, New York, Iowa, and further, being named at various stages of her life as Jyoti, Jasmine, Jazzy, Jase, and Jane, reflecting different ethnicities. As it emphasizes the migrant's agency and ability to cope with conditions of violence and abuse, its portrayal of the migrant has occasionally been criticized and seen as unrealistic. Look at the following excerpt commenting on migrants' journeys towards their dream destination and find examples of the ways in which hybrid identities are constructed through travel in the Third Space of in-between that is confusing and confused but may lead to a new identity.

There is a shadow world of aircraft permanently aloft that share air lines and radio frequencies with Pan Am and British Air and Air-India, portaging people who coexist with tourists and businessmen. But we are refugees and mercenaries and guest workers; you see us sleeping in airport lounges; you watch us unwrapping the last of our native foods, unrolling our prayer rugs, reading our holy books, taking out for the hundredth time an aerogram promising a letter or space to sleep, a newspaper in our language, a photo of happier times, a passport, a visa, a *laissez-passer.*

We are the outcasts and deportees, strange pilgrims visiting outlandish shrine, landing at the end of tarmacs, ferried in old army trucks where we are roughly handles and taken to roped-off corners where surly, barely wakened customs guards await their bribe. We are dressed in shreds of national costumes, out of season, the wilted plumage of intercontinental vagabondage. We ask only one thing: to be allowed to land; to pass through to continue. We sneak a look at the big departure board, the one the tourists use. Our cities are there, too, our destinations so close! But not yet, not so directly. We must sneak in, land by night in little-used strips. [...]

What country? What continent? We pass through wars, through plagues. I am hungry for news but the discarded papers are in characters or languages I cannot read.

The zig-zag route is straightest.

(Mukherjee 1991, 100–101)

Gloria Anzaldúa, Borderlands/La Frontera: The New Mestiza (1987)

Gloria Anzaldúa's book addressing is a genre hybrid, combining autobiography, LGBT theory, and mythology in the context of Chicana identity. It uses prose and poetry in both English and Spanish, and the work is nowadays considered a central text in the theorization of border identities. Read the following excerpts and think about what different kinds of borders and border-crossings the text imagines. How has hybridity been imagined by Anzaldúa? What different layers of hybrid identity do the passages reveal?

"Pocho, cultural traitor, you're speaking the oppressor's language by speaking English, you're ruining the Spanish language," I have been accused by various Latinos and Latinas. Chicano Spanish is considered by the purist and by most Latinos' deficient, a mutilation of Spanish.

But Chicano Spanish is a border tongue which developed naturally. Change, *evolución, enriquement de palabras nuevas por invención o adopción* have created variants of Chicano Spanish, *un nuevo lenguaje. Un lenguaje que corresponde a un modo de vivir.* Chicano Spanish is not incorrect, it is a living language. [...] A language which they can connect their identity to, one capable of communicating the realities and values true to themselves – a language with terms that are neither *español ni inglés*, but both.

(Anzaldúa 1987, 55)

As a *mestiza* I have no country, my homeland cast me out; yet all countries are mine because I am every woman's sister and potential lover. (As a lesbian I have no race, my own people disclaim me; but I am all races because there is the queer of me in all races.) I am cultureless, because, as a feminist, I challenge the collective cultural/religious male-derived beliefs of Indo-Hispanics and Anglos; yet I am cultured because I am participating in the creation of yet another culture, a new story to explain the world and our participation in it, a new value system with images and symbols that connects us to each other and the planet.

(Anzaldúa 1987, 80–81)

Gabriel García Márquez, "A Very Old Man with Enormous Wings" (1998; "Un señor muy viejo con unas alas enormes" [1968])

Gabriel García Márquez's story is often seen as a magic realist text since it portrays an unlikely series of events where an old man with angel's wings falls from the sky and ends up living in a chicken coop behind a farmer's house. From the perspective of hybridity, it can also be seen to problematize conventional classifications of natural beings and to address questions of fear of Otherness. Read the entire story and think about the following questions: How do the people of the village react to the difference the human-angel represents? In what ways does he break the boundaries between human and animal? What does the ending of the story say about hybridity and its potential? The story is widely available as it has been anthologized in *The Norton Introduction to Literature*.

References

Alibhai-Brown, Yasmine. 2010. *The Settler's Cookbook: A Memoir of Love, Migration and Food*. London: Portobello Books.

Anzaldúa, Gloria. 1987. *Borderlands/La Frontera: The New Mestiza*. San Francisco: Spinsters/Aunt Lute.

Appadurai, Arjun. 1996. *Modernity at Large: Cultural Dimensions of Globalization*. Minneapolis: University of Minnesota Press.

Ashcroft, Bill. 2009. *Caliban's Voice: The Transformation of English in Post-Colonial Literatures*. London: Routledge.

Ashcroft, Bill, Gareth Griffiths, and Helen Tiffin. 1989. *Empire Writes Back: Theory and Practice in Post-Colonial Literatures*. London: Routledge.

Ashcroft, Bill, Gareth Griffiths, and Helen Tiffin. 2000. *Post-colonial Studies: The Key Concepts*. 2nd ed. London: Routledge.

Bakhtin, Mikhail M. 1981. *The Dialogic Imagination: Four Essays*, edited by Michael Holquist. Translated by Caryl Emerson and Michael Holquist. Austin: University of Texas Press.

Bakhtin, Mikhail M. 1984. *Problems of Dostoyevsky's Poetics*, edited and translated by Caryl Emerson. Minneapolis: University of Minnesota Press.

Bhabha, Homi K. 1994. *The Location of Culture*. London: Routledge.

Boehmer, Elleke. 1995. *Colonial and Postcolonial Literature: Migrant Metaphors*. Oxford: Oxford University Press.

Brambilla, Chiara. 2015. "Exploring the Critical Potential of the Borderscapes Concept." *Geopolitics*, vol. 20, no. 1, pp. 14–34. https://doi.org/10.1080/14650045.2014.884561

Brathwaite, Edward Kamau. 1984. *History of the Voice: The Development of Nation Language in Anglophone Caribbean Poetry*. Boston: Beacon Press.

Bridges, Tristan, and C.J. Pascoe. 2014. "Hybrid Masculinities: New Directions in the Sociology of Men and Masculinities." *Sociology Compass*, vol. 8, no. 3, pp. 246–258. https://doi.org/10.1111/soc4.12134

Butler, Judith. 1990. *Gender Trouble: Feminism and the Subversion of Identity*. London: Routledge.

Castillo, Debra. 2007. "Borders, Identities, Objects." In *Border Poetics De-Limited*, edited by Johan Schimanski and Stephen Wolfe, 115–148. Hannover: Wehrhahn.

Chambers, Claire. 2019. *Making Sense of Contemporary British Muslim Novels*. London: Palgrave Macmillan. https://doi.org/10.1057/978-1-137-52089-0

Chávez, Denise. 1986. "Compadre." In *The Last of the Menu Girls*, by Denise Chávez, 139–190. Houston: Arte Público Press.

Chikwava, Brian. 2010 [originally published 2009]. *Harare North*. London: Vintage.

Davidson, Arnold E., Priscilla Walton, and Jennifer Andrews. 2003. *Border Crossings: Thomas King's Cultural Inversions*. Toronto: University of Toronto Press.

Davis, Rocío. 2001. *Transcultural Reinventions: Asian American and Asian American Short Story*. Toronto: TSAR.

DeLillo, Don. 2003. *Cosmopolis*. New York: Scribner.

Elze, Jens. 2017. *Postcolonial Modernism and the Picaresque Novel*. Cham: Palgrave Macmillan. https://doi.org/10.1007/978-3-319-51938-8

Erdrich, Louise. 1989 [originally published 1988]. *Tracks*. New York: Perennial.

Fellner, Astrid M. 2020. "Introduction: Narratives of Border Crossing X Border Crossing Narratives." In *Narratives of Border Crossings: Literary Approaches and Negotiations*, edited by Astrid M. Fellner, 7–19. Baden Baden: Nomos. https://doi.org/10.5771/9783748924005

Frears, Stephen, director. *My Beautiful Launderette*. 1986. Channel 4. 1 hr., 30 min.

Freud, Sigmund. 1998 [originally published 1919]. "The Uncanny." Translated by James Strachey. In *Literary Theory: An Anthology*, edited by Julie Rivkin and Michael Ryan, 154–167. Oxford: Blackwell.

Game, Ann. 2001. "Riding: Embodying the Centaur." *Body & Society*, vol. 7, no. 4, pp. 1–12. https://doi.org/10.1177/1357034X01007004001

García Márquez, Gabriel. 1998 [originally published 1968]. "A Very Old Man with Enormous Wings" ("Un señor muy viejo con unas alas enormes"). Translated by Gregory Rabassa. In *Norton Introduction to Literature*, 7th ed., edited by Jerome Beaty and J. Paul Hunter, 440–444. New York: Norton.

Gavaler, Chris. 2018. *Superhero Comics*. London: Bloomsbury Academic.

Ghasemi, Mehdi. 2022. "Post-postmodernism and Emergence of Heterolinational Literatures." *Contemporary Aesthetics*, vol. 20. https://contempaesthetics.org/2022/07/14/post-postmodernism-and-the-emergence-of-heterolinational-literatures/

Giddens, Anthony. 1990. *The Consequences of Modernity*. Oxford: Polity.

Gunn, Giles. 2001. "Introduction: Globalizing Literary Studies." *PMLA*, vol. 116, no. 1, pp. 16–31. https://doi.org/10.1632/pmla.2001.116.1.16

Gupta, Suman. 2009. *Globalization and Literature*. Cambridge: Polity.

Hamburger Kunsthalle. 2022. "On Hybrid Creatures: Sculpture in Modernism." https://www.hamburger-kunsthalle.de/en/exhibitions/hybrid-creatures

Haraway, Donna. 2008. *When Species Meet*. Minneapolis: University of Minnesota Press.

Haraway, Donna. 2016. *Manifestly Haraway*. Minneapolis: University of Minnesota Press.

Heilmann, Ann, and Margaret Beetham. 2012. "Introduction." In *New Woman Hybridities: Femininity, Feminism, and International Consumer Culture, 1880–1930*, edited by Ann Heilmann and Margaret Beetham, 1–14. London: Routledge.

Held, David, Anthony McGrew, David Goldblatt, and Jonathan Perraton. 1999. *Global Transformations: Politics, Economics and Culture.* Cambridge: Polity.

van Houtum, Henk. 2021. "Beyond 'Borderism': Overcoming Discriminate B/ordering and Othering." *Tijdschrift voor Economische en Sociale Geografie*, vol. 112, no. 1, pp. 34–43. https://doi.org/10.1111/tesg.12473

van Houtum, Henk, Olivier Kramsch, and Wolfgang Zierhofer. 2005. "Prologue: B/ordering Space." In *B/ordering Space*, edited by Henk van Houtum, Olivier Kramsch, and Wolfgang Zierhofer, 1–13. Aldershot: Ashgate.

Hulme, Peter. 1992. *Colonial Encounters: Europe and the Native Caribbean 1492–1776.* London: Routledge.

Hutnyk, John. 2005. "Hybridity." *Ethnic and Racial Studies*, vol. 28, no. 1, pp. 79–102. https://doi.org/10.1080/0141987042000280021

Ilott, Sarah. 2015. *New Postcolonial British Genres: Shifting the Boundaries.* Houndmills: Palgrave Macmillan. https://doi.org/10.1057/9781137505224

Ispa-Landa, Simone, and Mariana Oliver. 2020. "Hybrid Femininities: Making Sense of Sorority Rankings and Reputation." *Gender & Society*, vol. 34, no. 6, pp. 893–921. https://doi.org/10.1177/0891243220968882

Jay, Paul. 2001. "Beyond Discipline? Globalization and the Future of English." *PMLA*, vol. 116, no. 1, pp. 32–47. https://doi.org/10.1632/pmla.2001.116.1.32

Johnson, Linton Kwesi. 2002 [originally published 1980]. "Inglan Is a Bitch." In *Mi Revalueshanary Fren: Selected Poems*, by Linton Kwesi Johnson, 39–41. London: Penguin.

Johnson, Paul Christopher. 2017. "Syncretism and Hybridization." In *The Oxford Handbook of the Study of Religion*, edited by Michael Stausberg and Steven Engler, 754–772. Oxford: Oxford University Press. https://doi.org/10.1093/oxfordhb/9780198729570.013.50

Kay, Jackie. 1998. *Trumpet.* London: Picador.

Kenyeres, János. 2021. "Metamorphosis and Hybridity in Margaret Atwood's *Angel Catbird.*" *Central European Journal of Canadian Studies*, vol. 16, pp. 69–78. https://digilib.phil.muni.cz/_flysystem/fedora/pdf/144906.pdf

Kortekallio, Kaisa. 2020a. *Reading Mutant Narratives: The Bodily Experientality of Contemporary Ecological Science Fiction.* Helsinki: University of Helsinki. http://hdl.handle.net/10138/309144

Kortekallio, Kaisa. 2020b. "Becoming Instrument: Thinking with Jeff VanderMeer's *Annihilation* and Timothy Morton's *Hyperobjects.*" In *Reconfiguring Human, Nonhuman and Posthuman in Literature and Culture*, edited by Sanna Karkulehto, Aino-Kaisa Koistinen, Karoliina Lummaa, and Essi Varis, 57–75. London: Routledge. https://doi.org/10.4324/9780429243042

Kureishi, Hanif. 2000 [originally published 1995]. *The Black Album.* London: Faber and Faber.

Kymlicka, Will. 2001. *Politics in the Vernacular: Nationalism, Multiculturalism, and Citizenship.* Oxford: Oxford University Press. https://doi.org/10.1093/0199240981.001.0001

Leppänen, Sirpa. 2012. "Linguistic and Generic Hybridity in Web Writing: The Case of Fan Fiction." In *Language Mixing and Code-Switching in Writing:*

Approaches to Mixed-Language Written Discourse, edited by Mark Sebba, Shahrzad Mahoodian, and Carla Jonsson, 233–254. London: Routledge.

Mabardi, Sabine. 2000. "Encounters of a Heterogeneous Kind: Hybridity in Cultural Theory." In *Unforeseeable Americas: Questioning Cultural Hybridity in the Americas*, edited by Rita De Grandis and Zilá Bernd, 1–17. Amsterdam: Rodopi. https://doi.org/10.1163/9789004333802_001

Mackenthun, Gesa. 1996. "A Monstrous Race for Possession: Discourses of Monstrosity in *The Tempest* and Early British America." In *Writing and Race*, edited by Tim Youngs, 52–79. London: Longman.

Magoulick, Mary. 2018. "Trickster Lives in Erdrich: Continuity, Innovation and Eloquence of Troubling, Beloved Character." *Journal of Folklore Research*, vol. 55, no. 3, pp. 87–126. https://doi.org/10.2979/jfolkrese.55.3.04

McCafferty, Kate. 1997. "Generative Adversity: Shapeshifting Pauline/Leopolda in *Tracks* and *Love Medicine*." *American Indian Quarterly*, vol. 21, no. 44, pp. 727–751. https://doi.org/10.2307/1185722

McHugh, Susan. 2011. *Animal Stories: Narrating across Species Lines*. Minneapolis: University of Minnesota Press.

McLeod, John. 2004. *Postcolonial London: Writing the Metropolis*. London: Routledge.

Mears, Gillian. 2012 [originally published 2011]. *Foal's Bread*. London: Allen & Unwin.

Mohanram, Radhika. 1995. "Postcolonial Spaces and Deterritorialized (homo) Sexuality: The Films of Hanif Kureishi." In *Postcolonial Discourse and Changing Cultural Contexts*, edited by Gita Rajan and Radhika Mohanram, 117–134. Westport: Greenwood Press.

Montes-Alcalá, Cecilia. 2012. "Code-Switching in US–Latino Novels." In *Language Mixing and Code-Switching in Writing: Approaches to Mixed-Language Written Discourse*, edited by Mark Sebba, Shahrzad Mahoodian, and Carla Jonsson, 68–88. London: Routledge.

Moraga, Cherríe. 1995. "Art in America con acento." In *Latina: Women's Voices from the Borderlands*, edited by Lillian Castillo-Speed, 210–220. New York: Simon and Schuster.

Mukherjee, Bharati. 1991 [originally published 1989]. *Jasmine*. London: Virago.

Nederveen Pieterse, Jan. 2009. *Globalization and Culture: Global Mélange*. 2nd ed. London: Rowman and Littlefield.

Nyman, Jopi. 2019. *Equine Fictions: Human–Horse Relations in Twenty-first-century Writing*. Newcastle: Cambridge Scholars Publishing.

Padget, Martin. 2001. "Native American Fiction." In *Beginning Ethnic American Literatures*, by Helena Grice, Candida Hepworth, Maria Lauret, and Martin Padget, 10–63. Manchester: Manchester University Press.

Posthumus, Liane. 2011. "Hybrid Monsters in the Classical World: The Nature and Function of Hybrid Monsters in Greek Mythology, Literature and Art." M.Phil. thesis, Department of Ancient Studies, University of Stellenbosch. https://scholar.sun.ac.za/handle/10019.1/6865

Pratt, Mary Louise. 1992. *Imperial Eyes: Travel Writing and Transculturation*. London: Routledge.

Pykett, Lyn. 1995. *Engendering Fictions: The English Novel in the Early Twentieth Century*. London: Edward Arnold.

Quayson, Ato. 2021. *Tragedy and Postcolonial Literature*. Oxford: Oxford University Press. https://doi.org/10.1017/9781108921992

Rao, Raja. 1967 [originally published 1938]. *Kanthapura*. New York: New Directions.

Reeck, Laura. 2020. "Somewhere between 'French' and 'Francophone': Immigrant and Ethnic-minority Writing in France." In *Immigrant and Ethnic-minority Writers since 1945: Fourteen National Contexts in Europe and Beyond*, edited by Wiebke Sievers and Sandra Vlasta, 172–218. Amsterdam: Brill/Rodopi. https://doi.org/10.1163/9789004363243_008

Reichstein, Andreas. 1998. "Batman – An American Mr. Hyde?" *Amerikastudien/American Studies*, vol. 43, no. 2, pp. 329–350.

Rosello, Mireille, and Stephen F. Wolfe. 2017. "Introduction." In *Border Aesthetics: Concepts and Intersections*, edited by Johan Schimanski and Stephen F. Wolfe, 1–24. Oxford: Berghahn.

Sadowski-Smith, Claudia. 2008. *Border Fictions: Globalization, Empire, and Writing at the Boundaries of the United States*. Charlottesville: University of Virginia Press.

Salovaara, Harri. 2022. "'Nature Is Dope': Timothy Olson and Athletic Masculinity in Nature." *ISLE: Interdisciplinary Studies in Literature and Environment*, vol. 29, no. 2, pp. 323–340. https://doi.org/:10.1093/isle/isab048

Sanderson, Jay. 2013. "Pigoons, Rakunks, and Crakers: Margaret Atwood's *Oryx and Crake* and Genetically Engineered Animals in a (Latourian) Hybrid World." *Law and Humanities*, vol. 7, no. 2, pp. 218–240. http://dx.doi.org/10.5235/17521483.7.2.218

SBS. 2019. "Two Countries, Two Detectives and a Dead Body: The Worldwide Fascination with 'The Bridge.'" *sbs.com.au* (December 29, 2019). https://www.sbs.com.au/guide/article/2019/12/20/two-countries-two-detectives-and-dead-body-worldwide-fascination-bridge

Schemien, Alexia. 2013. "Hybrid Spiritualities in Ana Castillo's *The Guardians*." *Forum for Inter-American Research*, vol. 6, no. 1. http://interamericaonline.org/volume-6-1/schemien/

Schimanski, Johan, and Stephen Wolfe. 2007. "Entry Points: An Introduction." In *Border Poetics De-limited*, edited by Johan Schimanski and Stephen Wolfe, 9–26. Hannover: Wehrhahn.

Scott, Ridley, director. *Blade Runner*. Warner. 1982. 1 hr., 57 min.

Sievers, Wiebke, and Sandra Vlasta, eds. 2018. *Immigrant and Ethnic-minority Writers since 1945: Fourteen National Contexts in Europe and Beyond*. Amsterdam: Brill/Rodopi. https://doi.org/10.1163/9789004363243

Smith, Jeanne Rosier. 1997. *Writing Tricksters: Mythic Gambols in American Ethnic Literature*. Berkeley: University of California Press.

Stein, Mark. 2004. *Black British Literature: Novels of Transformation*. Columbus: Ohio State University Press.

Stein, Mark. 2008. "The Location of Transculture." In *Transcultural English Studies: Theories, Fictions, Realities*, edited by Frank Schulze-Engler and Sissy Helff, 251–266. Amsterdam: Rodopi. https://doi.org/10.1163/9789042028845_016

Stevenson, Robert Louis. 1886. *Strange Case of Dr Jekyll and Mr Hyde*. London: Longmans, Green, and Co.

Talib, Ismail S. 2002. *The Language of Postcolonial Literatures: An Introduction.* London: Routledge.

Tatonetti, Lisa. 2020. "Queer Sovereignty." In *The Cambridge History of Native American Literature*, edited by Melanie Benson Taylor, 379–394. Cambridge: Cambridge University Press. https://doi.org/10.1017/9781108699419

Tuhkanen, Mikko. 2009. "Queer Hybridity." In *Deleuze and Queer Theory*, edited by Chrysanthi Nigianni and Merl Storr, 97–114. Edinburgh: Edinburgh University Press.

VanderMeer, Jeff. 2014. *Annihilation.* New York: Farrar, Straus, and Giroux.

Vermeulen, Pieter. 2017. "'The Sea, Not the Ocean': Anthropocene Fiction and the Memory of (Non)human Life." *Genre: Forms of Discourse and Culture*, vol. 50, no. 2, pp. 181–200. https://doi.org/10.1215/00166928-3890028

Wilson, Thomas M., and Hastings Donnan. 2012. "Borders and Border Studies." In *A Companion to Border Studies*, edited by Thomas M. Wilson and Hastings Donnan, 1–25. Chichester: Wiley-Blackwell. https://doi.org/10.1002/9781118255223.ch1

Yekani, Elahe Haschemi. 2011. *The Privilege of Crisis: Narratives of Masculinities in Colonial and Postcolonial Literature, Photography, and Film.* Frankfurt am Main: Campus.

Young, Robert J.C. 1995. *Colonial Desire: Hybridity in Theory, Culture and Race.* London: Routledge.

Zabor, Rafi. 1999 [originally published 1998]. *The Bear Comes Home.* London: Vintage.

2

RACE, ETHNICITY, MIGRATION, AND HYBRIDITY

Jopi Nyman

Introduction

As the previous chapters have shown, the history of the concept of hybridity reveals how ideas of racial purity and ethnic authenticity have always been challenged by the different dimensions of hybridity. According to Robert Young (1995), the origins of the term are rooted in colonialism and binary thinking promoting fixed identities and borderings. As Young (1995) shows in his discussion of nineteenth-century colonialist discourses, the term indicates an undesired state of being: hybridity and hybrid beings are signs of impurity and of breaching of racial categories and are thus negative, a view that has been persistent well into the two subsequent centuries. However, this also shows that hybridity has the potential to question phenomena that have commonly been presented as clear-cut objects, divided into categories, and to problematize such age-old boundaries. In this chapter, we show how discourses concerning personal, cultural, and national identities have been affected by questions of hybridity and mixed-race subjectivity. This chapter starts with a discussion of the debate concerning the ideologies of purity and hybridity, continues by addressing hybridity as a means to challenge diverse essentialisms and nationalisms, as well as by explaining the role of migration and diaspora, and extends to reflections on debates concerning hybridity and cultural appropriation. The chapter closes with a discussion of the novel *The Translator* (1999) by the Sudanese British author Leila Aboulela.

DOI: 10.4324/9781003269670-3

Hybridity and Purity

While the history of hybridity discourse and the importance of racial purity and racialized boundaries extends to ancient societies and Imperial Rome, as Amar Acheraïou (2011) has suggested, contemporary understanding of such polarization is rooted in colonialism, the Enlightenment, and the binarisms they have generated (see Said 1978; Ashcroft, Griffiths, and Tiffin 2000). In providing further representations of hybridity and racial mixing challenging established power hierarchies and the alleged supremacy of white European colonizers, colonial discourse was allied with Western science, which produced nuanced racial taxonomies and hierarchies to construct racial difference as a fact. A famous chart of different racial descriptors presented by the Victorian explorer W.B. Stevenson in 1825 presents a detailed list of such pseudoscientific identity positions based on a child's paternity, including terms such as "zambo," "quinteron," and "mulatto" that indicate different degrees of racial mixing (qtd. in Loomba 1999, 120). As Sara Salih (2010, 2–3) writes in the context of the eighteenth and nineteenth centuries, such positions as the "mulatto" were legal entities and categories, rather than identities as such, revealing how colonial power worked, positioning humans differently through law and other discourses.

Colonial discourse sought to maintain the boundaries of such fixed categories as natural and true, and thus as unbreachable. In the view of Ania Loomba (1999, 116–118), the colonial discourse of race operated by means of three key ideas: (i) using a biological analogy, the different human 'races' were seen as species-like and their intermixing would result in undesired consequences; (ii) established stereotypes of non-Europeans as savage Others and non-civilized barbarians continued to be circulated in order to distinguish between European civilization and its counterposed Other; and (iii) the term 'race' was gradually associated with 'nation' to create a sense of togetherness, an "imagined community" (see Anderson 2006) with a shared racialized and moral identity. Under such conditions, any emerging form of hybridity – either biological or cultural – resulting from interchange between Europeans and non-Europeans was imagined in negative terms. In colonial discourse, non-European influence is a threat to the maintenance of white European identity and must be seen as inferior.

In the nineteenth century and later, literary representations of racialized hybridities, usually considered lacking, and termed "half-caste" or "half-breed," constructed their object as primarily negative and supported the moral supremacy of the white European untainted by non-European racial identity. Such discourse associates the position between the Western and non-Western worlds as one always prone to rupture and revert to its non-Western heritage. While also critiquing the stereotype, an example of such ideological oscillation is provided in Joseph Conrad's *Almayer's Folly* (1992). In this novel set in the Dutch East Indies, Nina, the daughter of the unsuccessful colonial merchant Kaspar Almayer and his Malay wife, a descendant of the "Sulu Pirates," abandons her father and adopts the values of her Malay lineage (see Yeow 2009, 137). Another literary example of the threat generated by such hybrid characters can be found in the wilderness narratives of the US naturalist writer Jack London in the early twentieth century. For example, in the short story "Bâtard" (1992), that is, "bastard," species interbreeding between dogs and wolves constructs the hybrid as an untrustworthy mongrel associated with racial degeneration (see Nyman 2003). In this story, both the dog and its French master are non-human beasts:

> The first time they met, Bâtard was a part-grown puppy, lean and hungry, with bitter eyes; and they met with a snap and snarl, and wicked looks, for Leclère's upper lip had a wolfish way of lifting and showing the white, cruel teeth.
>
> *(London 1992, 293)*

Such appeals to alleged purity and the need to maintain racial boundaries were popularized in discourses such as that of the early twentieth-century eugenics movement. This version of Social Darwinism aimed at creating what its proponents considered to be an improved 'race' by promoting particular dispositions of class and ethnicity as guiding the nation towards a desired future. By underlining the role of whiteness, eugenicists sought to introduce practices that would guarantee alleged racial purity associated with hegemonic national identity in many European countries and in the United States. With the aid of the period's racial science (e.g., phrenology, the study of skull shapes), non-white immigrants, the disabled, and the urban poor were excluded from the desired social formation through inhuman practices including sterilization programs and culminating in the Holocaust. Traces of such an attitude can still also be seen in such popular representations as the wizards' condescending attitude towards "half-bloods" and "mudbloods" in J.K. Rowling's Harry Potter series (1997–2007).

As these examples show, hybridity is a contested concept with a long and contested cultural history. As Nikos Papastergiadis (1997, 259) claims, "the hybrid is always positioned in relation to the value of purity, along axes of inclusion and exclusion." It has been used as a means of Othering to construct fixed identity positions where intercultural identities and cultural mixing have been seen as negative, but at the same time it challenges such discourses. In today's multicultural and transnational world, claims to purity and authenticity have been shown to rest on outdated thinking about race and ethnicity. Migration, mobility, and a revised understanding of the role of historical ethnic minorities have shown that ideas of romantic nationalism adopted by many nation-states emphasizing the monocultural unity of language and people are historical constructs that undermine the role of cultural diversity and contacts. More recent discussions take into account the concept of hybridity and its potential in addressing existing and emergent identities generated by diverse border-crossings and transnational linkages.

Hybridity as Critique of Power

The space of in-betweenness and ambiguity, understood by Homi K. Bhabha (1994) as elements of the insecurity of the Third Space where identity is reconstructed in ways that challenge the subject's previous identity, generates new meanings that transform cultural codes and enable the formation of collective politics in transcultural contexts. In other words, the contemporary understanding of hybridity emphasizes that the position in between different identifications, involving a refusal to accept fixedness, allows for the crossing of different cultural, national, and racial borders. In such situations, narrative strategies include mimicry and counter-discourse that challenge hegemonic values and show their constructedness. Mimicry, as defined by Bhabha (1994), is a way of imitating the colonizer with a difference aiming at revealing difference and fluidity in postcolonial identity. The concept is useful in understanding that any identity can be copied, and rather than authentic or fixed, identities are performed in different cultural and historical contexts. The novel *The Impressionist* (2003), by the postcolonial British writer Hari Kunzru, set in nineteenth-century India, provides a good example of identity as performative since its protagonist Pran Nath, also known as Pretty Bobby, is capable of adopting different identities (see Nyman 2009). He has a talent for copying the language and behaviour of the colonizer that serves his opportunism:

> Bobby's capacity for mimicry helps in his work. He can reduce British Other Ranks to fits by imitating regional accents. Oroight there mate? Och ye dinnae wanna worrit yersel'. Now then sirs, if you please to follow me I know a very good place [...] Bobby deals in stereotypes, sharply drawn.
>
> *(Kunzru 2003, 237)*

Another example of mimicry in contemporary writing can be found in the British writer Zadie Smith's *White Teeth* (2000), where the schoolboy

Magid Iqbal is sent by his father from Britain to Bangladesh to learn about his roots. However, in the colonial educational system that understands the centre as the model, Magid becomes "more English than the English" (Smith 2000, 365), a mimic who speaks Queen's English, desires bacon sandwiches upon his return, and chooses genetics and the natural sciences over religion and tradition.

The concept of mimicry as a means of challenging dominant hierarchies is related to the concept of passing that both Bobby and Magid perform, more or less successfully. In the context of race, the idea of passing often refers to a situation where a person with a racialized background passes as a white person, invariably in a society where whiteness is a social norm associated with class and prestige and interracial relations are either formally sanctioned or socially disapproved. The classic example is the novel *Passing* (1929) by the mixed-race US writer Nella Larsen, where one of the main characters adopts a white identity and hides her black background even from her husband. The idea of passing is linked with such figures as the "tragic mulatto[/a]," a stereotypical trope emerging in the mid-nineteenth-century United States to address issues concerning race and nation (Raimon 2004, 4) through light-skinned, biracial protagonists and their hardships in an antagonistic world of slavery, often ending tragically in desperation or in the death of the major character (2004, 7). Early examples of the genre include such works as Harriet Wilson's *Our Nig* (1859) and William Wells Brown's *Clotel* (1853). The pull of the idea of passing remains to the present owing to a variety of reasons. This major trope in African American literature has been applied in many works. These include Walter Mosley's detective novel *Devil in a Blue Dress* (1990), in which a black detective searches for a young white woman who turns out be passing amidst the racial categories of post-war Los Angeles, and Danzy Senna's novel *From Caucasia, with Love* (1998), which explores passing in the context of contemporary post-ethnicity through its adolescent protagonist as well as in works such as Philip Roth's *The Human Stain* (2000; see Moynihan 2010) and Brit Bennett's *The Vanishing Half* (2020). The trope has also been utilized by white writers passing as a member of another racialized group, as in the bestselling memoir *Lowest of the Low* (1988; orig. *Ganz Unten*, 1985), in which the German journalist Günter Walraff enters the world of Turkish migrant labour under an alias, and Ben Judah's report of ethnic transformation in contemporary London, *This Is London* (2016), where the British journalist becomes an Eastern European worker. In such cases, however, passing may also become a form of the white gaze objectifying and exoticizing the Other. In a larger context, Sinead Moynihan (2010, 5–6) suggests two reasons for the sustained interest in the multi-layered phenomenon in literature. First, view; at the global level, multiracial identity is more visible than before, without a similar stigmatization as in the past; and second, the idea of mixing and hybridizing appeals also to writers interested in developing self-reflexive textual forms such as metafiction – literature indeed consists of the interplay of black characters and a white surface (2010, 5–6).

Both mimicry and passing can be seen as ways of expressing hybrid, mixed-race subjectivity in culture, emphasizing the position of in-betweenness or what could also be termed as doubleness or *mestizaje*. Jonathan Brennan (2002, 9) suggests that "the term mixed race serve [*sic*] as a metaphor for cultural hybridity, the merging of more than one stream of cultural/literary tradition." Often addressed as hyphenated identities (e.g., Chinese American, German Turkish, Moroccan Dutch), such categories, as Brennan (2002, 9–10) claims, are cultural not racial, bringing together multiple identities and literary traditions. The traditional term to indicate the subject's location in more than one culture is of course W.E.B. Du Bois's (1903) notion of double consciousness that indicates the African American subject's doubleness, being both American (included) but black and African (excluded). The position at the border, however, provides a critical awareness of both cultures, and the concept has been developed by critics such as Nahum Welang (2018) into triple consciousness that emphasizes gender as a third element in African American identity formation. Such positions of liminality indicate hybrid identity and are recognizable in the sense of in-betweenness shared by many migrant groups and minorities that may generate critical and creative reflections on identity.

The terms *métissage* and *mestizaje* are, in Paul Christopher Johnson's (2017) view, originally associated with "processes of racial mixture." In describing cultural interchange and transformation, theorists have shown the usefulness of the terms and expanded their frame of reference. In the field of francophone studies, as Srilata Ravi (2007, 16) shows, the concept indicates encounters and mixing at levels extending from historical encounters to its use as a means of referring to an ideology, reaching as far as its literary usage:

> For example, Edward [*sic*] Glissant refers to the term primarily as ideology, while Maryse Condé considers it purely as textual practice, whereas Françoise Lionnet considers it a symbol of liberation, an ideology of subversion and a textual site of multiplicity.

In this sense, the concept is quite similar to that of *mestizaje*, widely used in the Spanish-speaking world to underline the formation of a new kind of identity as a result of cultural and ethnic intermingling in contrast to historical racial mixing. A particularly well-known example of this is Gloria Anzaldúa's (1987, 77) definition: "From the racial, ideological, cultural and biological cross-pollination, an 'alien' consciousness is presently in the making – a new *mestiza* consciousness, *una conciencia de mujer*. It is a consciousness of the Borderlands." Anzaldúa's (1987, 88) mestizaje combines several cultural traditions rather than simply two, Native American, Mexican, and Anglo, as an attempt "to juggle cultures," as her own work combining autobiographical and theoretical perspectives shows. As a result, hybridization reveals that, regardless of their claims of homogeneity and unity, all national and cultural ideals are constructs based on encounters and contacts.

Migration and Critique of Nationalism

As the section above has suggested, nations and cultures are not sealed containers, but such identities are in constant flux: they are hybridized through transnational processes such as migration and mobility, diaspora and exile, as well through transnational links between migrants' place of origin and destination. This shows how migration literature challenges the nation and its alleged homogeneity. Such a process is transnational, a term that, in current social theory, has challenged methodological nationalism, that is, a means of addressing socio-cultural phenomena in the context of the nation-state, rather than in their border-crossing contexts. As migration scholars have suggested, transnational connections have wide economic, political, and cultural consequences, a process that the German sociologist Ulrich Beck (2000, 11) has referred to as an element in globalization by suggesting that "sovereign national states are criss-crossed and undermined by transnational actors with varying prospects of power, orientations, identities and networks."

Such a concept of transnational networks and links is highly relevant for understanding literature and its multiple contexts. For instance, scholars of ethnic and minority literatures in the United States may need to address their topics in a way that takes into account the transnational status of the particular ethnic community with its members' links with the values, politics, and cultural life in their original homeland. Similarly, a full understanding of migrant identity may demand particular linguistic skills since migration literatures are not necessarily available in the language of the dominant culture. As the Norwegian American writer Ole Rølvaag, known for his migration epic *Giants in the Earth* (1927), which was originally written in Norwegian, has suggested: "We can call these works and poems provincial or emigrant literature, but then we give the child the wrong name. For they are not that: they are American literature in the Norwegian language" (qtd in Skårdal 1962, 14). This description shows how an understanding of culture, literature, and identity as transnational changes the established view of nation as closed unity; through transnational links, alliances, and communities, the nation is hybridized and is in continuous dialogue with other (always already hybridized) cultures. This is evident in the formation of ethnic and migrant literary traditions voicing the experiences of particular groups such as Jewish Americans, Finnish Swedes, Cypriot British, and Turkish Germans, each with their literary traditions. Such literatures often mix different cultural traditions to interrogate nationalism and its official narrative to show what the hegemonic discourse suppresses and silences. As Bhabha (1990, 5) has suggested, there is no single narrative of a nation but discourses of nation remain unstable and ambiguous, selective and forgetting, and that "the origins of national traditions turn out to be as much acts of affiliation and establishment as they are moments of disavowal, displacement, exclusion and cultural contestation." Transnational literary connections also reveal how much the insistence on national purity has affected the formation of literary canon through selection and exclusion, making it difficult for postcolonial and migrant writers to gain acceptance.

The critic Paul Jay (2021, 10) understands such dialectics, links beyond the nation, as a key element in transnational literature: while mobility and migration link people with other parts of the world, such "transnational forces" affect the formation of national cultures so that "transnational spaces form a kind of crossroads." Such transnational spaces can be located in literatures telling of global mobility, as shown in the works of the South Asian American author Bharati Mukherjee that link South Asia with the United States. Transnational alliances and networks are also influential in the formation of border-crossing literary movements that challenge the categorizations of conventional nation-based literary histories. For example, the critic Brent Hayes Edwards (2003) has shown how the Harlem Renaissance associated with black US culture in the 1920s and 1930s benefits from the writers' links and connections with francophone intellectuals in Paris. Similarly, the network of the nineteenth-century anti-slavery writers and publishers in Britain and the United States, including figures such as William Wells Brown, the author of the first African American novel, and his British publisher Charles Gilpin, constructed a transatlantic protest literature where literature, politics, and publishing were united in a common cause (Drescher 2016).

Transnational identities have often been discussed in the context of cosmopolitanism. While the concept is often associated with selected citizens of the world, an elite, with experiences detached from the nation-state and its commitments and serving a worldwide community (Robbins 1998, 1–2), it is now also used in a different sense. Beck (2006, 9, 103), for instance, uses the notions of "contemporary cosmopolitanization" and "cosmopolitanism from below," which link it more with everyday border-crossings such as diverse modes of working, staying, and studying away from one's original country. An example of such labourers can be seen in the description of the migrant workers, European and African, working in the kitchen of the Imperial Hotel restaurant in London, as portrayed in Monica Ali's novel *In the Kitchen* (2009, 99–100):

> Every corner of the earth was represented here. Hispanic, Asian, African, Baltic and most places in between. Oona had taken on a new dishwasher, from Somalia or somewhere pretty much like that. The other one was Mongolian and the third was from – where? – the Philippines? Gabe had worked in places where porters came as a job lot, the first bringing along a cousin who recommended a brother-in-law who also brought his friend. Before you knew it there was a gang of them, and that only spelled trouble ahead. The room-service guy was fresh from Chile and Gabriel doubted that his English extended beyond fries and burgers and whatever else was on the menu. He'd fitted in all right. It was touching, really, to watch them all, every race, every colour, every creed.

As the passage indicates, the space of the restaurant kitchen shows the importance of globalization and the pull of global cities such as London. The presence of different languages and cultures in the same space indicates multiculturalism and hybridity – one could think about what kind of hybrid cooking such a team may create.

The experience of everyday cosmopolitanism is present in the recent notion of Afropolitanism, a concept that the postcolonial theorist Achille Mbembe (2007, 28) has described as "[a]wareness of the interweaving of the here and there, the presence of the elsewhere in the here and vice versa" to indicate how processes of globalization and immigration involve African mobilities and diasporas. An example of this can be seen in the experience of Afroeuropeans, a transnational community seeking common ground in the legacies of European colonialism and resistance to its racializing practices, shown, for instance, in the observations on contemporary black Europeans in novels such as Chika Unigwe's *On Black Sisters' Street* (2009), portraying the life of African prostitutes in Antwerp, Belgium, and their desire to be free.

In addition to texts addressing contemporary diasporas and mobilities, as in the passage from Monica Ali's novel referred to above, transnational histories and hybrid pasts are also common themes in migration literatures. In addressing such topics, texts often rely on tropes of memory and alternative histories to counter and challenge the views of the national canon, frequently using strategies such as intertextuality and tropes such as the palimpsest to signify how histories are transnational rather than national, yet often "multiply written and erased" (Kalogeras et al. 2021, 8). For instance, ethnic and postcolonial texts revisit and hybridize the past to voice what has been suppressed in nationalist historiography by showing how different histories affect each other, as in such well-known historical novels as Salman Rushdie's *The Moor's Last Sigh* (1995) and Caryl Phillips's *Crossing the River* (1993) (see Narain 2006; Ledent 2002). When Phillips rewrites historical sources such as slave merchant journals in his *Crossing the River*, fiction hybridizes the alleged historical truth and asks what has been forgotten or left out. In so doing, narratives uncover silenced pasts and hybridize national (hi)stories with their fixed positions of identity, showing the exclusionary character of the national narrative. Further examples of such historical narratives include Toni Morrison's novels *Beloved* (1987) and *Mercy* (2008), revisiting US cultural memories of slavery in different historical contexts. The attention to the past and the role of journeying is reflected in the way the spatio-temporality of migration is often addressed using such tropes as memory, home, and return that link the presence of the migrant with the past and the way migration has changed the journey and complicates belonging and the formation of a new identity (see Nyman 2024).

Transnational and Translational Identities

The notion of transnationalism is closely linked with the concept of diaspora, rooted in the Greek expression *diaspeirein* (διάσπείρειν) meaning dispersion (Oxford Reference 2022). While the term is often associated with historical diasporas such as those of the Jews and the Armenians, postcolonial diaspora theory has used the concept in other contexts to discuss a hybrid identity where the migrant's past experience of home culture continues to affect their migrant identity in the present but not necessarily in the sense of victimization (Cohen 2001; see also Tölölyan 1991). Because of this collective idea of a homeland and its transgenerational significance for their members, diasporas should be distinguished from more conventional migration where a similar unifying factor may not be found. Similarly, diaspora is not a synonym for exile, a term often used in reference to cosmopolitan modernist writers, who may find the experience of being cut off from their homeland inspiring, offering moments of creativity. Such a view has been suggested by Edward W. Said (2003, 181), who writes that "'exile' carries with it, I think, a touch of solitude and spirituality." Hybrid and diasporic space, however, challenges such an emphasis on aestheticized space and places the forming identity in diverse mobilities and encounters. Diaspora texts problematize the fixedness of any identity as well as ideas of home and belonging, revealing that the "[h]ome in the immigrant genre is a fiction that one can move beyond or recreate at will" (George 1996, 200). In the view of Avtar Brah (1996, 192–193; emphasis original), diaspora identity is based on what she calls "homing desire" that can be defined as a way of navigating between "the discourse of 'home' and 'dispersion' [...], *inscribing a homing desire while simultaneously critiquing discourses of fixed origins.*" Diaspora literature becomes involved in such mappings of identity by rewriting home and imagining ways of coping with its loss, as Susheila Nasta (2002, 7–8) has suggested.

Suggesting that diasporas are changing as part of increasing globalization, Robin Cohen (2001, xii) addresses more recent diasporas such as that of the Caribbeans, in the context of hybridization, as "a cultural diaspora" since it is produced also through cultural expressions (music, literature) and the migration experience. In his famous essay "Cultural Identity and Diaspora," the cultural critic Stuart Hall (2021a, 258) presents a similar view as he argues that cultural identity should not be understood as a reflection of a "collective 'one true self'" providing a stable sense of identity. Rather, cultural and especially diasporic identity as it is formed in the Caribbean as a result of various encounters is constantly changing. As Hall (2021a, 269; emphasis original) writes, it

> is defined, not by essence or purity, but by the recognition of a necessary heterogeneity and diversity; by a conception of 'identity' which lives with and through, not despite, difference; by *hybridity*. Diaspora identities are those which are constantly producing and reproducing themselves anew, through transformation and difference.

In Hall's (2021a, 269) view, Caribbean diaspora identity is, then, one that is based on "blends" and "mixes," both historical, cultural, racial, linguistic, involving narratives and cultural practices and leading to a hybrid "diaspora aesthetic" where it is possible to "see and recognise the different parts and histories of ourselves" that make and mark cultural identity (2021a, 270). For Hall (2021b), such ways of combining different histories of migration and cultural representation create something new through a process which he terms "diapora-isation" (or diasporization). In analyzing emergent black British films in the 1980s, including the documentary *Handsworth Songs* by the Black Audio Film Collective (1986), exploring black British life in the context of the 1980s civil disturbances, and the Kureishi–Frears films *My Beautiful Laundrette* (1985) and *Sammy and Rosie Get Laid* (1987), Hall (2021b, 253–254) argues that, by combining African and Caribbean experiences with Third World cinema and African and Asian aesthetics, such cultural texts are also involved in redefining Britishness rather than propagating a return to pure identities or "the ancestral past." Such processes reveal the extent to which hybridity is generated through global mobility, where established categories and national identities are challenged by the presence of different diasporic groups and taken in new directions.

Paul Gilroy's (1993) theory of the Black Atlantic has been particularly important in understanding the formation of cultural hybridity in the context of the black diasporic experience. Referring to this cultural formation as modernity's counterculture, Gilroy claims that, following slavery, a black diaspora community has formed around the Atlantic, from West Africa to the Caribbean and Britain, and to the United States. Rather than being excluded from modernity, blacks have contributed to its making in diverse ways. For instance, the work of the African American abolitionist Frederick Douglass should be examined in the context of British radicalism; similarly, the African American writer Richard Wright's view of black identity is produced in response to both the period's black identity politics and also Euro-American modernism. Gilroy's (1993) theory aims at the deconstruction of nationalisms and their insistence on allegedly pure identities. By showing how cultures and histories are embedded in each other and that mobilities and flows produce hybrid forms of culture, Gilroy (1993, 190) critiques essentialisms and argues that musical forms such as tango and jazz are not authentic or "Africentric" but formed through cultural contact, expressing "the flows, exchanges, and in-between elements that call the very desire to be centred into question." The idea of music as a metaphor of cultural hybridity has been applied by many texts such as Toni Morrison's *Jazz* (1993) and Jackie Kay's *Trumpet* (1998), but it plays a particularly emphatic role in *Drifting Latitudes* (2006), by the Sudanese/British/European writer Jamal Mahjoub. The novel shows a 1950s Liverpool jazz club as a location of cultural interchange and hybridity, allowing for a transformation of identity: "Once the music began to flow you could be anything or anyone you wanted to be" (Mahjoub 2006, 82). In the passage below, the global flows enter the contact zone of the port of Liverpool through different genres of music, transforming the harbour workers into musicians involved in appropriating foreign sound and, in so doing, changing it. Such hybridity is linked with the explicitly mentioned genres of fado, tango, and rembetika, all of which are historically formed through cultural encounters. To quote the novel:

> The music of a cacophony of places and styles from every corner of the plane. Most of the time it was just plain old Dixieland waterfront jazz. Out-of-tune four-piece combos of machine fitters and stevedores, off-duty tug pilots who could manage a passable imitation of New Orleans syncopation. Those were the regulars. On other nights there was a steady

stream of musicians passing through, bringing with them mournful songs from other ports. One night it might be Portuguese fado, the next night it would be a tango trio from Buenos Aires, or a bouzouki troupe from Piraeus; an Icelandic ragtime pianist; a nineteen-piece orchestra complete with tuba, all the way from Turku; Brazilian crooners nobody could understand until they started moving their hips; once even a trio of mournful zither players from the Black Sea.

(Mahjoub 2006, 41)

Through such global encounters, the novel also argues how Europe is a part of wider cultural flows. Each group of migrants brings something new and is thus involved in recasting the continent's history and identity (see Nyman 2017).

In processes of hybridization, formerly established identities and their locations become spaces of in-betweenness and sites of new meaning-making. In a reading of Bhabha, the translation theorist Susan Bassnett (2013, 342; emphasis original) sees the former's understanding of migration as "a *translational* phenomenon – a state in which meaning is constantly remade through encounters with other cultures." Such "cultural translation" has led to a wide-spread use of translation as a metaphor in migrant writing where cultural and geographical transitions involve elements of (non-)translatability (Bassnett 2013, 342). Examples of this range from Salman Rushdie's (1991, 17) claim that all migrants "having been borne across the world, are translated men" to texts foregrounding language barriers, translation, and problems of intercultural communication, such as Xiaolu Guo's *A Concise Chinese–English Dictionary for Lovers* (2007), Leila Aboulela's *The Translator* (1999), and the film *Lost in Translation* (dir. Sofia Coppola, 2003). While Coppola's film foregrounds the central characters' linguistic alienation, loneliness, and displacement in a foreign city and culture, Guo's diary novel focuses on language through its protagonist Z's persistent comparisons of Chinese, her first language, and English, the object of her learning, and the related world views that the protagonist considers contradictory. As critics such as Ulla Rahbek (2011) have noticed, Guo's novel narrates cultural translation, shown in Z's words that locate her transforming linguistic and cultural identity in the English language she gradually learns to master: "I steal your words. I steal all your beautiful words. I speak your language" (Guo 2008, 293). While the thematization of language and translation is often emphasized in postcolonial and border-crossing literatures, as in the play *Translations* (1980), by the Irish dramatist Brian Friel, focusing on the translation of local placenames by the colonizer in the process of map-making, the phenomenon that foregrounds translation and cross-cultural and cross-linguistic contacts is more general and is known as "translational literature" (Hassan 2008, 304) or transfiction (Kaindl 2014, 4). The reading of Aboulela's novel at the end of this chapter will explore the theme in more detail.

Migration and Displacement

While the previous sections have concentrated on narratives of diaspora and migration where hybridity emerges as an opportunity and may lead to empowerment, some experiences of migration are strongly marked by displacement and loss, telling of frustrating journeys and the impossibility of being accepted in destination countries. Displacement is often addressed in narratives of forced migration where the decision to leave one's home is not voluntary and where the experience of exile does not offer moments of creative solitude but traumatic memories and a lack of agency. An example of this can be seen in refugee writing, a genre in which the experience of exclusion is strongly present. This can be seen, for example, in the depiction of a group of refugee women in Sylvia Hoffmann's compilation "Swansea Collage," which appeared in the anthology *Between a Mountain and a Sea: Refugees Writing in Wales* (2003), a collection that includes many texts written by Welsh-based refugees themselves (see Nyman 2017). As Jopi Nyman (2017) has shown, a short poem included in "Swansea Collage" portrays a group of women gathered at the library who wish to communicate by email but have only each other to send messages to in this safe place (see Hoffman, comp. 2003, 77).

Frequently, refugee narratives place their subjects in conditions of what the Italian philosopher Giorgio Agamben (2000, 21–23) calls "bare life" or "naked life," in refugee camps or detention centres, to show spaces that are liminal, in-between, and do not allow for mobility and border-crossings, revealing the nightmarish and uncanny elements of the Third Space. In such conditions, as Nyman (2021) has shown, the act of doing turns into waiting, and activity into passivity, as expressed by the central character in Annie Holmes's (2016, 138) short story set in the 'Jungle,' the notorious refugee camp near Calais, France:

> Always night. [...] Always darkness. [...] The mortar blowing up the neighbours' house in the night in Hasakah. The boat from Turkey across the sea to Greece. All those nights waiting for trucks or waiting in trucks or running from trucks. Darkness!

Similarly, the first volume of the anthology series *Refugee Tales* contains several short stories where waiting is associated with insecurity and threatening deportation, as in Maria Lewycka's "The Dependant's Tale"

(2016; see Nyman 2020). Telling of a family facing forced return to their country of origin, Lewycka's story uses a child's perspective to narrate anxiety and emerging mental disorders, transforming the centre into an uncanny site of terror (see Nyman 2020):

> The nightmare always starts in the same way: a big man standing at the foot of my bed, shouting at me. "Get up! Hurry hurry hurry! Pack up your stuff! We've come to take you away." I call out to my parents, but they have disappeared. My little brother starts yelling, but the man just shouts again.
> Sometimes it's a nightmare, and sometimes it's for real.
>
> *(Lewycka 2016, 85)*

While narratives of forced migration and the refugee experience often foreground experiences of displacement and racism, as in Caryl Phillips's *A Distant Shore* (2003), a novel culminating in the violent death of its black protagonist at the hands of thugs in a town in the North of England, their power counters the stereotypical representations of popular media that often imagine forced migrants as a mass (see Marfleet 2006; Nyman 2017, 15–35). In Phillips's novel, the reader learns of its protagonist's personal history as a soldier and his attempt to start a new life in Britain. Through ideas of displacement and removal, refugee narratives voice questions of unbelonging and exclusion, as in Lewycka's text, shown also in their incarceration and exclusion from public space, but such narratives also imagine the possibilities for belonging and transnational alliances. Hybridity, then, has a double function: for the dominant discourse, it emerges as a threat to national unity, but the presence of the migrant also transforms the established identity of the nation by functioning as an agent of diasporization in the sense suggested by Hall (2021b).

Encounters: Hybridity and Appropriation

The encounters generated by migration and other cross-cultural encounters may be understood positively or negatively, and they extend well beyond literature to questions of power and cultural rights. We have already commented briefly on the role of music in the context of hybridity, suggesting that musical genres can be formed in response to cultural contacts, as in the case of jazz and blues. Such a process is, however, continuous, and, as an example, several scholars have looked at the influence of African American music and dance at European music cultures, finding such hybridization, as the essay collection *Blackening Europe: The African American Presence* (Raphael-Hernandez, ed. 2004) shows, in cases such as black dance culture in modernist Paris and post-World War II Germany, in Soviet jazz sub-cultures, and in local versions of hip-hop and rap in Hungary and France, to mention only a few examples. Rather than merely being local versions of American globalization, such responses are translocal in the sense proposed by Jan Nederveen Pieterse (2009, 85; emphasis original), involving "an *outward looking* sense of place" in their combination of the local and the global elements. The resulting cultural product is indeed more than the sum of its parts and involves negotiation.

Another significant example of cultural appropriation worth discussing in this context concerns dress and fashion, which play a role in several post-colonial debates concerning migration and ethnic minorities. First, clothing and the use of traditional clothing constitute a marker of migrant visibility and difference, which are often treated with suspicion or non-acceptance. A particular case in point concerns Muslim women's dress and the veil in particular, shown in the French ban on covering one's face in public places. While the practice of the hijab has different discursive meanings, serving as a marker of Orientalism and sensualism but also as a sign of patriarchal subjection of women, its function of marking belonging to a religious community may also be empowering and signalling resistance to Western values and discourses (Pereira-Ares 2018, 152–153). Fashion and dress can be examined from the perspective of cultural hybridity, including, for instance, the phenomenon of Islamic fashion that brings together Western and Muslim practices and creativities (see Tarlo and Moors 2013). Second, postcolonial fashion scholars have also shown how the process of forming black identity through fashionable dress can be traced in magazine debates in 1930s France and also in Du Bois's 1900 photography exhibition "The American Negro" revealing the extent to which African Americans used fashion as "an emancipatory self-fashioning strategy" (Gaugele and Titton 2019, 23). In literature, such postcolonial self-fashioning can be located in representations of African and, in particular, Caribbean migrants, as shown in Christine Checinska's (2019) reading of the figure of Sir Galahad in Sam Selvon's migrant novel *The Lonely Londoners* (1956). In Checinska's (2019, 85–86) view, Sir Galahad exhibits the Windrush Generation's awareness of style, being highly aware of the latest fashion and cuts, preferring a "zoot" approach and style over practicality and discretion. A similar attention to dress can be traced in the ageing Jamaican protagonist in Bernardine Evaristo's (2013, 109) *Mr Loverman*, with his "gold cufflinks," "starched white shirt," and a suit tailored by Levinsky in Golders Green, the only remaining tailor able to "make a suit in authentic fifties style without charging Savile Row prices." Third, the dominant culture's interchange with minority culture has also been addressed from a critical perspective and is regarded quite negatively as a form of cultural appropriation where the dominant culture is seen to capitalize on marginalized groups and their cultural traditions. Such instances are widely debated in the social and other media and often addressed simplistically (see Lenard and Balint 2020).

What distinguishes such situations from acts of appropriation performed by postcolonial writers and artists is the role of power and prestige. From the perspective of the marginalized, involvement in appropriating the dominant culture and its symbolic power is a way to resist hegemonies and established hierarchies. In the case of the dominant culture adopting and appropriating the symbols and practices of the subordinate group, the case is more complex since it may involve economic benefits or inability to reflect on the cultural and symbolic value that the traditional headdress or clothing may have for a particular ethnic group. A good example of this concerns the traditional Sámi dress, which has often been appropriated for commercial, entertainment, and touristic purposes by Finnish and other companies and public personalities. From the perspective of the indigenous Sámi, as Piia Nuorgam (2017, 23–23) writes, such appropriations remain negligent and unaware of the collective meaning of the dress as a marker of cultural heritage and community identity and also of individual identity.

In a discussion of cultural appropriation in the context of music, James O. Young (2011, 183–185) suggests that appropriation emerges as problematic in two central ways: one concerning the appropriation as a misrepresentation promoting stereotypical views of the other culture, and the second pointing to its potentially harmful effects on the minority and indigenous cultures involved, such as assimilation and loss of cultural heritage. Young (2011, 185) underlines the ethical role of artists borrowing from other cultures, urging them to avoid representing their hybrid art as emerging from within the culture and not to engage in offensive appropriation of, for instance, sacred objects and practices. What is important to recognize in this context is that appropriation and cultural borrowing are not necessarily condemnable, if they do not involve "cultural offence and cultural misrepresentation" (Lenard and Balint 2020, 332), but may also lead to aesthetically and cultural relevant hybrids, especially in the arts, as Young's (2011) discussion of examples ranging from Mozart to white blues musicians shows. In other words, all cultural exchanges are located in historical and cultural contexts that need to be taken into account when examining their particular features.

To conclude, the discussion of hybridity in the context of race, ethnicity, and migration in this chapter has shown that the concept is a useful tool to challenge fixed ideologies and discourses of nationalism and purity and may function as a form of counter-discourse (Tiffin 1987). Tools and tropes such as mimicry and passing call dominant hierarchies into question and provide alternative perspectives for understanding the identities of different migrants and minorities. Similarly, transnationalism, transcultural, and translational connections between cultures, languages, and diasporas open up identifications that cannot be bordered or limited to any one nation. The counter-discursive role of hybridity is also relevant as a means to understand different forms of appropriation and their varied contexts.

Textual Analysis: Leila Aboulela, *The Translator* (1999)

The Translator (2008), by the Sudanese-born Scottish Muslim writer Leila Aboulela, foregrounds issues of migration, diaspora, and cultural translation in many ways that are relevant to the concerns of this chapter. The novel focuses on cultural encounters through the experiences of Sammar, a Muslim migrant from Sudan who works as a translator at a university in Aberdeen and falls in love with Rae Isles, a professor of Middle Eastern Studies, for whom she translates various Arabic documents. Through Sammar and the problematic romance, the novel addresses questions of identity in migration and the possibility of cross-cultural understanding and relationships. The novel is structured in two parts: the first part focuses on Sammar's developing relationship and life in Scotland, while the second part shows her return to Sudan to be with her son and family following the rift between Rae and herself that has caused her to demand that Rae should convert to Islam so that they can get married. The final chapters provide a happy ending to the situation.

Migration is central to the world of Aboulela's novel, extending in time from Sammar's parents' studying in London and Rae's personal history, including years of working in Morocco and memories of an uncle who has emigrated to Egypt and converted to Islam, to contemporary migrations such as that of Sammar and her husband, and also labour migration to Qatar, which many of the minor characters find attractive. The experience of migration is central for Sammar, who lives the lonely life of a widow in Aberdeen, far from her family in Sudan. Having arrived in Scotland several years earlier with her Sudanese husband Tarig, who has wished to attend medical school, her life has drastically changed upon his accidental death and the consequent change in her life. For the past four years, Sammar has lived alone in Aberdeen, while her son has been raised by her aunt and her mother-in-law Mahasen in Khartoum. The representation of Sammar's migration combines her traumatized experience of her husband's death with a generally negative attitude towards her host country and its estranging culture. Her contacts with Scotland are practically limited to her place of employment, where she interacts primarily with other migrant workers and with department members and PhD students.

Owing to her past migration history, UK passport, and excellent command of English, Sammar's position is exceptional as she does not need to worry about work and residence permits. On a general level, multiculturality is recognized by her host society and its institutions, seen in several attempts to understand and recognize minority cultures, including the university's specially designated prayer rooms for Muslims and the hospital's provision of expert help upon her husband's death. The description of the small mosque on the university campus, "a room given over to the Muslim students" and located "in another building, older and more beautiful than the modern building where her department was" (Aboulela 2008, 72), shows that space is hybridized, allowing for different faiths and practices and forming a space of conviviality and tolerance, but also indicating the minority culture's need to form a community as is evident in her wish to join communal prayers. Sammar's integration, her involvement with the project at the university, and her collaboration with Rae are signs of her hybridity, as is also her eventual marriage to him. For many migrants, however, to attain such belonging is difficult since the prevailing media discourse provides negative views of Muslims as Other. This is evident in the view of her Pakistani-born friend Yasmin, Rae's secretary, who in her views distinguishes between the values of the British and those of migrants: "'We are not like them', or 'We have close family ties, not like them'" (Aboulela 2008, 11).

Diaspora and migration literatures often focus on home and its reconstruction in the conditions of global mobility. In the case of Sammar, regardless of her lengthy stay in Scotland, it is not represented as a home that can offer proper belonging. The small apartment where she has lived following Tarig's death is portrayed as a "hospital room" with "ugly curtains" and a "faded bed-spread" (Aboulela 2008, 65), reflecting her trauma and over-extended mourning. The city is described as a space that she feels estranged from, both physically and mentally:

> She was afraid of rain, afraid of the fog and the snow which came to this country, afraid of the wind even. At such times she would stay indoors and wait, watching from her window people doing what she couldn't do.
>
> *(Aboulela 2008, 3)*

For Sammar, this place is an example of not-home, without the sun, warmth, and family networks associated with Sudan. For her, the migration has generated a persistent culture shock where Otherness is constantly present and prevents her from integrating into the host culture: "She had stacked the differences; the weather, the culture, the modernity, the language, the silence of the muezzin, then found that the colours of mud, sky and leaves were different too" (Aboulela 2008, 43). Similarly, the behaviour and values of the people contrast with her ideas: students are disrespectful towards their professors, men wear earrings, and public spaces display advertising for cigarettes, lingerie, and nightclubs (see Aboulela 2008, 68). Through such images, the text shows how Sammar's relationship with secular Britain and its inhabitants is rooted in cultural difference, where her positionality as a Muslim is constantly present and supported by the novel's detailed descriptions of religious rituals such as praying and fasting that indicate Sammar's faith (see Aboulela 2008, 35–36). For her, Muslim identity is personal since it generates what Wail S. Hassan calls "a sense of wholeness" (2008, 311), and it is also cultural, serving as a link to the larger community of Muslims and offering a possibility to construct a transnational identity that may serve as a counterpoint to the dominant Britishness. This is visible in her comment that she has "gradually" understood "that she was not alone, that not everyone believed what the billboards said" (Aboulela 2008, 68), which Waïl S. Hassan (2008, 316) calls "a reverse-Eurocentrism." She also finds a sense of belonging in a shop run by a Bengali migrant, where she can find halal food, tins with Arabic script, and even "a packet of falafel mix" from Alexandria (Aboulela 2008, 64), a further example of the novel's method of foregrounding cultural hybridity and appropriation.

As is the case in many migration narratives, the previous home location and its associated past play a significant role. While Sammar's memories of home appear to be represented in a positive light, it is not represented as a site of mere nostalgia but one that also involves contradictions and conflicts. This becomes clear on her return to Sudan following her confrontation with Rae and her misreading of his emotions. Initially, the return restores her sense of self, the heat being good for "her bones" and restoring her youthfulness: the body and skin "cleared and forgot […] wool and gloves" (Aboulela 2008, 132). In this space of home, she feels welcome, finding belonging in the networks of family, friends, and neighbours. However, the home that she shares with her in-laws contains memories of a painful past and is signified in the photograph of Tarig, which generates emotional responses and tears. The contradictions surface in her mother-in-law's comments that hurt Sammar: Mahasen attacks her verbally, seeing her as useless and a burden on the family finances, which culminates in her act of blaming Sammar for Tarig's death and urging her to return to Scotland (see Aboulela 2008, 165–167). This estrangement from home and the family is further addressed in Sammar's continuous feelings for Rae, which she cannot suppress, to the extent that home turns into a form of "exile from him" (Aboulela 2008, 160). Through the emerging sense of not-home, Sammar's story shows how migration and diaspora literatures may use the trope of return in a way that is not a solution to the migrant's loss but juxtaposes imagined and nostalgic pasts with hard realities (Boehmer 1995, 201). This reveals how Sammar's position is insecure in both countries, showing a sense of non-belonging that return mobility cannot solve.

However, in-betweenness and the problem of belonging appear to connect Sammar to Rae, who is represented as a typical middle-class academic working at a Scottish university, divorced, with a daughter at a public school and an ex-wife working for the United Nations in Geneva. While he enjoys a reputation as a media expert on the Middle East, he also has a more futile background that has made him sensitive to the question of being a migrant in a foreign culture. The novel reveals that Rae lived in Morocco for a period of several years after his first degree and this experience provided him with insight into the politics and culture of the region. Working in a crafts shop frequented by European expatriates and diplomats, and "Surrounded by calligraphy, arabesque [...], Rae learnt what he had not learnt in university nor in the debating society" (Aboulela 2008, 57). As he mixes more with the local young people, learning the local language and living with Air Maroc pilots, he is considered to be transgressive by many Europeans, including his first wife, the sheltered Anglo-Spanish Amelia, who has grown up in Morocco: "there was something *Arab* about this young Scottish man. Something Arab that Amelia had wanted for years" (Aboulela 2008, 59; emphasis original). By exoticizing Rae, the novel places him in the space of hybridity and hints at his potential to leave the values of white European culture, which appeals to Sammar, who cannot marry a Christian and ponders upon his potential conversion (see Aboulela 2008, 21). For Sammar, the title of Rae's book, *The Illusion of an Islamic Threat*, seems to distinguish his values from the majority and to indicate a potential border-crossing.

As a hybrid text, *The Translator* appropriates the literary tradition. It writes back to Tayeb Salih's *Season of Migration to the North* (1969), a Sudanese novel in which the protagonist travels to Europe and back, involving himself in acts of gendered violence that lead to despair. Its emphasis on the migrant's failure is challenged by Aboulela's focus on religion and its potential for redemption (Hassan 2008, 300). More significantly, it appropriates the genre of the romantic novel, and, written by a Muslim woman, it exemplifies a recent trend in which the conventions of the romance are hybridized to discuss an identity characteristic of the contemporary world that is both intimate and located socio-politically (Stotesbury 2005). In an interview, Aboulela offers the following view:

> I saw *The Translator* as being a Muslim *Jane Eyre*. The problem in *Jane Eyre* is that Mr Rochester can't marry both Bertha and Jane at the same time. As a Muslim I was reading it, and from an Islamic point of view

there *is* no problem, because he can be married to both women at the same time.

(Chambers 2011, 109; emphasis original)

While the novel does not discuss polygamy, the romance is strongly anchored in Islamic beliefs that Sammar cannot transgress. Marriage with a non-believer is impossible, which leads to her return home. The narrative is full of romantic expectations and tropes. Sammar aches to meet with Rae, wishing that they would continue their intimate discussion in the office. Similarly, Rae wants to show her places that link Scotland and Sudan: "Show her a bend in the Dee and she would see the Nile, show her a house with a flat roof, a lighthouse that looked like a white minaret" (Aboulela 2008, 55). She also imagines a shared future where she will perform a traditional female role and cook for Rae. Rae's daughter Mhairi would also live them, and the women would shop together for "pretty things, soap that smelt of raspberries and ribbons of different widths for her [Mhairi's] hair" (Aboulela 2008, 115). When back in Sudan, rather than forgetting him, Sammar keeps dreaming of Rae and feels rejected by him in her dreams. The final chapters of the novel reveal Rae's conversion, conveyed to Sammar in a letter by Rae's Muslim friend Fareed, that leads to Sammar's message to Rae and his arrival in Khartoum, culminating in the decision to marry and return to Scotland with her son Amir as a family.

In Aboulela's novel, the romance plot is, however, also a narrative device that tells of cultural border-crossings and is part of its thematic of cultural encounters and of translation in particular (see Cooper 2006; Hassan 2008). At the textual level, the English-language novel contains many Arabic words and Islamic terms, which underlines that migrants' texts are not pure either linguistically or ideologically but foreground their hybrid origins in many ways. In this novel, it is through translation that the difficulties in understanding the other can be relieved even though perfect equivalent meanings do not exist. Here Sammar's profession as a translator is particularly relevant, and her sensitivity to language is frequently shown in her pondering on words, phrases, and their meanings. The two languages are both present in the text, often defamiliarizing the text but also indicating the gap between the two worlds and their linguistic codings that need to be bridged. A good example of this is Sammar's search for a particular spice she needs when cooking for Rae but whose English name she does not know:

Spice that she had to search for, the name unknown in English, not in any of the Arabic-English dictionaries that she had. *Habbahan, habbahan.* She must walk around the supermarket, frantically searching for something she could not ask about, and she was a translator, she should know. *Habbahan*. Without it, the soup would not taste right, would not be complete. At last, she found the *habbahan*. It existed, it had a name: whole green cardamom.

(Aboulela 2008, 94)

Significantly, the multiplicity of meanings extends to the names of the central characters that have different meanings in different languages. In addition to the naming of Rae and Sammar discussed in the novel, other names, including Mahasen (beauty; merits), Tarig (striker), and Amir (prince; ruler) are also relevant. In the case of two romance protagonists, their naming is discussed from the perspective of ambiguity, thus adding to the theme of translation. In the case of Rae, the double meanings of his name are evoked explicitly: "'Rye, *rai*?' [...] *Rai*' was opinion in Arabic. 'Yes, [...] he has lots of opinions'" (Aboulela 2008, 150). Similarly, the pronunciation and meanings of Sammar are also directly addressed and mentioned to be different in Arabic and English:

"Do you pronounce it like the season, summer?" Rae asked the first time she had met him. "Yes, but it does not have the same meaning." And because he wanted to know more, she said, "It means conversations with friends, late at night. It's what the desert nomads liked to do, talk leisurely by the light of the moon, when it was no longer so hot and the day's work was over."

(Aboulela 2008, 5)

The novel uses the idea of translation in both linguistic and cultural contexts. As Brenda Cooper (2006, 327) suggests, Sammar struggles when translating the realities of the host country into her world, and the resultant images are referred to as hallucinations in which, if the translation is successful, the worlds fuse into each other. When she finds a solution to translate "the Qudsi Hadiths" (Aboulela 2008, 40) and climbs the stairs to her apartment so that she can read her version to Rae, she enters "a hallucination in which the world had swung around. Home and the past had come here and balanced just for her" (Aboulela 2008, 40). What the passage indicates is that she is entering a state of cultural hybridity where a new, balanced identity is constructed, linking her past self with a new identity, translating her into something else. Similarly, her task in the novel is to translate Rae, not only to translate for him, and play an active role in his transformation and acceptance of a Muslim identity that link them with each other (see Chambers 2011, 107–108). This shows how translation leads to border-crossing hybridity where characters who occupy liminal positions in their respective societies – Sammar as a North African migrant who questions the dominant discourse and meanings that English provides, Rae as a Western academic who has devoted his career to understanding and defending the Other – are able to make sense of their in-betweenness.

To conclude, through its narratives of diaspora and migration, the novel functions as a transformative narrative and "inserts and reinforces heterogeneity" (Stein 2004, 54) in contemporary Britain, thus hybridizing conventional narratives of national identity based on alleged uniformity and exclusion. In addition to representing the construction of Sammar's and Rae's identities as hybrid, and their return as a way to settle in, and "reterritorialize," Britain, it reveals the transformation of Western societies and the need to accommodate alternative experiences.

Further Reading

Bassnett, Susan. 2013. "Postcolonialism and/as Translation." In *The Oxford Handbook of Postcolonial Studies*, edited by Graham Huggan, 340–358. Oxford: Oxford University Press.

Gilroy, Paul. 1993. *The Black Atlantic: Modernity and Double Consciousness*. London: Verso.

Jay, Paul. 2021. *Transnational Literature: The Basics*. New York: Routledge.

Nederveen Pieterse, Jan. 2009. *Globalization and Culture: Global Mélange*. 2nd ed. London: Rowman and Littlefield.

Nyman, Jopi. 2017. *Displacement, Memory, and Travel in Contemporary Migrant Writing*. Leiden: Brill.

Further Exercises

Faïza Guène, Kiffe Kiffe Tomorrow (2006; Kiffe kiffe demain [2004])

Guène's novel, originally written in French, approaches the migrant's experience from the contemporary perspective of fifteen-year-old Doria, a French Moroccan girl living with her mother in the suburbs of Paris. Employing a sardonic voice, Doria comments on her family, school, and social life from a migrant's point of view. What does the following passage say about migrants and stereotypes? How does it challenge them? How does it describe the state of multiculturalism in Doria's surroundings?

Ramadan started a little over a week ago. I made Mom sign a form saying why I wouldn't be eating in the cafeteria. When I gave it to the principal, he asked if I was trying to put one over on him. His name is Monsieur Loiseau. He's fat, he's stupid, he smokes a pipe, and when he opens his mouth it reeks of cheap wine. At the end of the day, his big sister picks him up out front of school in a red hatchback. So when he wants to play the big boss, he's got a real credibility problem.

Anyway, M. Loiseau asked me if I was taking him for a ride because he thought I'd forged my mom's name on the paper. He's an idiot. If I'd wanted to fake a signature, I'd have made it look like a real one. On this thing Mom just made a kind of squiggly line. She's not used to holding a pen. The jerk didn't even think about that, didn't even ask himself why her signature might be weird. He's one of those people who think illiteracy is like AIDS. It only exists in Africa.

Not very long ago Mom started working. She cleans rooms at the Formula 1 Motel in Bagnolet while she's waiting to find something else, soon I hope. Sometimes, when she gets home late at night, she cries. She says it's from feeling so tired. She struggles even harder during Ramadan, because when it's time to break the fast, around 5:30 P.M., she's still at work. So if she wants to eat, she has to hide some dates in her smock. She even sewed an inside pocket so she can be sly about it, because if her boss saw her he'd be totally pissed. Everyone calls her "Fatma" at the Formula 1. They shout at her all the time, and they keep a close watch on her to make sure she doesn't steal anything from the rooms. Of course, Mom's name isn't Fatma, it's Yasmina. It must really give Monsieur Winner a charge to call all the Arabs "Fatma," all the blacks "Mamadou," and all the Chinese "Ping-Pong." Pretty freaking lame.

(Guène 2018, 2)

Gish Jen, Mona in the Promised Land *(1996)*

Jen's comic novel, set in the late 1960s, focuses on the hybridization of identity through the Chinese American Chang family who move to live in a multicultural (mainly Jewish) neighbourhood in New York. The following passage focuses on the exchange between Helen Chang and her adolescent daughter Mona who has decided to be Jewish. Read through the passage and think about its discussion of ethnic and cultural identity. Is group identity a choice or a performance? What does it say about the making of Americanness, the promised land of the novel? What is the relationship between 'race' and ethnicity? How would the passage read in the context of mimicry or cultural appropriation?

"You are the one who brought us up to speak English. You said you would bend like bamboo instead of acting like you were planted by Bell Telephone. You said we weren't pure Chinese anymore, the parents had to accept we would be something else."

"American, not Jewish." Helen assigns Mona a piece of pork to slice while she herself cleans the fish, and it calms them both down to see what a nice job Mona can still do – thin, and across the grain. (Lucky for them, Mona is the reformed kind of Jew that does not observe the many rules regarding fins and hoofs, mollusks and ruminants.)

"Jewish is American," Mona says. "American means being whatever you want, and I happened to pick being Jewish."

"Since when do children pick this, pick that? You tell me. Children are supposed to listen to their parents. Otherwise, the world become crazy. Who knows? Tomorrow you will come home and tell me you want to be black."

"How can I turn black? That's a race, not a religion." (Mona says this even though she knows some kids studying to be Bobby Seale [an African American Black Panther activist]. They call each other brother, and eat soul food instead of subs, and wear their hair in the baddest Afros they can manage.)

"And after that you're going to come home and tell me you want to be a boy instead of a girl." […] "And after that you are going to come home and tell me you want to be a tree."

(Jen 1996, 49)

James Mercer Langston Hughes, "Cross" (1994 [1926])

The text of Langston Hughes's short poem can be found in *The Collected Poems of Langston Hughes* (1994) or online (https://www.poetryfoundation.org/poems/150989/cross). Published originally in 1926, this poem by the African American writer addresses its speaker's mixed-race background with mixed feelings. Read the poem and discuss ways in which the position between two cultures and racialized groups is negative and/or positive for the speaker. How has the background affected his experience of racial exclusion and inability to identify with either ethnicity?

Gogol Bordello, "Immigraniada (We Comin' Rougher)" (2012)

The New York-based rock band Gogol Bordello, led by the Ukrainian-born singer Eugene Hütz, consists of musicians representing different countries, cultures, and musical traditions. Watch the music video of their immigration-focused "Immigraniada (We Comin' Rougher)," available on their official website www.gogolbordello.com, and discuss the following questions: How are migration and cultural hybridity represented visually, musically, and textually in the song lyrics? How does the text play with iconic images and symbols of migration? How does it comment on politics and nationalism in the context of the United States?

References

Aboulela, Leila. 2008 [originally published 1999]. *The Translator.* Edinburgh: Polygon.

Acheraïou, Amar. 2011. *Questioning Hybridity, Postcolonialism and Globalization.* Houndmills: Palgrave Macmillan. https://doi.org/10.1057/9780230305243

Agamben, Giorgio. 2000 [originally published 1996]. *Means without End: Notes on Politics.* Translated by Vincenzo Binetti and Cesare Casarino. Minneapolis: University of Minnesota Press.

Ali, Monica. 2009. *In the Kitchen.* London: Doubleday.

Anderson, Benedict. 2006 [originally published 1983]. *Imagined Communities: Reflections on the Origin and Spread of Nationalism.* 2nd rev. ed. London: Verso.

Anzaldúa, Gloria. 1987. *Borderlands/La Frontera: The New Mestiza.* San Francisco: Spinsters/Aunt Lute.

Ashcroft, Bill, Gareth Griffiths, and Helen Tiffin. 2000 [originally published 1998]. *Post-colonial Studies: The Key Concepts.* 2nd ed. London: Routledge.

Bassnett, Susan. 2013. "Postcolonialism and/as Translation." In *The Oxford Handbook of Postcolonial Studies,* edited by Graham Huggan, 340–358. Oxford: Oxford University Press. https://doi.org/10.1093/oxfordhb /9780199588251.013.0022

Beck, Ulrich. 2000 [originally published 1997]. *What Is Globalization?* Translated by Patrick Camiller. Cambridge: Polity.

Beck, Ulrich. 2006 [originally published 2004]. *The Cosmopolitan Vision.* Translated by Ciaran Cronin. Cambridge: Polity.

Bhabha, Homi K. 1990. "Introduction." In *Nation and Narration,* edited by Homi K. Bhabha, 1–7. London: Routledge.

Bhabha, Homi K. 1994. *The Location of Culture.* London: Routledge.

Boehmer, Elleke. 1995. *Colonial/Postcolonial Literature: Migrant Metaphors.* Oxford: Oxford University Press.

Du Bois, W.E.B. 1903. *The Souls of Black Folk.* Chicago: A. C. McClurg.

Brah, Avtar. 1996. *Cartographies of Diaspora: Contesting Identities.* London: Routledge.

Brennan, Jonathan. 2002. "Introduction." In *Mixed Race Literature,* edited by Jonathan Brennan, 1–56. Stanford: Stanford University Press.

Chambers, Claire. 2011. *British Muslim Fictions: Interviews with Contemporary Writers.* Houndmills: Palgrave Macmillan.

Chechinska, Christine. 2019. "(Re-)fashioning African Diasporic Masculinities." In *Fashion and Postcolonial Critique,* edited by Elke Gaugele and Monica Titton, 74–89. Berlin: Sternberg Press. https://doi.org/10.21937 /9783956794650

Cohen, Robin. 2001 [originally published 1997]. *Global Diasporas: An Introduction.* London: Routledge.

Conrad, Joseph. 1992 [originally published 1895]. *Almayer's Folly,* edited by Jacques Berthoud. Oxford: Oxford University Press.

Cooper, Brenda. 2006. "Look Who's Talking? Multiple Worlds, Migration and Translation in Leila Aboulela's *The Translator*." *The Translator*, vol. 12, no. 2, pp. 323–344. https://doi.org/10.1080/13556509.2006.10799221

Coppola, Sofia, director. *Lost in Translation*. 2003. American Zoetrope. 1 hr., 42 minutes.

Drescher, Michael Rodegang. 2016. "The Publishing of Protest: Brown, Pennington, and Gilpin's Network of Dissent." In *Racial and Ethnic Identities in the Media*, edited by Elefheria Arapoglou, Yiorgos Kalogeras, and Jopi Nyman, 59–76. London: Palgrave Macmillan. https://doi.org.10.1057/978-1-137-56834-2_4

Edwards, Brent Hayes. 2003. *The Practice of Diaspora: Literature, Translation, and the Rise of Black Internationalism*. Cambridge: Harvard University Press.

Evaristo, Bernardine. 2013. *Mr Loverman*. London: Penguin.

Gaugele, Elke, and Monica Titton. 2019. "Fashion and Postcolonial Critique: An Introduction." In *Fashion and Postcolonial Critique*, edited by Elke Gaugele and Monica Titton, 10–37. Berlin: Sternberg Press. https://doi.org/10.21937/9783956794650

George, Rosemary Marangoly. 1996. *The Politics of Home: Postcolonial Relocations and Twentieth-century Fiction*. Cambridge: Cambridge University Press.

Gilroy, Paul. 1993. *The Black Atlantic: Modernity and Double Consciousness*. London: Verso.

Gogol Bordello. 2012 [originally published 2010]. "Immigraniada (We Comin' Rougher)." http://www.gogolbordello.com/

Guène, Faïza. 2006 [originally published 2004]. *Kiffe Kiffe Tomorrow (Kiffe kiffe demain)*. Translated by Sarah Adams. Orlando: Harcourt.

Guo, Xiaolu. 2008. *A Concise Chinese–English Dictionary for Lovers*. London: Vintage.

Hall, Stuart. 2021a [originally published 1990]. "Cultural Identity and Diaspora." In *Selected Writings on Race and Difference*, by Stuart Hall, edited by Paul Gilroy and Ruth Wilson Gilmore, 257–271. Durham: Duke University Press.

Hall, Stuart. 2021b [originally published 1992]. "New Ethnicities." In *Selected Writings on Race and Difference*, by Stuart Hall, edited by Paul Gilroy and Ruth Wilson Gilmore, 246–256. Durham: Duke University Press.

Hassan, Waïl S. 2008. "Leila Aboulela and the Ideology of Muslim Immigrant Fiction." *Novel: A Forum on Fiction*, vol. 41, no. 2–3, pp. 298–319. https://doi.org/10.1215/ddnov.041020298

Hoffmann, Sylvie, comp. 2003. "Swansea Collage." In *Between a Mountain and a Sea: Refugees Writing in Wales*, edited by Eric Ngalle Charles, Tom Cheesman, and Sylvie Hoffman, 74–81. Swansea: Hafan Books.

Holmes, Annie. 2016. "Oranges in the River." In *Breach*, by Olumide Popoola and Annie Holmes, 125–139. London: Peirene Press.

Hughes, Langston. 1994. "Cross." In *The Collected Poems of Langston Hughes*, by Langston Hughes, edited by Arnold Rampersad and David Roessel, 58. New York: Knopf.

Jay, Paul. 2021. *Transnational Literature: The Basics*. New York: Routledge.

Jen, Gish. 1996. *Mona in the Promised Land*. London: Granta Books.

Johnson, Paul Christopher. 2017. "Syncretism and Hybridization." In *The Oxford Handbook of the Study of Religion*, edited by Michael Stausberg and Steven Engler, 754–772. Oxford: Oxford University Press. https://doi.org /10.1093/oxfordhb/9780198729570.013.50

Kaindl, Klaus. 2014. "Going Fictional! Translators and Interpreters in Literature and Film: An Introduction." In *Transfiction: Research into the Realities of Translation Fiction*, edited by Klaus Kaindl and Karlheinz Spitzl, 1–26. Amsterdam: John Benjamins. https://doi.org/10.1075/btl.110.01kai

Kalogeras, Yiorgos, Johanna C. Kardux, Monika Mueller, and Jopi Nyman. 2021. "Introduction." In *Palimpsests in Ethnic and Postcolonial Literature and Culture: Surfacing Histories*, edited by Yiorgos Kalogeras, Johanna C. Kardux, Monika Mueller, and Jopi Nyman, 1–17. Cham: Palgrave Macmillan. https://doi.org/10.1007/978-3-030 -64586-1_1

Kunzru, Hari. 2003 [originally published 2002]. *The Impressionist.* London: Penguin.

Ledent, Bénédicte. 2002. *Caryl Phillips.* Manchester: Manchester University Press.

Lenard, Patti Tamara, and Peter Balint. 2020. "What Is (the Wrong of) Cultural Appropriation?" *Ethnicities*, vol. 20, no. 2, pp. 331–352. https://doi.org/10 .1177/1468796819866498

Lewycka, Marina. 2016. "The Dependant's Tale." In *Refugee Tales*, edited by David Herd and Anna Pincus, 85–91. Manchester: Comma.

London, Jack. 1992 [originally published 1902]. "Bâtard." In *Call of the Wild, White Fang, and Other Stories*, edited with an Introduction by Earle Labor and Robert C. Leitz, III, 293–307. Oxford: Oxford University Press.

Loomba, Ania. 1999. *Colonialism/Postcolonialism.* London: Routledge.

Mahjoub, Jamal. 2006. *The Drift Latitudes.* London: Chatto and Windus.

Marfleet, Phil. 2006. *Refugees in a Global Era.* Houndmills: Palgrave Macmillan.

Mbembe, Achille. 2007 [originally published 2006]. "Afropolitanism." Translated by Laurent Chauvet. In *Africa Remix: Contemporary Art of a Continent*, edited by Simon Njami, 26–30. Johannesburg: Jacana Media.

Moynihan, Sinead. 2010. *Passing into the Present: Contemporary American Fiction of Racial and Gender Passing.* Manchester: Manchester University Press.

Narain, Mona. 2006. "Re-Imagined Histories: Rewriting the Early Modern in Rushdie's *The Moor's Last Sigh*." *Journal for Early Modern Cultural Studies*, vol. 6, no. 2, pp. 55–68. https://www.jstor.org/stable/40339573

Nasta, Susheila. 2002. *Home Truths: Fictions of the South Asian Diaspora in Britain.* London: Palgrave. https://doi.org/10.1007/978-1-4039-3268-6

Nederveen Pieterse, Jan. 2009 [originally published 2003]. *Globalization and Culture: Global Mélange.* 2nd ed. London: Rowman and Littlefield.

Nuorgam, Piia. 2017. "Wider Use of Traditional Sámi Dress in Finland: Discrimination against the Sámi." In *Indigenous People's Cultural Heritage: Rights, Debates, Challenges*, edited by Alexandra Xanthaki, Sanna Valkonen, Leena Heinämäki, and Piia Nuorgam, 229–252. Leiden: Brill. https://doi .org/10.1163/9789004342194_012

Nyman, Jopi. 2003. *Postcolonial Animal Tale from Kipling to Coetzee*. New Delhi: Atlantic Publishers and Distributors.

Nyman, Jopi. 2009. *Home, Identity, and Mobility in Contemporary Diasporic Fiction*. Amsterdam: Rodopi.

Nyman, Jopi. 2017. *Displacement, Memory, and Travel in Contemporary Migrant Writing*. Leiden: Brill.

Nyman, Jopi. 2020. "Narratives of Contemporary Im/Mobility: Writing Forced Migration in the Borderscape." In *Mobile Identities*, edited by Kamal Sbiri, Jopi Nyman, and Rachida Yassine, 15–34. Newcastle: Cambridge Scholars Publishing.

Nyman, Jopi. 2021. "Borderscapes of Calais: Images of 'The Jungle' in *Breach* by Olumide Popoola and Annie Holmes." In *Border Images, Border Narratives: The Political Aesthetics of Boundaries and Crossings*, edited by Johan Schimanski and Jopi Nyman, 187–205. Manchester: Manchester University Press.

Nyman, Jopi. 2024. "Identity and Migration Literature." In *Routledge Companion to Migration Literature*, edited by Rebecca Fasselt et al. Abingdon: Routledge.

Oxford Reference. 2022. "diaspora." 24 February 2022. Online. https://www.oxfordreference.com/view/10.1093/oi/authority.20110803095716263

Papastergiadis, Nikos. 1997. "Tracing Hybridity in Theory." In *Debating Cultural Hybridity: Multi-Cultural Identities and the Politics of Anti-Racism*, edited by Pnina Werbner and Tariq Modood, 257–281. London: Zed Books.

Pereira-Ares, Noemí. 2018. *Fashion, Dress and Identity in South Asian Diaspora Narratives: From the Eighteenth Century to Monica Ali*. Cham: Palgrave Macmillan. https://doi.org/10.1007/978-3-319-61397-0

Rahbek, Ulla. 2011. "When Z Lost Her Reference: Language, Culture, and Identity in Xiaolu Guo's *A Concise Chinese–English Dictionary for Lovers*." *Otherness: Essays and Studies*, vol. 3, no. 1. https://otherness.dk/fileadmin/www.othernessandthearts.org/Publications/Journal_Otherness/Otherness_3.1new/Rahbek.pdf

Raimon, Eve Allegra. 2004. *The 'Tragic Mulatta' Revisited: Race and Nationalism in Nineteenth-century Antislavery Fiction*. New Brunswick: Rutgers University Press.

Raphael-Hernandez, Heike, ed. 2004. *Blackening Europe: The African American Presence*. With a Foreword by Paul Gilroy. London: Routledge.

Ravi, Srilata. 2007. "*Métisse* Stories and Ambivalent Desire for Cultural Belonging." *Journal of Intercultural Studies*, vol. 28, no. 1, pp. 15–26. https://doi.org/10.1080/07256860601082905

Robbins, Bruce. 1998. "Introduction: Part I: Actually Existing Cosmopolitanism." *Cosmopolitics: Thinking and Feeling beyond the Nation*, edited by Pheng Cheah and Bruce Robbins, 1–19. Minneapolis: University of Minnesota Press.

Rushdie, Salman. 1991. *Imaginary Homelands: Essays and Criticism 1981–1991*. Harmondsworth: Penguin.

Said, Edward W. 1978. *Orientalism: Western Conceptions of the Orient*. London: Penguin.

Said, Edward W. 2003. *Reflections on Exile and Other Essays*. Cambridge: Harvard University Press.

Salih, Sara. 2010. *Representing Mixed Race in Jamaica and England from the Abolition Era to the Present*. New York: Routledge. https://doi.org/10.4324/9780203843499

Skårdal, Dorothy Burton. 1962. "The Scandinavian Immigrant Writer in America." *Norwegian–American Studies*, vol. 21, pp. 14–53. https://www.jstor.org/stable/45221253

Smith, Zadie. 2000. *White Teeth*. London: Penguin.

Stein, Mark. 2004. *Black British Literature: Novels of Transformation*. Columbus: Ohio State University Press.

Stotesbury, John A. 2005. "Genre and Islam in Recent Anglophone Romantic Fiction." In *Refracting the Canon in Contemporary British Literature and Film*, edited by Susana Onega and Christian Gutleben, 69–82. Amsterdam: Rodopi. https://doi.org/10.1163/9789401208307_005

Tarlo, Emma, and Annelies Moors, eds. 2013. *Islamic Fashion and Anti-Fashion: New Perspectives from Europe and North America*. London: Bloomsbury.

Tiffin, Helen. 1987. "Post-colonial Literatures and Counter-Discourse." *Kunapipi*, vol. 9, no. 3, pp. 17–34.

Tölölyan, Khachig. 1991. "The Nation-State and Its Others: In Lieu of a Preface." *Diaspora: A Journal of Transnational Studies*, vol. 1, no. 1, pp. 3–7. https://doi.org/10.1353/dsp.1991.0008

Welang, Nahum. 2018. "Triple Consciousness: The Reimagination of Black Female Identities in Contemporary American Culture." *Open Cultural Studies*, vol. 2, pp. 296–306. https://doi.org/10.1515/culture-2018-0027

Yeow, Agnes S.K. 2009. *Conrad's Eastern Vision: A Vain and Floating Appearance*. Houndmills: Palgrave Macmillan.

Young, James O. 2011. "Appropriation and Hybridity." In *Routledge Companion to Philosophy and Music*, edited by Theodore Gracyk and Andrew Kania, 178–186. London: Routledge.

Young, Robert J.C. 1995. *Colonial Desire: Hybridity in Theory, Culture and Race*. London: Routledge.

3

HYBRIDITY IN POSTCOLONIAL LITERARY CONTEXTS

Joel Kuortti

Introduction

Hybridity is one of the major thematic axes of the discourse of postcolonial cultures. It functions as an operational articulation of ambiguity and changeability, showing the dynamics of opposition and resistance to the dominant ideological and cultural colonial hegemony, and offering a break with the insistence on duality and opposition. From this creative field grows the discourse of postcolonial literature as a hybrid that goes beyond inert and monolithic identities. As one of the most recurrent concepts in postcolonial literature, hybridity represents itself in the contact zones between the colonized and the colonizer and their mutual interdependence. In contrast to Orientalist assumptions, founded on binary oppositions between East and West, we show how the hybrid epistemology is formed based on the dynamic mixture of cultures, languages, and histories. Postcolonial studies is maybe the most prominent field where the notion of hybridity has been discussed and applied, and therefore, at the heart of this chapter is the discussion of theoretical discourses with a special focus on a number of related key ideas developed especially by Homi K. Bhabha such as 'ambivalence,' 'mimicry,' 'Third Space,' 'in-betweenness,' 'liminality,' and 'hybrid identities.' This chapter maps the close connections between hybridity and postcolonial literary studies. It discusses various aspects of hybridity, how it affects emerging cultures, and how it relates to postcolonial literature. As postcolonial literature is related to literature preceding the postcolonial era, we first chart briefly the prehistory of postcolonial literature through the periods of colonization and decolonization. In this chapter, we aim to

DOI: 10.4324/9781003269670-4

demonstrate also the wide variety of colonial and postcolonial theorization, as the historical, social, cultural, linguistic, and ethnic contexts of colonization vary immensely, although many elements are also shared across these contexts.

The theories of hybridity are then applied to the poem "Unhybrid" (2000) by the Indian Danish author Tabish Khair. For further study we offer four practical exercises.

Colonial Baggage: *Ambivalence* of Colonial Literature and Hybridity

Colonialism in its modern sense began in the early fifteenth century and the European overseas conquests. Earlier ancient and mediaeval colonial expansion and settlements by such a variety of peoples as, for example, the Phoenicians, the Greeks, the Etruscans, the Romans, the Vikings, the Arabs, the Crusaders, the Pisans, and the Russians are generally regarded as fundamentally different from modern colonization (see, e.g., Chronopoulos et al. 2021; Lee 2018, 438). Furthermore, imperialist expansions beyond the European, the Levantine, and the Middle Eastern contexts by, for example, the Chinese, the Incas, or the Malians are also commonly excluded from the discourse on colonialism (see, e.g., Jones and Phillips 2005). Colonialism and colonial literature remain vague notions as they cannot be contained in geographic, chronologic, or linguistic terms, as Ania Loomba (2015, 20) comments: "Colonialism was not an identical process in different parts of the world but everywhere it locked the original inhabitants and the newcomers into the most complex and traumatic relationships in human history" (cf. Veracini 2010, 2–6). Furthermore, Nancy Shoemaker (2015) defines as many as twelve different types of colonialism: settler, planter, extractive, trade, transport, imperial power, not-in-my-backyard, legal, rogue, missionary, romantic, and postcolonial colonialism (cf. Carrillo Rowe and Tuck 2017, 4–6). Colonial literature, then, in briefest terms, refers to literature from the time of colonization, where the point of view is typically that of the colonizers. It would be important to understand further the continuities and discontinuities of pre-modern colonialism as well as the different types of colonialism, but for this chapter, we restrict our discussion of colonial/postcolonial literature to the modern, European colonialism and its aftereffects.

Elleke Boehmer (2005, 2) differentiates between 'colonial' and 'colonialist' literature, of which the first is *about* the colonial conditions (e.g., *The Light That Failed* [1890] by Rudyard Kipling), and the second is written *for* the supremacist status of the colonizers (e.g., *Lord Jim* [1900] by Joseph Conrad). It was often the colonizers themselves who produced colonialist literature, whereas colonial literature was written "mainly by metropolitans, but also by creoles and indigenes." Even though the colonial contexts vary greatly, "the West established its sovereignty by defining its colonies as 'others,' with all the accompanying significations of lesser, effeminate, savage, monstrous, expendable, which that concept bears" (Boehmer 1998, xxii–xxiii).

The colonial, and colonialist, mindset was incumbent for the colonization process, to sustain a continuous supremacy over the 'other' "by always self-legitimizing disparagements of the colonized" (Memmi 2000, 105). This included also the fear of miscegenation based on the idea of incommensurability of identities of 'self' and 'other.' In his discussion of colonial discourse as colonial stereotypical discourse, Homi K. Bhabha (2003, 153, 148) mentions "the fear/desire of miscegenation" that is a symptom of "the force of ambivalence that gives the colonial stereotype its currency." Caliban in William Shakespeare's *The Tempest* (III, ii, l. 1531) can be, and often is, seen as the archetypal demonized, colonized 'other,' who causes fear: "Art thou afeard?" (cf. Spivak 2003, 117). When Prospero accuses Caliban for an attempted rape of Miranda, Caliban taps on the fear of miscegenation and snaps irreverently that had Prospero not interrupted, "I had peopled else / This isle with Calibans" (*The Tempest*, I, ii, ll. 502–503). While Gayatri Chakravorty Spivak (2003, 117–118) criticizes the postcolonial critics' too easy identification of "Calibán as an inescapable model" postcolonial, Caliban's figure remains a powerful representation of postcolonial circumstances.

Discussing Franz Fanon's "search for a conceptual form appropriate to the social antagonism of the colonial relation," Bhabha (1990, 184) identifies how "the stereotype of the native [is] fixed at the shifting boundaries between barbarism and civility." Here, Bhabha's use of the notion of *ambivalence* is crucial. Although Bhabha (1988, 21) applies his reading of ambivalence especially to the colonial discourse, it is even more pervasive as "all cultural statements and systems are constructed in th[e] contradictory and ambivalent space of enunciation" because "hierarchical claims to the inherent originality or 'purity' of cultures are untenable." In the colonial situation, this ambivalence is, however, more pronounced as the participants in the discourse are at the outset in a hierarchically unequal relationship, as is the case with J.M. Coetzee's seminal novel *Waiting for the Barbarians* (1980).

Colonial ambivalence emerges, or is present, at the border of such contact between cultures, groups, and individuals, because there the distance is (perceived as) extensive and "we find ourselves in the moment of transit where space and time cross to produce complex figures of difference and identity, past and present, inside and outside, inclusion and exclusion"

(Bhabha 2004, 1). It is, in Franz Fanon's (1963, 227; 2002, 215) terms, "the zone of occult instability" ("ce lieu de déséquilibre occulte"), the "fluctuating movement" that "will be the signal for everything to be called in question." Both Bhabha's "moment of transit" and Fanon's "fluctuating movement" indicate a liminality, an "interstitial passage between fixed identifications [that] opens up the possibility of a cultural hybridity that entertains difference without an assumed or imposed hierarchy" (Bhabha 2004, 4).

The *Third Space*, then, is, like ambivalence, more general than simply a colonial condition but "represents both the general conditions of language and the specific implication of the utterance in a performative and institutional strategy of which it cannot 'in itself be conscious'" (Bhabha 1988, 20). Applied to analysis of the colonial discourse, the ambivalence of enunciation irrevocably breaks the idea of homogeneity and continuity of culture and nation – or rather, is a reminder of this irrevocability, "that even the same signs can be appropriated, translated, rehistoricized, and read anew" (Bhabha 1988, 21). Here, we can refer back to the Heraclitean idea of 'panta rei' (πάντα ῥεῖ), that everything flows and nothing ever stays the same. It is a radical idea in opposition to fixed identities, and it is at the heart of understanding colonial connection as ambivalent. It manifests complex mixed feelings and continual fluctuations in the relationship between the colonizer and the colonized. This ambiguity can be seen in cultural works that portray times of colonialism.

As examples of colonialist literature and discourse in general, we may mention such colonialist literary works on Africa as the English writer H. Rider Haggard's novel *King Solomon's Mines* (1885) and the Southern African writer Olive Schreiner's *Story of an African Farm* (1883; written customarily under a male nom de plume, Ralph Iron). Even between Haggard and Schreiner we can see a continuum, where one end is more colonialist and the other end less so. While in Haggard, the adventurers depict Zulus as savages who must be governed by civilized Europeans for their own good, Schreiner's "feminist settler novel" focuses on the white, mainly British, South Africans, paying very little attention to the native Africans, accepting "white dominance as part of the order of things" (Boehmer 2005, 83). Haggard based his text on his brief, seven-year stay in Africa, and on other adventurers' experiences, contributing to "a system of signs, values, and hierarchies that enables him, and others like him, to write white, Christian, English, heterosexual identity into perpetual supremacy" (Kaufman 2005, 519), and his romances "illustrate a total mentality, a philosophy of life, an idea of humankind completely in harmony with the imperial ideology" (Katz 2010, 4). Later in life, before his death in 1925, Haggard turned his interest in agriculture, gardening, and land reform (see

Watts 2022). Schreiner, then, was born on a Mission in the Cape Colony, in what is in present-day Lesotho, and she envisioned a South African nation where the British and the Boers could live as "one white race in the land of many African races" (Krebs 1997, 427). However, as Dorothy Driver (2019) notes, by the time of her death in 1920, Schreiner was "one of the boldest and most far-sighted white critics of contemporary colonialist and industrial racist capitalism the Cape Colony had [..., and] a radical thinker whose anti-racism informed her anti-imperialist, socialist, and feminist views."

Commenting on Driver's analysis of Schreiner's works, Valerie L. Stevens adds that Schreiner's ecological thinking posits her "as a proto-ecofeminist thinker" (in Nivesjö and Barend 2021, 49). As these two examples indicate, pigeonholing writers and literary works in a simplistic manner may reduce them to emblems that evade their complexity. This is one reason why, for example, literary works need to be re-evaluated. Such frequent re-evaluation is done for William Shakespeare's *The Tempest* (1611), Aphra Behn's *Oroonoko* (1688), Joseph Conrad's *Heart of Darkness* (1899), Edgar Rice Burroughs's Tarzan novels (first, *Tarzan of the Apes* 1912/1914), and other works from the colonial period.

From Colonialism to Decolonization – *Mimicry* and *Hybrid Identity*

Gradually also indigenous African writers emerged who began to write literary works under colonial rule. While African literary traditions had in pre-colonial times been largely oral (Joseph 2013, 371–379; Owomoyela [1993, 3] notes that 'oral literature' is an oxymoron), there were several pre-colonial written African literatures – most notably in Ge'ez (Ethiopia), Hausa (Nigeria), Zulu (Southern Africa), Swahili (coastal East Africa), Wolof (Senegal), and Somali (Somalia). As Oyekan Owomoyela (1993, 3) notes, this serves as "a useful reminder that another Africa exists besides the one that normally preoccupies the world's attention, and that it also produces noteworthy literatures." While the African context is here used as an example, parallel developments took place elsewhere, in South Asia, South East Asia, Latin America, the Caribbean, the Pacific, Australia, and New Zealand.

With the introduction of Christianity and Islam in Africa, several new literary languages were introduced, especially Arabic (e.g., in the Maghreb and the Sahel) and colonial European languages, with varying levels of mixing between them and the vernaculars and pidgins: English (in West Africa: Nigeria, Ghana, Gambia, Sierra Leone, Liberia, and Cameroon; in East Africa: Uganda, Kenya, Tanzania [previously Tanganyika and Zanzibar], Sudan, South Sudan, Mauritius, and Seychelles; in Southern Africa: South Africa, Namibia, Zambia, Zimbabwe, Botswana, Lesotho, Malawi, and

Eswatini [previously Swaziland]); French (Algeria, Benin, Burkina Faso, Burundi, Cameroon, Central African Republic, Chad, Comoros, The Republic of Congo, Democratic Republic of Congo, Côte d'Ivoire, Djibouti, Gabon, Guinea, Madagascar, Mali, Mauritania, Morocco, Niger, Rwanda, Senegal, Togo, and Tunisia); Portuguese (Cape Verde, Guinea-Bissau, Sao Tomé and Príncipe, Angola, and Mozambique); Afrikaans/Dutch (South Africa and Namibia); and, to a lesser extent, German (Namibia) and Spanish (Equatorial Guinea) (Owomoyela 1993, 3; Grunebaum 1964; Senghor 1948; Andrade, ed. 1958; Van Coller 1998; Warmbold 1989; Ngom Faye 1996). Suffice it to say that this colonial linguistic spread in the African context alone makes it impossible to meaningfully encapsulate the development of colonial literatures in any brief manner. The hybrid forms these literatures have taken are myriad in the particular contexts the languages, peoples, and cultures have converged over time.

The emergence of African native writers was not straightforward. The publications were mostly in the colonial languages. Furthermore, the publishing houses were usually located in the colonial and other Western metropolitan centres such as London, Paris, and New York (see Zell 1993, 369; Currey 2003) or in missionary stations, such as the Lovedale Press, founded in 1861, of the Lovedale Missionary Institute in Alice (i.e., eDikeni) in Eastern Cape (Shepherd 1970, 15), which meant that the publications were administered by colonialists seeking to fulfil missionary aims. Thus, for example, Amos Tutuola's *The Palm-Wine Drinkard and His Dead Palm-Wine Tapster in the Dead's Town* (1952) was published in London by Faber & Faber and in New York by the Grove Press (1953). Tutuola's eccentric novel is often regarded as the first African novel in English. It received good reviews in Europe, and in his review, Dylan Thomas (1952, 7) called it a "brief, thronged, grisly and bewitching story." Especially Thomas's review paved the way for the fame of Tutuola's book, although many African critics found its 'falsified' depiction of Africa objectionable (Salamone 2010, 146; cf. Tobias 1999, 67–74). In Thomas's (1952, 7) view, the novel was "written in young English," as Tutuola mixed modernist literary expression with Yoruba folklore and used a hybrid form of English, a kind of "creolized Yoruba English" (Hannerz 2022, 30). However, Molara Ogundipe (1969, 105) finds it less structural and more idiosyncratic, "as something of his own making, forged from scraps of language such as officialese, journalese, ungrammatical English formations superimposed on his own rendition in English words of the Yoruba language" (see also Nyamnjoh 2015, 7). Tutuola's colleague, the Nigerian poet John P. Clark (1962, 80), then, criticized him for using "other man's tongue he little knew."

Clark's criticism illustrates one aspect of what in (post)colonial criticism is, following Bhabha (1984, 126; emphasis original), discussed in terms of *mimicry*: "Colonial mimicry is the desire for a reformed, recognizable Other, as *a subject of difference that is almost the same, but not quite.*" Crucial in this mimicry is the ambivalent difference with which the colonized 'mimic men' "pretended to be real, to be learning, to be preparing ourselves for life, we mimic men of the New World, one unknown corner of it, with all its reminders of the corruption that came so quickly to the new" (Naipaul 1967, 146). The desired imitation of the colonizer and their ostensibly more advanced culture necessarily produces, in Bhabha's (1984, 126) terms, "its slippage, its excess, its difference." V.S. Naipaul's ironic view on such failed imitation in *Mimic Men*, quoted above, is seconded in Salman Rushdie's novel *Midnight's Children* (1981), where on the eve of India's independence, the departing Englishman William Methwold is selling his estate to the parents of the protagonist, Saleem Sinai. The trick with the sale is that the

> Estate was sold on two conditions: that the houses be bought complete with every last thing in them, that the entire contents be retained by the new owners; and that the actual transfer should not take place until midnight on August 15th.
>
> *(Rushdie 1991, 109)*

This arrangement metaphorically captures the postcolonial Indian situation: India was trapped into a situation where it continued the same practices the colonial power had done, repressing its own culture.

The ambivalence between colonial desire and alienation is present also in two other major African novels, *Things Fall Apart* (1958) by the Nigerian novelist Chinua Achebe and *The River Between* (1965) by the Kenyan novelist Ngũgĩ wa Thiong'o. Achebe and Ngũgĩ have been important polar figures in the debate over the position of the English language in Africa (Achebe 1965; Ngũgĩ 1986; Saro-Wiva 1992; Marzagora 2015). The underlining difference between Achebe's and Ngũgĩ's positions, or the polarity fashioned around their stands, focuses on the rejection or acceptance of the use of a colonial language (excluding Arabic; Ngũgĩ 1986, 30, note 1; Makoni et al. 2012, 536–540), between singularity and plurality, between purity and hybridity, to put it bluntly. The debate was intensified in and after a literary conference in Makerere, Uganda, in 1962, and Obiajunwa Wali's (1963, 14) article "The Dead End of African Literature," where he argued that

> the whole uncritical acceptance of English and French as the inevitable medium for educated African writing, is misdirected, and has no chance of advancing African literature and culture. In other words, until these

writers and their Western midwives accept the fact that any true African literature must be written in African languages, they would be merely pursuing a dead end, which can only lead to sterility, uncreativity and frustration.

Ngũgĩ, who started his writing career under his birth name James Ngũgĩ, changed his name to Ngũgĩ wa Thiong'o and began writing in his native language, Kikuyu/Gĩkũyũ. His views are presented in the aptly titled book *Decolonising the Mind: The Politics of Language in African Literature* as follows: "The choice of language and the use to which language is put are central to a people's definition of itself in relation to its natural and social environment" (Ngũgĩ 1986, 109) Achebe's (1965, 28) view, then, was pragmatic in commenting that "those African writers who have chosen to write in English or French are not unpatriotic smart alecs, with an eye on the main chance – outside their own countries."

In India, then, the novelist Raja Rao (1970b, 5–6) pondered about the way Indian writers used English in his debut novel *Kanthapura* (1938):

One has to convey in a language that is not one's own the spirit that is one's own. One has to convey the various shades and omissions of a certain thought-movement that looks maltreated in an alien language. I use the word 'alien', yet English is not really an alien language to us. [...] We cannot write like the English. We should not. We cannot write only as Indians. We have grown to look at the world as part of us. Our method of expression therefore has to be a dialect which will some day prove to be as distinctive and colourful as the Irish or the American.

Rao describes the Indian writer as encompassing "the world," and English as a dialect that would evolve into a new hybrid form in India. The language debate does not concern only English but it is common to all colonial linguistic contexts (Innes 1990, 105–106). In the French-speaking context, 44 French writers issued a manifesto in 2007 – "Pour une 'littérature-monde' en français" (Barbery et al. 2007), declaring the "end of 'francophone' literature – and the birth of a world literature in French" (Barbery et al. 2009, 54). These writers were concerned about the absence of "the world" from French literature, in contrast with English literature that had in the preceding decades experienced the emergence of

an impressive hubbub, a series of noisy, versicolored, métis novels that proclaimed, with a rare force and new vocabulary, the din of these exponential foreign cities where the cultures of all the continents collided, reshuffled, and mingled with one another.

("Toward," 2009, 55; Chatzidimitriou 2015)

Colonization meant subjugation for the colonized people, but it was never just a one-way traffic as Christopher J. Lee (2018, 438) notes: "Local responses to foreign intrusion and colonial rule were immediate, frequent, and ongoing." As Lee's comment suggests, decolonization is not something that started with independence struggles but began already with the colonial contact itself. Bhabha discusses this in the Indian setting in his article on the introduction of the Bible to an Indian crowd in 1817. The people understand the "word of God" in their own way, not in the way one of the earliest Indian Christian catechists would want them to perceive it. The inadvertently irreverent interpretation of the crowd subverts the intended message, demonstrating how "the colonial presence is always ambivalent, split between its appearance as original and authoritative and its articulation as repetition and difference" (Bhabha 1985, 150). Such irreverence is not (inevitably) a political act but, rather, an "effect of an ambivalence produced within the rules of recognition of dominating discourses as they articulate the signs of cultural difference" (Bhabha 1985, 153).

We can find expressions of anti-colonial ideology in various directions: the first anti-colonial revolution that broke the United States off from Britain in 1776 (Bailyn 1992, 286; Paine 1776); in Latin America, Creole people fought for national liberation, with Haiti being the first to gain independence in 1803 (Aristide 2008, vii; Toussaint 2008, 2), the anti-slavery movement gradually achieved global abolition (Drescher 2009, 461–462; Douglass 1845, 41–42); in India, Mohandas Gandhi (1938; Rao 1970a, 22–23, 176–177) led the non-violent resistance, *satyagraha*, against British Rule; and after the 1955 Afro-Asian Conference at Bandung, Indonesia, and the Cuban Revolution in 1959, Che Guevara and Fidel Castro organized the Tricontinental Conference in 1966, in Havana, Cuba, for Latin American, African, and colonial Asian countries (Parrott 2022; Guevara 1967, 55). Colonial domination was not established peacefully, and as the above examples show, its dismantling was not peaceful, either.

A further example of decolonization is the *négritude* movement. It was initiated especially by the Senegalese poet Léopold Sédar Senghor (1964a, 9; Hiddleston 2014), the Guyanese surrealist Léon-Gontran Damas (1947, 13; Racine 1982), and the Martinican poet Aimé Césaire (1935, 1; Rexer 2013) in the 1930s in Paris. They outlined an anti-racist and anti-colonial philosophy. Damas (1947, 7) outlines a new literary history for poetry in French with his anthology of colonial poets, *Latitudes françaises: Poètes d'expression Française*. The emergence of these overseas poets "finished the reign of the imitation, of the decalcomania!" (Damas 1947, 9). While arguing for *cultural* emancipation, Césaire (1935, 1) criticizes the assimilationist black for mimicking the whites, for being a "sterile imitative monkey!" ("singe stérilement imitateur"). Instead, he called for recognition of one's

inner self, one's *negritude*, and to break the enslaving bonds of the paralyz-
ing white 'civilization.' This seemingly essentialist position on negritude
(Lane 2013, 94; Hiddlestone 2014, 40–41) is interpreted in a wider sense
by Senghor (1964a, 9), who sees negritude as "a knot of realities" – "un
nœud de réalités" – a composite of values, a hybrid identity. He describes the
francophone black writers in terms of "bicéphalisme," as bilingual "cultural
crossbreeds" (Senghor 1964c, 225). Such crossbreeding is evident in creol-
ity (*criollismo; créolité*), most notably in the Caribbean, where the various
colonial powers settled with the indigenous population and the enslaved
people.

As with literature, analogous developments of hybridization of culture
can be seen in music. These developments "were irreducibly mixed, hybrid,
syncretic, in-between, impure. And this is one of the enduring effects of
colonialism" (Agawu 2003, 15). Already in 1937, Senghor (1964b, 19)
wrote about jazz (or *hot-jazz*) as an expression of the "black soul" that
Western instruments could not capture. The new contrapuntal polyrhyth-
mic form of music that jazz represented combined the West African musical
traditions with the European folk music traditions, and American motifs.
Furthermore, it was also an expression of black consciousness through,
for example, the valorization of jazz in the Harlem Renaissance, although
the sentiment was not shared by all (Martin 2021, 348). In his poem, "A
New York (pour un orchestre de jazz: solo de trompette)," Senghor (1956)
returns to the jazz theme in the form of a love poem for the city of New
York that turns into a tribute to its heart in Harlem, beating in the black
rhythm. For Senghor, jazz signalled the possibility of a tradition that could
proudly claim African heritage in a mixed form. In fiction, Toni Morrison's
novel *Jazz* (1992) talks about the contextual conditions that paved the
way for jazz. A telling example of the cultural amalgamation is the jazz
icon Josephine Baker and her bold performative of black subjectivity in
the French cultural context (Edwards 2003, 162), where her *danse sau-
vage*, wild dance, both enthralled European audiences and created suspicion for 'selling out.' Such embracing of hybridity creates an ambivalent
dilemma between essential authenticity and performance of identity (for
Paul Gilroy's critique of essentialism in relation to music, see Chapter 1).
Despite how authentic or subversive Baker might have been, Samir Dayal
(2004, 50) argues that "her presence in that scene brought to the fore how
intimately 'blackness' was sutured to the construction of modern white
European subjectivity." Colonial history had irrevocably interwoven the
metropole with the colonies.

The development of music in Algeria in the 1970s stemmed from different roots. Raï music developed from the multicultural environment created
after the colonization of Algeria in 1830, when people of various cultures

immigrated there. The classical Islamic *andalusi* music of the elite was challenged by the Bedouin *melhun* style (Noor Al-Deen 2005, 597–598). Under the French colonial oppression, a new form began to emerge in the 1920s when women singers, *cheikhas*, began to perform lewd and daring songs. Gradually this became to be known as raï, a musical form of resistance and expression of the trauma of the Algerian War of Independence. In the multicultural city of Oran (Wahran in Arabic), the traditional forms of *andalusi*, *melhun*, and *raï* evolved into *wahrani* that "was like a musical melting pot" (Noor Al-Deen 2005, 602). From this mélange emerged modern raï that was banned by the Algerian government after the independence in 1962 and until 1985. By then, raï had developed into a very popular dance and pop music, together with its controversial side, by combining various musical styles and traditions.

The hybrid forms can, in music as in other cultural creations, be produced in two contrasting modalities, in Bakhtinian terms as organic, unconscious hybrids or as non-organic, "deliberate artistic device" (Featherstone 2005, 45). Simon Featherstone (2005) discusses the intentional hybridity in 'world music' especially in relation to Ry Cooder and his project with Wim Wenders in recording the *Buena Vista Social Club* (1999) music documentary. If Paul Simon's earlier work, such as *Graceland* (1986) that appropriated black South African music, could be seen as an "example of exploitative cultural tourism" (Featherstone 2005, 43), Cooder and Wender exploit economically the aestheticized non-Western Cuban music in ambivalent political terms. The transatlantic music travelled across the Black Atlantic, between Europe, Africa, and the United States. As in jazz and raï, the influences and hybridities were exchanged in all directions, and new hybrid styles emerged: Sahara blues, Cuban son, Trinidadian calypso, rap, and so on. There were, of course, developments also beyond the transatlantic connections. One particularly influential, globally popular music style is *bhangra*, a hybrid form combining Punjabi folk music, traditional ghazals, modern pop music, and, quite spectacularly, Bollywood-style dance. A popular example can be seen in a significant scene of the British Asian director Gurinder Chadha's film *Bend It Like Beckham* (2002). In the scene, Jess Bhamra (acted by Parminder Nagra), the younger daughter of a British Indian Punjabi Sikh family, sneaks out from her sister Pinky's wedding to play with her football team in a crucial match. The scene cuts between the wedding celebration with a full flare of bhangra music and dance and the match where Jess excels by "bending it like Beckham," scoring the critical winning goal. The scene ends with cross-cuts from the wedding where the new husband lifts Pinky up and the team hoists Jess up in celebration.

Hybridity and Postcolonial Literatures and Theory

As the previous sections demonstrate, the roots of postcolonial literature and criticism lie deep in colonial history. The experiences of slavery,
diaspora, subalternity, exploitation, and alterity have shaped the cultures
and peoples under colonialism in profound ways. With this background
in mind, it is difficult to determine when postcolonial theory got started.
The Palestinian critic Edward Said's pivotal work *Orientalism* (1978) is
usually considered as the birth of postcolonial theory. It prompted further analyses of the colonial condition, as well as criticism of his analyses.
However, Said's book was preceded by many works that discussed similar
topics, such as *Contrapunteo cubano del tabaco y el azúcar* (1940; *Cuban
Counterpoint: Tobacco and Sugar*) by Fernando Ortiz from Cuba, *Peau
noire, masques blancs* (1952; *Black Skin, White Masks*) by Franz Fanon from
Martinique, *Portrait du colonisé, précédé de portrait du colonisateur* (1957;
The Colonizer and the Colonized) by Albert Memmi from Tunisia, *Pedagogy
of the Oppressed* (1970; *Pedagogia do oprimido*) by Paolo Freire from Brazil,
and *Guiné-Bissau: Nação africana forjada na luta* (1974; Guinea-Bissau:
African Nation Forged in the Struggle) by Amílcar Cabral from Guinea-
Bissau. Much of the development of postcolonial theory took, however, its
cue from Said.

One of Said's main points was that the West had looked at the Orient in
a certain, skewed light. By claiming to know the Orient, Occidentals took
epistemological control over the Orientals, establishing a hegemonic binarism between the two cultural spheres (Said 1978, 3). Despite the assumed
superiority within this binary structure, the division was never real but carried with it an accidental ambiguous relationship of mimicry and desire: the
Oriental mimicry of the West, and the Occidental desire for, and cultural
appropriation of, the exoticized Orient. While postcolonial theory in this
manner successfully reveals, as one of its methods, the structure of epis-
temic, cultural, economic, and military domination, it also often bypasses
the hybridities that the setting enabled and created. Through and with
colonial contacts, various forms of in-betweenness emerged in languages,
literatures, ethnicities, and other social formations.

An example of such epistemological control can be found in Benedict
Anderson's discussion of the colonial census practices. Anderson (2006,
169) describes how the colonial officials, in their desire to control the
colonized, "tried carefully to count the objects of its feverish imagining,"
forcing people to be catalogued into "a maze of grids" by ignoring the multiplicity of reality. An illustration of such incommensurable categorization
is in Jorge Luis Borges's (1942) classic essay "The Analytical Language of
John Wilkins." In the essay, he refers to a fictional Chinese encyclopaedia,

"Celestial Empire of Benevolent Knowledge" that presents a taxonomy of animals with fourteen peculiar categories:

> (a) belonging to the Emperor, (b) embalmed ones, (c) those that are trained, (d) suckling pigs, (e) mermaids, (f) fabulous ones, (g) stray dogs, (h) those that are included in this classification, (i) those that tremble as though they were mad, (j) innumerable ones, (k) those drawn with a very fine camel's-hair brush, (l) others, (m) those that have just broken a flower vase, (n) those that resemble flies from a distance.
>
> *(Borges 1964, 103)*

The irony of Borges's (1964, 104) text is directed at the always already vain attempt to complete knowledge, as "there is no classification of the Universe that is not arbitrary and full of conjectures." The categorization impulse of the colonizers also created anti-colonial nationalist movements by identifying people into groups that had not before identified themselves together (Anderson 2006, 170).

The ambiguous colonial situation was echoed in culture, and, for example, in literature, 'writing back' became one way of expressing the new-found self-reliance of the colonized or newly independent people. A classic example is Jean Rhys's rewriting of Charlotte Brontë's *Jane Eyre* (1847) in *Wide Sargasso Sea* (1966). Instead of the colonialists' perspective, Rhys adopts the perspective of Bertha Mason, who in Brontë's book is a mad woman, but in the revisioning is Antoinette Cosway, a resourceful Creole woman (Spivak 2003, 114–132). 'Writing back' is still used as a method of cultural counterbalancing of the effects of colonization as the colonial period is not fully over yet, and new forms of neocolonial domination have emerged. 'Writing back' developed into a term after the publication of one of the most influential postcolonial books, *The Empire Writes Back* by Bill Ashcroft, Gareth Griffiths, and Helen Tiffin (1989). The title is adopted from Salman Rushdie's (1982, 3) article, "The Empire Writes Back with a Vengeance," where he writes:

> The language, like much else in the newly independent societies, needs to be decolonized, to be remade in other images, if those of us who use it from positions outside Anglo-Saxon culture are to be more than artistic Uncle Toms.

In Ashcroft, Griffiths, and Tiffin (1989), language is taken up as an important dimension for postcoloniality, as we have argued in Chapter 1, about the crossing of borders of language to construct plurilingual spaces through untranslated expressions, code-switching, and nation-languages.

Ashcroft, Griffiths, and Tiffin (1989, 8) argue, for example, in favour of 'englishes' instead of 'English,' that the formerly peripheral regions and language forms were "the site of some of the most exciting and innovative literatures of the modern period." Another key idea was the Caribbean Creole continuum, the polyglossic or polydialectical reality of the region that undermined the idea of linguistic homogeneity, acknowledged "language as practice," and bestowed subjectivity to the speakers (Ashcroft, Griffiths, and Tiffin 1989, 44–45).

Furthermore, by affirming the plurality of practice, the linguistic theory of the Creole continuum offers a paradigmatic demonstration of the abrogating impetus in postcolonial literary theory. Rushdie's and Raja Rao's views on language confirm the pluralistic position and express a counter-mimetic statement, a call for new ways of creating culture. This does not mean that writers invent the language they use in their writing (although idiosyncratic lexis and structure may be adopted) but they tap into the surrounding linguistic resources, "the irreducible hybridity of all language" (Spivak 2003, 163).

To conclude, in this chapter, we have outlined the emergence of postcolonial literature and theory and how hybridity is embedded in the practice of postcoloniality in many significant ways. As the postcolonial era is not a straightforward period, we have discussed the colonial conditions as well as the decolonization processes that preceded and coincided with the postcolonial. Such concepts as "ambivalence," "mimicry," "Third Space," "in-betweenness," "liminality," and "hybrid identities" were discussed as they challenge the tendency for binarization of identities, cultures, and literatures. The "postcolonial condition" (Young 2012, 600) is "a colonial effect of belatedness that continues to link colony and metropole under its common shadow," under which Europe as the former colonial centre is in a temporal deferral of postcoloniality due to the lingering effects of colonialism: diaspora, migration, hybridity, creolization, transculturation.

Textual Analysis: Tabish Khair, "Unhybrid"

In this model analysis, we offer a detailed textual interpretation of the Indian Danish author Tabish Khair's poem "Unhybrid" (2000) from his poetry collection *Where Parallel Lines Meet* (2000). The book has an oxymoronic title. In conventional Euclidean geometry, parallel lines are parallel just because they do *not* meet; they stay at a fixed distance from each other, as in the frequently cited first line of Rudyard Kipling's (1892, 3, l. 1) classic poem "The Ballad of East and West" (1889): "Oh, East is East, and West is West, and never the twain shall meet." Khair's collection is structured around geometrical sets: "Squares and Circles," "Straight Lines and Triangles," and "Other Geometries." These sets represent the various settings with which a diasporic person's life is bound; they could also be named "home," "away," and "elsewhere," but Khair does not settle with such a clear-cut framework, as the book's title already suggests.

The structure of the collection challenges the Euclidean perception by suggesting an elliptic geometry where conventional axioms and roles do not hold. The same is true also in Kipling's (1892, 3, ll. 3–4) poem, although this is often overlooked, for the poem continues by challenging the parallel postulate: "But there is neither East nor West, Border, nor Breed, nor Birth, / When two strong men stand face to face, tho' they come from the ends of the earth!" Here, (ethnic) difference is erased, the border dismantled, between East and West in a context of equality. If Kipling's context is that of courage and camaraderie at times of war, Khair is more mundane, describing illiterate subalterns in contact with the world of learning over bread (ll. 14–15), East meeting with West.

"Unhybrid," from the "Squares and Circles" set, is a free-verse poem with eleven three-line stanzas. The theme that the speaker of the poem ponders about is the applicability of the concept of hybridity in an Indian context. The first stanza offers a comment on the general arbitrariness of language that "overflows with meanings" (l. 2) in linguistic terms, how vowels and stress patterns (l. 1) change the meaning of similar-looking, homonymic words: "Kal, kali, kalá, kálá, káli, kál" (l. 3). These words, used in several Indian languages, such as Sanskrit, Hindi and Urdu, are then given translations in the next stanza: tomorrow/yesterday (Hindi 'kal,' कल) and (eternal) time ('kál,' काल) (l. 4); buds ('kali,' कली), art ('kalá,' कला), blackness ('kálá,' काला), goddesses ('káli,' काली) (l. 6). The third stanza then extends the scope, indicating, in a poststructuralist manner, the infinity of meaning in/of language.

The subject position in the poem is not straightforward. There are present-passive pronouns – "our cup" (l. 2; with a Biblical allusion to Psalms 23:5), "we" (l. 7), and "You" (l. 9) – which turn into active identificational ones: "We have not always grown up with many languages" (l. 10), and "If you throw hard words at us" (l. 13). The us/them binary establishes a distance between the speaker and the addressee, "You." This binary is, however, broken as the speaker splits the "us" into "The literate" and "The illiterate" (ll. 14–15). Furthermore, the speaker dissociates themselves from the illiterate by using the pronoun "their": "their lost Portuguese to your learnt English" (l. 16). Here, "your" refers to the educated Indians, but perhaps more specifically to Indian writers writing in English, whose work Khair discusses in the book *Babu Fictions: Alienation in Contemporary*

Indian English Novels (2001). In an interview, Khair comments that his audience is this kind of educated segment, he writes for "South Asians who read English and for the significant minority of western readers interested in going beyond the west's dominant discourses" (Ravindran 2007). The speaker, then, identifies themselves self-ironically in the self-reflective phrase as "a suited-booted babu" (l. 18), an educated sharp-dressed bureaucrat, making also a parodic ("my humble self," l. 26) metatextual comment on the hybrid position of the Indian Danish author himself (Kuortti 2019, 151–152).

The Babu is a recurring, notable figure in Indian literature and society (Srivastava 2007, 55). In the colonial setting, the Babus were English-educated middlemen who functioned between the British colonizers and the indigenous population as clerks and officials. The original signification of respect was altered to a pejorative meaning for "characterizing a superficially cultivated, but too often effeminate, Bengali" (Yule and Burnell 2010, 31; also Srivastava 2007, 56–57; Hankin 1992, 24), a 'mimic man.' Against this historical background, the use of the word 'babu' in the poem is ambiguous: in addition to its pejorative use, it refers to people who are "middle or upper class, mostly urban (at times cosmopolitan), Brahminized and/or 'westernized', and fluent in English" (Khair 2001, ix). The non-Babus, "the Coolies," then, are "non-English speaking, not or not significantly 'westernized,' not or less Brahminized, economically deprived, culturally marginalized and, often, rural or migrant-urban populations" (Khair 2001, ix).

This social differentiation between Babus and Coolies lies also at the bottom of "Unhybrid." The speaker comments that the literate Babus would (mis)understand the "hard" word 'hybrid,' thrown at them as "hai bread," with amused puzzlement, for – as an interlingual composite of, e.g., Hindi/Urdu and English – it would translate as 'have bread' (ll. 13–14, 19–20). The illiterate Coolies, then, would not understand the word at all – until a Babu like the speaker "publish/ This lament for bread" (ll. 18–19). For the illiterate, bread would be "pauroti," i.e., 'bread,' in "their lost Portuguese" (ll. 15–16). 'Hybrid' reveals the underlying chasm in both theoretical and practical terms, discussed here in terms of ordinary bread: whether the literate (mis-)understanding of 'hybrid' as bread, or the illiterate not understanding it at all, as for them bread would be *pauroti*. 'Roti' in *pauroti* is a common Indian term for many types of bread, while 'pau' is derived from the Portuguese *pāo* for a loaf of bread, originating from the times Portuguese had colonial footholds in India – especially Goa – until 1961 ("Goans are so fond of bread that Indians from other regions call them *pau wallahs* (bread men)" (Boileau 2010, 217; also Achaya 2009, 236). Like many postcolonial works, "Unhybrid" is a linguistic hybrid, using several languages in creating its setting. Here it is not just postmodern playfulness but, rather, a factual representation of the multilingual reality of India.

The speaker continues that instead of using the elevated language of literary theory and a word like 'hybrid,' one should have used "Some other language, Hindi, for example, or Urdu, / Which is what we ought to speak but we don't" (ll. 21–22). This is also a (self-)critical commentary on the way educated (diasporic) scholars have adopted English as their active language. However, even by using Hindi one would not be able to convey the meaning of 'hybrid,' as the illiterate, the subaltern "*they*" speak is a dialect, "The only language most of them wish to speak" – dialect "so thick you can cut / Cross-sections of it" (ll. 23–27). Someone outside of that speaking community (for it is sometimes a language without "existence in writing," l. 12) would not see how these people understand (or do not) words like 'hybrid': "Hybrid's not really the word for them," and they do not pay attention to languages they do not know.

Towards the end, the speaker comments on the preference of people (not necessarily, or only, illiterate subalterns) who do not speak the language of high theory and share the idea of arbitrariness of language: "If they had their way / Language would not overflow with meanings" (ll. 30–31). The challenge of postcolonial theorists is, thus, to find ways of discussing the relevant topics in a language that would be understood also by the non-experts. The call for an ethical encounter with the other that Gayatri Chakravorty Spivak made already in 1985 in her article "Can the Subaltern Speak?" has not lost its currency. For further consideration, think about the use of different languages in the poem. You may reflect on what the last two lines on languages growing up with us, rather than us growing up with any language, might mean.

Further Reading

Dwivedi, Om Prakash, ed. 2013. *Tabish Khair: A Critical Companion*. Kolkata: Roman Books.

Gámez-Fernández, Cristina M., and Om Prakash Dwivedi, eds. 2012. *Tabish Khair: Critical Perspectives*. Newcastle: Cambridge Scholars Publishing.

Khair, Tabish. 2001. *Babu Fictions: Alienation in Contemporary Indian English Novels*. New Delhi: Oxford University Press.

Kuortti, Joel. 2019. "The Ordinariness of the Diasporic Kitchen." In *Thinking with the Familiar in Contemporary Literature and Culture 'Out of the Ordinary'*, edited by Joel Kuortti et al. Leiden: Brill, pp. 135–160. DOI: https://doi.org/10.1163/9789004406742_009

Kuortti, Joel, and Jopi Nyman, eds. 2007. *Reconstructing Hybridity: Post-colonial Studies in Transition*. Amsterdam: Rodopi.

Tabish Khair, "Unhybrid" (reprinted with the author's permission)

A vowel here, a stress there, that's all
And our cup of sound overflows with meanings:
Kal, kali, kalá, kálá, káli, kál …

So many, from the yesterday that is tomorrow
To the Time that is all in all. And in between,   5
Buds, art, blackness, goddesses, more

If we bring in a long vowel like 'ee'
Or a short 'oo'. In which case it could mean
A nail, a lineage or only. You see.

We have not always grown up with many languages   10
(Some of us have not grown up with any language
That can attest to its existence in writing).

If you throw hard words at us like 'hybrid',
The literate among us will hear 'hai bread'
(The illiterate call bread 'pauroti' which   15

Is their lost Portuguese to your learnt English –
So they will hear nothing till others publish
This lament for bread by a suited-booted babu),

And will be a little bit mystified,
Hugely amused. You could have tried   20
Some other language, Hindi, for example, or Urdu,

Which is what we ought to speak but we don't. Not
All, not *them*: what: what *they* speak is so thick you can cut
Cross-sections of it, mount it and fail to see

What sense they make of it. Even Hindi won't help.   25
Dialect's the language they know and, unlike my humble self,
The only language most of them wish to speak.

Hybrid's not really the word for them. They don't
Attach much importance to what other people say
In tongues strange and so funny. If they had their way   30

Language would not overflow with meanings. You see
Most of us have not grown up with any language – only,
It seems, many languages have grown up with us.

Further Exercises

Jamaica Kincaid, My Garden (Book) *(1999)*

The Antiguan American author Jamaica Kincaid's *My Garden (Book)* is a memoir that chronicles Kincaid's experiences with gardening both in her native Antigua and in the United States, where she immigrated at the age of seventeen. In her writing, Kincaid mixes styles – autobiography, magical realism, and postcolonial counter-writing – with criticism of the colonial legacies in the colonies as well as in the metropolises. How does the following excerpt describe the ambivalence of the colonial situation? In what ways can Kincaid's views of gardening be interpreted as a critique of colonialism? Postcolonial theory is often intersectional, combining various analytical strands. Furthermore, think how the excerpt can be read in terms of postcolonial ecocriticism (Huggan and Tiffin 2015).

> I must have been about ten years old when I first came in contact with cold air; where I lived the air was only hot and then hotter, and if sometimes, usually only in December, the temperature at night got to around 75 degrees, everyone wore a sweater and a flannel blanket was placed on the bed. But once, the parents of a girl I knew got a refrigerator, and when they were not at home, she asked me to come in and put my hand in the freezer part. I became convinced then (and remain so even now) that cold air is unnatural and man-made and associated with prosperity (for refrigerators were common in the prosperous North) and more real and special than the warm air that was so ordinary to me; and then I became suspicious of it, because it seemed to me that it was also associated with the dark, with the cold comes the dark, in the dark things grow pale and die; no explanation from science or nature of how the sun can shine very brightly in the deep of winter has ever been satisfactory to me; in my heart I know the two cannot be, the cold and the bright light, at the same time.
>
> And so between the end of summer and the shortest day of the year I battle a constant feeling of disbelief; everything comes to a halt rapidly, they die, die, die, the garden is all brown stalks and the ground tightening; the things that continue to grow and bloom do so in isolation; all the different species of chrysanthemums in the world grouped together (and some of them often are on display in a greenhouse at Smith College), all the sedum, all the rest of it, is very beautiful and I like it very much, but it doesn't really do, because it's against a background of dead or almost dead.
>
> *(Kincaid 1999, 70–71)*

Patricia Grace, Potiki *(1986)*

The novel *Potiki* by the Māori writer Patricia Grace from New Zealand
Aotearoa is a story about a threat to a local Māori by the land developer
"Dollarman." The narrative point of view changes throughout the novel
but the main narrator is Roimata, mother of a Māori family. One focal element in the novel is the ancestral Māori meeting house, *wharenui*, which
the developer sets to fire to drive the locals from the land. The difficulties of
mixing traditional and modern ways of life become acute in the context of
indigenous land rights, as well as combining traditional and modern education. The striking realism is combined with the magical in the prophet-child
Tokowaru-i-te-Marama's special power of knowing. In the following excerpt,
Roimata's husband Hemi is pondering about the changes in the Māori community and how traditions could be upheld and transformed. What does
the excerpt tell about how indigenous people cope with the colonial legacy?

Then apart from the land and the sea, apart from the survival things,
there were their songs and their stories. There was their language. There
would be more opportunity now to make sure that they, the older ones,
handed on what they knew.

Kids were different these days. They wanted knowledge of their own
things, their own things first. They were proud and didn't hide their
culture, and no one could bullshit them either.

In his day they had been expected to hide things, to pretend they
weren't what they where. It was funny how people saw each other. Funny
how you came to see yourself in the mould that others put you in, and
how you began not to believe in yourself. You began to believe that you
should hide away in the old seaweed like a sand flea, and that all you
could do when disturbed was hop about and hope you wouldn't get
stood on. But of course you did get stood on.

Well their ancestors had been rubbished in schools, and in books,
and everywhere. So were their customs, so was their language. Still
were rubbished too, as far as he could see. Rubbished or ignored. And
if those things were being rubbished, then it was an attack on you, on
a whole people. You could get weak under the attack, then again you
could become strong.

The kids these days were strong, well some of them were. Others were
lost and without hope. But the strong ones? They were different, tougher
than what his lot had been as kids. They didn't accept some of the messages they were receiving about themselves, couldn't afford to if they
wanted to stay on the face of the earth.

(Grace 1986, 64–65)

Benjamin Zephaniah, Refugee Boy (2001)

The novel *Refugee Boy* by the black British writer Benjamin Zephaniah describes ambivalence and in-betweenness of refugee experiences in England. On arrival in England, in the beginning of Chapter One, the fourteen-year-old Alem is perplexed by the sight of a white British officer. What was to be Alem's holiday trip turns into a story of refuge as his father leaves him in London to be cared for by the Refugee Council. Alam is the son of an Ethiopian father and an Eritrean mother, and he is regarded as a mongrel in both countries. With both countries at war, the parents feel that it would be safer for Alam to be a refugee in Britain. How does the following excerpt reflect issues related to hybridity?

> "Welcome to England, Mr Kelo," said the immigration officer as he handed back the passports to Alem's father.
>
> Alem stared up at the tall officer; the officer looked down at Alem. "Have a good holiday now."
>
> "Thank you," said Alem's father. He took Alem's hand and began to head for the baggage-reclaim area.
>
> Alem jerked his father's hand and stopped suddenly. "Abbaye, yaw teguru tekatlowal," he said, brimming with excitement.
>
> His father turned to him and spoke as if he was trying to shout quietly. "What did I tell you? From now on you must try to speak English, you must practise your English – all right, young man?"
>
> Alem panicked. "Ishi abbaye," he said.
>
> His father's response was swift. "English, I said."
>
> "Yes, Father."
>
> "Now what did you say?"
>
> Alem looked back towards passport control. "Father, that man who looked at the passports, what was wrong with him?"
>
> "He looked all right to me."
>
> "I think something was wrong with his hair, he looked burned. Did you see his hair? It was red, red like sunset, he looked hot, he looked burned."
>
> His father shook his head and they continued to walk. "No, nothing is wrong with him. This type of hair is called ginger. In England you will see many people with this colour hair – and you must not say burned, you must say burnt – the word is 'burnt.'"
>
> *(Zephaniah 2001, 11)*

Gurinder Chadha, Bride and Prejudice *(2004)*

The movie *Bride and Prejudice* (2004), directed by the British Asian director Gurinder Chadha, is a Bollywood-style adaptation of Jane Austen's novel *Pride and Prejudice* (1813). Chadha is one of the first female directors of Indian origin, and the themes in her movies include gender, ethnicity, and challenges of diasporic life. Watch the movie and consider how it 'writes back' to the canon by reversing roles, settings, and perspectives. Think also about the representations of ethnicity and gender in the film; how are various elements of hybridity presented in, for example, music, dress, and language?

References

Achaya, K.T. 2009. *The Illustrated Foods of India A–Z.* New Delhi: Oxford University Press.

Achebe, Chinua. 1958. *Things Fall Apart.* London: William Heinemann.

Achebe, Chinua. 1965. "English and the African Writer." *Transition*, no. 18, pp. 27–30. https://doi.org/10.2307/2934835

Agawu, Kofi. 2003. *Representing African Music: Postcolonial Notes, Queries, Positions.* New York: Routledge.

Anderson, Benedict. 2006 [originally published 1983]. *Imagined Communities: Reflections on the Origin and Spread of Nationalism*, 2nd rev. ed. London: Verso.

Andrade, Mario Pinto de, ed. 1958. *Antologia da poesia negra de expressão portuguesa.* Paris: P. J. Oswald.

Aristide, Jean-Bertrand. 2008. "Introduction." In *Toussaint L'Ouverture: The Haitian Revolution*, edited and translated by Nick Nesbitt, vii–xxxiii. London: Verso.

Ashcroft, Bill, Gareth Griffiths, and Helen Tiffin. 1989. *The Empire Writes Back: Theory and Practice in Post-colonial Literatures.* London: Routledge.

Bailyn, Bernard. 1992 [originally published 1967]. *The Ideological Origins of the American Revolution.* Enlarged edition. Cambridge: Belknap Press.

Barbery, Muriel, et al. 2007. "Pour une 'littérature-monde' en français." *Le Monde* (March 16), pp. 1–3. https://www.lemonde.fr/livres/article/2007/03/15/des -ecrivains-plaident-pour-un-roman-en-francais-ouvert-sur-le-monde_883572 _3260.html

Barbery, Muriel, et al. 2009. "Toward a 'World-Literature.'" Translated by Daniel Simon, *World Literature Today*, vol. 83, no. 2, pp. 54–56. https://doi.org/10 .1353/wlt.2009.0214

Bhabha, Homi K. 1984. "Of Mimicry and Man: The Ambivalence of Colonial Discourse." *October*, no. 28 (Discipleship: A Special Issue on Psychoanalysis), pp. 125–133. http://www.jstor.org/stable/778467

Bhabha, Homi K. 1985. "Signs Taken for Wonders: Questions of Ambivalence and Authority under a Tree outside Delhi, May 1817." *Critical Inquiry*, vol. 12, no.

1 ('Race', Writing, and Difference), pp. 144–165. https://www.jstor.org/stable /1343466. [In Bhabha 1994, 145–174.]

Bhabha, Homi K. 1988. "The Commitment to Theory." *New Formations*, no. 5, pp. 5–23. [In *Questions of Third Cinema*, edited by Jim Pines and Paul Willemen. London: British Film Institute 1989, 111–132. In Bhabha 1994, 19–39.]

Bhabha, Homi K. 1990. "Interrogating Identity: Frantz Fanon and the Postcolonial Prerogative." In *Anatomy of Racism*, edited by David Theo Goldberg, 183–209. Minneapolis: University of Minnesota Press. [In Bhabha 1994, 40–65.]

Bhabha, Homi K. 2004 [originally published 1994]. *The Location of Culture*. 2nd ed. London: Routledge.

Bhabha, Homi K. 2003 [originally published 1982]. "The Other Question: Difference, Discrimination and the Discourse of Colonialism." In *Literature, Politics and Theory: Papers from the Essex Conference 1976–1984*, edited by Francis Barker, Peter Hulme, Margaret Iversen, and Diana Loxley, 148–172. London: Routledge. [In Bhabha 1994, 66–84.]

Boehmer, Elleke. 1998. "Introduction." In *Empire Writing: An Anthology of Colonial Literature 1870–1918*, edited by Elleke Boehmer, xv–xxxvi. Oxford: Oxford University Press.

Boehmer, Elleke. 2005 [originally published 1995]. *Colonial and Postcolonial Literature: Migrant Metaphors*. 2nd ed. Oxford: Oxford University Press.

Boileau, Janet P. 2010. "A Culinary History of the Portuguese Eurasians: The Origins of Luso-Asian Cuisine in the Sixteenth and Seventeenth Centuries." PhD Diss. University of Adelaide, School of History and Politics. https://hdl .handle.net/2440/77948

Borges, Jorge Luis. 1964 [originally published 1942]. "The Analytical Language of John Wilkins (El idioma analítico de John Wilkins)." In *Other Inquisitions 1937–1952*, by Jorge Luis Borges, translated by Ruth L.C. Simms, 101–105. Austin: University of Texas Press.

Brontë, Charlotte [Currer Bell]. 1847. *Jane Eyre*. London: Smith, Elder & Co.

Cabral, Amílcar. 1974. *Guiné-Bissau: Nação africana forjada na luta*. Lisboa: Nova Aurora.

Carrillo Rowe, Aimee, and Eve Tuck. 2017. "Settler Colonialism and Cultural Studies: Ongoing Settlement, Cultural Production, and Resistance." Editorial for special issue. *Cultural Studies/Critical Methodologies*, vol. 17, no. 1, pp. 3–13. https://doi.org/10.1177/1532708616653693

Césaire, Aimé. 1935. "Conscience raciale et révolution sociale." *L'Etudiant noir: Journal Mensuel de l'Association des Étudiants Martiniquais en France*, vol. 1, no. 3, pp. 1–2. https://letudiant-noir.webs.com

Chadha, Gurinder, dir. 2002. *Bend It Like Beckham*. Fox Searchlight Pictures.

Chadha, Gurinder, dir. 2004. *Bride and Prejudice*. Miramax Films.

Chatzidimitriou, Ioanna. 2015. "'Pour une "littérature-monde" en français': The End of the Francophone World as We Know It?" *The French Review*, vol. 88, no. 4 (Francophonie[s]), pp. 101–115. https://www.jstor.org/stable/24549634

Chronopoulos, Dimitris K., Sotiris Kampanelis, Daniel Oto-Peraliás, and John O.S. Wilson. 2021. "Ancient Colonialism and the Economic Geography of the

Mediterranean." *Journal of Economic Geography*, vol. 21, no. 5, pp. 717–759. https://doi.org/10.1093/jeg/lbaa028

Clark, John P. 1962. "Our Literary Critics." *Nigeria Magazine*, no. 74, pp. 79–82.

Conrad, Joseph. 1899. *Heart of Darkness, Blackwood's Magazine*, no. 1,000. [Repr. in *Youth: A Narrative, and Two Other Stories*, by Joseph Conrad, 49–182. Edinburgh and London: Blackwood & Sons.]

Currey, James. 2003. "Chinua ̄ Achebe, the African Writers Series, and the Establishment of African Literature." *African Affairs*, vol. 102, no. 409, pp. 575–585. https://doi.org/10.1093/afraf/adg067

Damas, Léon-Gontran. 1947. "Introduction." In *Latitudes françaises: Poètes d'expression Française: D'Afrique Noire, Madagascar, Réunion, Guadeloupe, Martinique, Indochine, Guyane, 1900–1945*, edited by Léon-Gontran Damas, 7–16. Paris: Éditions du Seuil.

Dayal, Samir. 2004. "Blackness as Symptom: Josephine Baker and European Identity." In *Blackening Europe: The African American Presence*, edited by Heike Raphael-Hernandez, 57–74. New York: Routledge.

Douglass, Frederick. 1845. *Narrative of the Life of Frederick Douglass, an American Slave, Written by Himself.* Boston: Anti-Slavery Office.

Drescher, Seymour. 2009. *Abolition: A History of Slavery and Antislavery.* Cambridge: Cambridge University Press. https://doi.org/10.1017/CBO9780511770555.016

Driver, Dorothy. 2019. "Invoking Indigeneity: Olive Schreiner and the Poetics of Plants." *Journal of Commonwealth Literature*, vol. 56, no. 1, pp. 61–76. Online first. https://doi.org/10.1177/0021989419842319

Edwards, Brent Hayes. 2003. *The Practice of Diaspora: Literature, Translation, and the Rise of Black Internationalism.* Cambridge: Harvard University Press.

Fanon, Franz. 2002 [originally published 1961]. "Sur la culture nationale." In *Les Damnés de la terre*, by Franz Fanon, 195–235. Paris: Éditions La Découverte & Syros.

Fanon, Franz. 1963 [originally published 1961]. "On National Culture." In *The Wretched of the Earth*, by Frantz Fanon, 166–199. Translated by Constance Farrington. Harmondsworth: Penguin.

Featherstone, Simon. 2005. "Music." In *Postcolonial Cultures*, by Simon Featherstone, 33–64. Edinburgh: Edinburgh University Press.

Freire, Paolo. 1970 [originally published 1968]. *Pedagogy of the Oppressed.* Translated by Myra Bergman Ramos. New York: Herder and Herder.

Gandhi, Mohandas K. 1938. [originally published 1909]. *Hind Swaraj, or Indian Home Rule.* Ahmedabad: Navajivan Publishing House. [As હિંદ સ્વરાજ in *Indian Opinion* (Natal), (11 & 18 December)] [In English translation by Mohandas Gandhi (Phœnix, Natal: International Press, 1910)].

Grace, Patricia. 1986. *Potiki.* Auckland: Penguin.

Grunebaum, Gustave Edmond Von. 1964. *French African Literature: Some Cultural Implications.* Paris: Mouton.

Guevara, Ernesto 'Che'. 2020 [1967]. "Create Two, Three … Many Vietnams, That Is the Watchword: Message to the Tricontinental." In *On Socialism and Internationalism*, by Ernesto 'Che' Guevara, 39–62. New Delhi: Left Word Books. https://thetricontinental.org/wp-content/uploads/2020/10/Che_Guevara

_On_Socialism_and_Internationalism_EN.pdf. [Originally as "Crear dos, tres, muchos Vietnam, esa es la convigua: Mensaje a los pueblos del mundo a través de la Tricontinental," *Tricontinental* magazine, suplemento especial (16 April); English translation by the Executive Secretariat of the Organization of the Solidarity of the Peoples of Africa, Asia, and Latin America (OSPAAAL), *Tricontinental* magazine, no. 1 (July–August) 1967; Repr. Bogotá: Ocean Sur, 2007. https://www.oceansur.com/uploads/catalogue/publications/files/crea-dos-tres-vietnam.pdf]

Haggard, H. Rider. 1907 [originally published 1885]. *King Solomon's Mines.* 1907 edition. London: Cassell and Company. https://www.gutenberg.org/files/2166/2166-h/2166-h.htm

Hankin, Nigel. 1992. *Hanklyn-Janklin: A Stranger's Rumble-Tumble Guide to Some Words, Customs, and Quiddities Indian and Indo-British.* New Delhi: Banyan.

Hannerz, Ulf. 2022. "Palm Wine, Amos Tutuola, and a Literary Gatekeeper." In *Afropolitan Horizons: Essays toward a Literary Anthropology of Nigeria*, by Ulf Hannerz, 28–37. New York: Berghahn Books.

Hiddleston, Jane. 2014. "Léopold Sédar Senghor: Politician and Poet between Hybridity and Solitude." In *Decolonising the Intellectual: Politics, Culture, and Humanism at the End of the French Empire*, by Jane Hiddleston, 38–74. Liverpool: Liverpool University Press.

Huggan, Graham, and Helen Tiffin. 2015 [originally published 2006]. *Postcolonial Ecocriticism: Literature, Animals, Environment.* 2nd ed. London: Routledge.

Innes, Catherine Lynnette. 1990. "The Novelist as Critic: Politics and Criticism, 1960–1988." In *Chinua Achebe*, by Catherine Lynnette Innes, 102–120. Cambridge: Cambridge University Press. https://doi.org/10.1017/CBO9780511554407.008

Jones, Rhys, and Richard Phillips. 2005. "Unsettling Geographical Horizons: Exploring Premodern and Non-European Imperialism." *Annals of the Association of American Geographers*, vol. 95, no. 1, pp. 141–161. https://doi.org/10.1093/jeg/lbaa028

Joseph, George. 2013. "African Literature." In *Understanding Contemporary Africa*, edited by April A. Gordon and Donald L. Gordon, 371–416, 5th ed. London: Lynne Rienner.

Katz, Wendy Roberta. 2010. *Rider Haggard and the Fiction of Empire: A Critical Study of British Imperial Fiction.* Cambridge: Cambridge University Press.

Kaufman, Heidi. 2005. "King Solomon's Mines? African Jewry, British Imperialism, and H. Rider Haggard's Diamonds." *Victorian Literature and Culture*, vol. 33, no. 2, pp. 517–539. https://doi.org/10.1017/S1060150305050965

Khair, Tabish. 2000. "Unhybrid." In *Where Parallel Lines Meet*, by Tabish Khair, 32–33. London: Viking.

Khair, Tabish. 2001. *Babu Fictions: Alienation in Contemporary Indian English Novels.* New Delhi: Oxford University Press.

Kincaid, Jamaica. 1999 [originally published 1993]. "The Garden in Winter." In *My Garden (Book)*, by Jamaica Kincaid, 65–76. New York: Farrar, Straus, and Giroux.

Kipling, Rudyard. 1892 [originally published 1889]. "The Ballad of East and West." In *Ballads and Barrack-room Ballads*, by Rudyard Kipling, 3–11. London: Macmillan and Co.

Krebs, Paula M. 1997. "Olive Schreiner's Racialization of South Africa: Document View." *Victorian Studies*, vol. 40, no. 3, pp. 427–444. https://www.jstor.org/stable/3829293

Kuortti, Joel. 2013. "'No need to be called by another name': Multilingual Challenge to Global English in Tabish Khair's Novel *The Bus Stopped*." In *Tabish Khair: A Critical Companion*, edited by Om Prakash Dwivedi, 48–57. Kolkata: Roman Books.

Kuortti, Joel. 2019. "The Ordinariness of the Diasporic Kitchen." In *Thinking with the Familiar in Contemporary Literature and Culture 'Out of the Ordinary'*, edited by Joel Kuortti, Kaisa Ilmonen, Elina Valovirta, and Janne Korkka, 137–160. Leiden: Brill. https://doi.org/10.1163/9789004406742_009

Lane, Jeremy F. 2013. "Jazz as Antidote to the Machine Age: From Hugues Panassié to Léopold Sédar Senghor." In *Jazz and Machine-Age Imperialism: Music, Race, and Intellectuals in France, 1918–1945*, by Jeremy Lane, 90–125. Ann Arbor: University of Michigan Press.

Lee, Christopher J. 2018. "Anti-Colonialism: Origins, Practices, and Historical Legacies." In *The Oxford Handbook of the Ends of Empire*, edited by Martin Thomas and Andrew S. Thompson, 436–452. Oxford: Oxford University Press (continuous publication). https://doi.org/10.1093/oxfordhb/9780198713197.013.24

Loomba, Ania. [1998] 2015. *Colonialism/Postcolonialism*. 3rd ed. London: Routledge.

Makoni, Sinfree, Busi Makoni, Ashraf Abdelhay, and Pedzisai Mashiri. 2012. "Colonial and Post-colonial Language Policies in Africa: Historical and Emerging Landscapes." In *The Cambridge Handbook of Language Policy*, edited by Bernard Spolsky, 523–543. Cambridge: Cambridge University Press. https://doi.org/10.1017/CBO9780511979026.032

Martin, Wendy. 2021. "Jazz and the Harlem Renaissance." In *A History of the Harlem Renaissance*, edited by Rachel Farebrother and Miriam Thaggert, 345–360. Cambridge: Cambridge University Press. https://doi.org/10.1017/9781108656313.021

Marzagora, Sara. 2015. "African-Language Literatures and the 'Transnational Turn' in Euro-American Humanities." *Journal of African Cultural Studies*, vol. 27, no. 1, pp. 40–55. https://doi.org/10.1080/13696815.2014.926450

Memmi, Albert. 2000 [originally published 1982]. *Racism*. Translated by Steve Martinot. Minneapolis: University of Minnesota Press.

Naipaul, V.S. *The Mimic Men*. London: Penguin, 1967.

Ngom Faye, Mbaré. 1996. *Diálogos con Guinea: Panorama de la literatura guineoecuatoriana de expresión castellana a través de sus protagonistas*. Madrid: Labrys 54 Ediciones.

Ngũgĩ, James [Ngũgĩ wa Thiong'o]. 1965. *The River between*. London: William Heinemann.

Ngũgĩ wa Thiong'o. 1986. *Decolonising the Mind: The Politics of Language in African Literature*. London: James Currey.

Nivesjö, Sanja, and Heidi Barend. 2021. "Current Perspectives on Olive Schreiner's *From Man to Man, or Perhaps Only —*." Interview with Angelo Fick, Jade Munslow Ong, and Valerie L. Stevens. *Journal of Commonwealth Literature*, vol. 56, no. 1, pp. 44–60. https://doi.org/10.1177/0021989418824360

Noor Al-Deen, Hana. 2005. "The Evolution of Rai Music." *Journal of Black Studies*, vol. 35, no. 5, pp. 597–611. https://www.jstor.org/stable/40034339

Nyamnjoh, Francis B. 2015. "Amos Tutuola and the Elusiveness of Completeness." *Stichproben: Wiener Zeitschrift für kritische Afrikastudien/Vienna Journal of African Studies*, vol. 15, no. 29, pp. 1–47. https://doi.org/10.25365/phaidra .360_01

Ogundipe, Molara. 1969. "*The Palm Wine Drinkard*: A Reassessment of Amos Tutuola." *Présence Africaine*, no. 71, pp. 99–108. http://www.jstor.org/stable /24348749

Ortiz, Fernando. 1940. *Contrapunteo cubano del tabaco y el azúcar*. La Habana: Ciencias Sociales.

Owomoyela, Oyekan. 1993. "Introduction." In *A History of Twentieth-Century African Literatures*, edited by Oyekan Owomoyela, 1–8. Lincoln: University of Nebraska Press.

Paine, Thomas [published anonymously]. 1776. *Common Sense*. Philadelphia: R. Bell.

Parrott, R. Joseph. 2022. "Introduction: Tricontinentalism and the Anti-Imperial Project." In *The Tricontinental Revolution: Third World Radicalism and the Cold War*, edited by R. Joseph Parrott and Mark Atwood Lawrence, 1–40. Cambridge: Cambridge University Press. https://doi.org/10.1017 /9781009004824.002

Racine, Daniel L. 1982. "The Aesthetics of Léon-Gontran Damas." *Présence Africaine*, no. 121/122, pp. 154–165. http://www.jstor.org/stable/24351278

Rao, Raja. 1970a [originally published 1938]. *Kanthapura*. Delhi: Hind Pocket Books.

Rao, Raja. 1970b [originally published 1938]. "Foreword." In *Kanthapura*, by Raja Rao, 5–6. Delhi: Hind Pocket Books.

Ravindran, Shruti. 2007. "'Hybrid and Exile Can Become Glib Words...': Shruti Ravindran Interviews Tabish Khair." *Outlook Web* (July 19), online. https:// www.outlookindia.com/website/story/hybrid-and-exile-can-become-glib -words/235121

Rexer, Raisa. 2013. "Black and White and Re(a)d All over: *L'Étudiant noir*, Communism, and the Birth of Négritude." *Research in African Literatures*, vol. 44, pp. 1–14. https://doi.org/10.2979/reseafrilite.44.4.1

Rhys, Jean. 1966. *Wide Sargasso Sea*. London: André Deutsch.

Rushdie, Salman. 1991 [originally published 1981]. *Midnight's Children*. New York: Penguin.

Rushdie, Salman. 1982. "The Empire Writes Back with a Vengeance." *The Times* (July 3), p. 8.

Said, Edward. 1978. *Orientalism*. New York: Pantheon Books.

Salamone, Frank. 2010 [originally published 2007]. "The Depiction of Masculinity in Classic Nigerian Literature." In *Bloom's Modern Critical Interpretations: Chinua Achebe's Things Fall Apart*, edited by Harold Bloom, 141–150. New York: Infobase Publishing. [Orig. *JAL: The Journal of the African Literature Association*, vol. 1, no. 1, pp. 202–213.]

Saro-Wiwa, Ken. 1992. "The Language of African Literature: A Writer's Testimony." *Research in African Literatures*, vol. 23, no. 1, pp. 153–157. https://www.jstor.org/stable/3819957

Schreiner, Olive [pseudonym Ralph Iron]. 1883. *Story of an African Farm*, vols I–II. London: Chapman & Hall. https://www.gutenberg.org/files/1441/1441-h/1441-h.htm

Senghor, Léopold Sédar. 1948. *Anthologie de la nouvelle poésie nègre et malgache de langue française*. Paris: Presses Universitaires de France.

Senghor, Léopold Sédar. 1956. "A New York (pour un orchestre de jazz: solo de trompette)." In *Éthiopiques*, by Léopold Sédar Senghor, 53–57. Paris: Éditions du Seuil.

Senghor, Léopold Sédar. 1964a. "Introduction." In *Liberté 1: Négritude et humanisme*, by Léopold Sédar Senghor, 8–10. Paris: Éditions du Seuil.

Senghor, Léopold Sédar. 1964b [originally published 1937]. "Le Problème Culturel en A.O.F." In *Liberté 1: Négritude et humanisme*, by Léopold Sédar Senghor, 11–21. Paris: Éditions du Seuil.

Senghor, Léopold Sédar. 1964c [originally published 1956]. "Comme les lamantins vont boire à la source." In *Liberté 1: Négritude et humanisme*, by Léopold Sédar Senghor, 218–227. Paris: Éditions du Seuil.

Shakespeare, William. 2003 [originally published 1611]. *The Tempest*. Open Source Shakespeare (OSS). George Mason University. https://www.opensourceshakespeare.org/views/plays/playmenu.php?WorkID=tempest

Shepherd, Robert H.W. 1970 [originally published 1945]. *Lovedale and Literature for the Bantu: A Brief History and a Forecast*. New York: Negro Universities Press.

Shoemaker, Nancy. 2015. "A Typology of Colonialism." *Perspectives on History* (1 October). American Historical Association. https://www.historians.org/publications-and-directories/perspectives-on- history/october-2015/a-typology-of-colonialism

Spivak, Gayatri Chakravorty. 1985. "Can the Subaltern Speak? Speculations on Widow Sacrifice." *Wedge*, no. 7/8, pp. 120–130.

Spivak, Gayatri Chakravorty. 2003 [originally published 1999]. "Literature." In *A Critique of Postcolonial Reason: Toward a History of the Vanishing Present*, by Gayatri Chakravorty Spivak, 112–197. New York: Harvard University Press.

Srivastava, Neelam. 2007. "'Pidgin English or Pigeon Indian?' Babus and Babuisms in Colonial and Postcolonial Fiction." *Journal of Postcolonial Writing*, vol. 43, no. 1, pp. 55–64. https://doi.org/10.1080/17449850701219876

Thomas, Dylan. 1952. "Blithe Spirits." Review of Amos Tutuola's *The Palm-Wine Drinkard*. *The Observer* (June 6), p. 7.

Tobias, Steven M. 1999. "Amos Tutuola and the Colonial Carnival." *Research in African Literatures*, vol. 30, no. 2, pp. 67–74. https://doi.org/10.2979/RAL.1999.30.2.66

Toussaint L'Ouverture. 2008 [original in 1793]. "Proclamation, 29 August 1793." In *Toussaint L'Ouverture: The Haitian Revolution*, edited and translated by Nick Nesbitt, 1–2. London: Verso.

Tutuola, Amos. 1952. *The Palm-Wine Drinkard and His Dead Palm-Wine Tapster in the Dead's Town*. London: Faber & Faber.

Van Coller, Hennie P., ed. 1998. *Perspektief en profiel: 'n Afrikaanse literatuurgeskiedenis*. Pretoria: J.L. Van Schaik.

Veracini, Lorenzo. 2010. *Settler Colonialism: A Theoretical Overview*. Houndmills: Palgrave Macmillan UK.

Wali, Obiajunwa. 1963. "The Dead End of African Literature." *Transition*, no. 10, pp. 13–15. https://www.jstor.org/stable/2934441

Warmbold, Joachim. 1989. *Germania in Africa: Germany's Colonial Literature*. Frankfurt am Main: Peter Lang.

Watts, James. 2022. "Land Reform, Henry Rider Haggard, and the Politics of Imperial Settlement, 1900–1920." *The Historical Journal*, vol. 65, no. 2, pp. 415–435. https://doi.org/10.1017/S0018246X21000613

Young, Robert J.C. 2012. "The Postcolonial Condition." In *The Oxford Handbook of Postwar European History*, edited by Dan Stone, 600–612. Oxford: Oxford University Press, online ed. https://doi.org/10.1093/oxfordhb /9780199560981.013.0030

Yule, Henry, and Arthur Coke Burnell. 2010 [originally published 1886]. *Hobson-Jobson: Being a Glossary of Anglo-Indian Colloquial Words and Phrases and of Kindred Terms Etymological, Historical, Geographical and Discursive*. Cambridge: Cambridge University Press. https://doi.org/10.1017/CBO9781139197922

Zell, Hans M. 1993. "Publishing in Africa: The Crisis and the Challenge." In *A History of Twentieth-Century African Literatures*, edited by Oyekan Owomoyela, 369–387. Lincoln: University of Nebraska Press.

Zephaniah, Benjamin. 2001. *Refugee Boy*. London: Bloomsbury.

4

ECHOES OF HYBRIDITY IN POSTMODERN LITERATURE

Mehdi Ghasemi

Introduction

With its decentered subject and boundary disruption, postmodernism creates a space wherein nothing feels pure and original, and texts host varied and even oppositional multitudes within themselves. As Fredric Jameson (1981, 95) observes, "texts emerge in a space in which we may expect them to be crisscrossed and intersected by a variety of impulses from contradictory modes of cultural production all at once." By the same token, with its subversive agency, hybridity, which brings together cultural mixings and categorical oppositions, suggests "the impossibility of essentialism" (Young 1995, 27). Accordingly, postmodern literature is also marked with hybridity, and a number of postmodern techniques, including bricolage, collage–montage, decanonization, double-coding, exhaustion and replenishment, faction, historiographic metafiction, hyperreality, indeterminacy, intertextuality, magical realism, omnitemporality, palimpsest, parody, participation, polyvocality, simulation, and spatiotemporality, catalyze ethos of hybridity in literary texts. The use of these postmodern techniques destabilizes the dominant concepts of assimilation, authenticity, centrism, essentialism, linearity, purity, stability, and univocal identity.

Shalini Puri (2004, 19) believes that "hybridity in postmodern academy has been to correct purist, essentialist, and organicist conceptions of culture. More specifically, postmodern theories of cultural hybridity have been mobilized to critique […] modern conceptions of a stable unitary subject." Likewise, Joel Kuortti and Jopi Nyman (2007, 3) note that "hybridity is a site of transformation and change where fixed identities based on

DOI: 10.4324/9781003269670-5

essentialisms are called into question." Thus, marked by the combination of different and in cases incongruous components, postmodern hybridity is associated with relativism and dynamism which licence the production of more inclusive products. In the present chapter, we first outline in theory a number of techniques that are most appropriate to our readings of hybridity in postmodern literature and then trace them in Michelle Cliff's novel *No Telephone to Heaven* (1987), Suzan-Lori Parks's play *The Death of the Last Black Man in the Whole Entire World* (1990) and Salman Rushdie's novel *The Satanic Verses* (1988). We aim to show how these authors embody the potential of postmodern hybridity to gear towards questioning hegemonic power structures, essentialism, and fundamentalism and to induce scepticism of social, cultural, historical, and religious grand narratives. We also explore how Cliff, Parks, and Rushdie benefit from the potential of postmodern hybridity to promote the development of a political agenda and incorporate their own mininarratives in the dominant discourses. Since the theories and techniques of postmodern hybridity are diverse, and one text alone does not include and reflect a major number of them, we analyze three texts in the textual analysis section of this chapter to offer better pictures of the hybrid postmodern techniques in practice.

Language and Text Hybridity

In *The Savage Mind*, the French anthropologist Claude Lévi-Strauss used the word "bricolage" to describe the process of deploying the remaining diverse range of fragments from former cultural formations and combining them to create something new. In fact, bricolage forms a mosaic out of the juxtaposition of several fragments, namely "the remains and debris of events" (Lévi-Strauss 1996, 21). As Lévi-Strauss (1996, 21) further explains, bricolage "provides a way to think without establishing a new center, a privileged reference, an origin, a truth. It also inspires creativity [...], making possible new ways of putting things together." In this climate, bricolage problematizes the purity, integrity, and originality of literary works and questions the stability and unity of their components. For example, the postmodern technique of linguistic bricolage typifies the juxtaposition of different terms and phrases, collected from different languages and dialects, which together create syntactical breaks and disintegrate the homogeneity of language. The employment of linguistic bricolage also promotes language fluidity which blurs the defined boundaries between high and low cultures and languages. The simultaneous presentation of different language sounds in one text also brings about indeterminacies, "a combination of trends that include openness, fragmentation, ambiguity, discontinuity, decenterment, heterodoxy, pluralism, deformation" (Hassan 1993,

282). Consequently, indeterminacies, which complicate readers' comprehension, leave the meanings open to different interpretations. Linguistic hybridity extends beyond the mimetic as shown in the use of neologisms, mixed languages, and even invented expressions by innovative writers such as Salman Rushdie and Amitav Ghosh. While Ghosh's historical works, including *Sea of Poppies* (2008), utilize the languages and expressions of India under the British Empire, Rushdie's works, including *Midnight's Children* and *The Satanic Verses*, as we discuss later in this chapter, use diverse linguistic strategies. As critics like O.P. Dwivedi (2008) have shown, Rushdie employs various linguistic tactics and layers as he mixes English with other languages, including Hindi and Urdu, as well as with slang to create hybrid verbal expressions and compounds suitable for addressing a multicultural nation.

In postmodern literature, bricolage is also affected by intertextuality, defined as an implicit or explicit reference to, and interrelationship between, different texts. Intertextuality is formed based on the combination or relations between different canons, discourses, and narratives, and it contributes to the creation of a heterogeneous climate. As Umberto Eco (1984, xxiv) puts it, "books always speak of other books, and every story tells a story that has already been told." In this light, "intertextuality represents a process of repetition and revision. [...] A number of shared structural elements are repeated, with differences that suggest familiarity with other texts" (Gates, Jr. 1988, 60). This device, which adds alternative perspectives to literary works, links a text to other subtexts and provides the ground for readers to, for instance, compare the present conditions with the past or touch upon the roots of some ideologies. Moreover, entrance into "multifaceted relationships with other texts" (Schmidt 2005, 37) defies notions of originality and replaces it with recycling different texts and contexts, ideas and ideologies. In this climate, intertextuality suggests that postmodern authors cannot claim that they are the sole proprietor of their works, because their works function as parodies, borrowing from a variety of texts from different areas and eras (Ghasemi 2016, 86). Moreover, the repetition and revision of a wide variety of fictional and nonfictional intertexts or hybrids provide authors with an opportunity to examine old metanarratives, add their own mininarratives into the new context, and offer a rereading of previous works from new perspectives which "fill readers with new significations" (Ghasemi 2014, 7).

As a result of mixing different texts and languages, hybrid postmodern literature functions to challenge the dominant orders of established hierarchies in an effort to free thoughts from outworn ideologies and metanarratives. According to the French literary theorist Jean-François Lyotard (1984, 60), in postmodernity, faith in metanarratives has ebbed, and thus, knowledge has had to seek its legitimation not universally but locally. Building on Lyotard's definition, Linda Hutcheon (1989, 39) argues that postmodernism "is characterized by no grand totalizing master narrative but by smaller and multiple narratives which do not seek (or obtain) any universalizing stabilization or legitimation." Based on these observations, postmodern hybridity is characterized by a rebuttal of metanarratives and an inclusion of provisional, contingent, and relational mininarratives. This is to say, postmodern hybridity "disrupts the boundaries between the dominant and the marginal, high and popular cultures through mixing of different ideologies, religions, cultures, discourses, and languages with the dominant ones, which in some cases is riddled with contradictions" (Ghasemi 2019, 168). In this light, the plurality of discourses and narratives in postmodern literature creates incredulity towards the total absolute concepts of Identity, History, and Truth, replacing them with multiple identities, histories, and truths, preparing the ground for the arrival of multiple (counter)narratives.

Hybridity of Time/Space and Fact/Fiction

The interference of a wide variety of (counter)narratives from different settings to the host texts creates spatiotemporality wherein time and place become dislodged and multiperspectival. Joanna P. Sharp (1994, 65) writes that "[h]ybridity is a spatial condition produced through attachment to multiple places." The creation of such spatiotemporality, which also brings about deliberate anachronism, enables postmodern writers to blend different times and host several characters from different eras and areas in their fictions. In this hybrid climate, the employment of temporal distortion defies "linearity in favor of a representation of time as a disjointed and highly fragmented collage of events yielding dispersed identities made up of multiple, often disconnected elements" (Strongman 2007, 97). Through using collage–montage technique, postmodern writers transfer and juxtapose different materials and borrowings from a number of heterogeneous contexts in their own texts. The collage–montage assemblage technique and temporal distortion enable postmodern writers to invite, for example, historical figures from different locations and times to their works and meet with their fictional counterparts. The use of historical figures along with fictional characters creates a stylistic and spatial hybridity, while also creating the ground for the creation of "historiographic metafiction."

Historiographic metafiction, which embeds elements of history and fiction, enhances hybridity in postmodern literature. Historiographic metafiction "problematises historical veracity in favour of metafictional self-reflexivity and intertextuality" (Pettersson 2013, 98) and "plays upon the truth and lies of historical records" (Hutcheon 1995, 114). Thus, a number of postmodern writers make use of the potential of historiographic metafiction to rethink and rework history contents, challenge the monologic discourses of history, and include repressed subgroups' mininarratives in the texture of history. As literary theorist Brian McHale (1987, 87; emphasis original) observes, a number of historical fictions "treat the interior life of historical figures as dark areas – logically enough, since the 'official' historical record cannot report on what went on *inside* a historical figure without fictionalizing to some extent." Hence, historiographic metafiction reimagines and invents dialogues, interior monologues, soliloquies, and even documentation to restore missing, subjugated, and silent historical moments within literary texts. To illuminate dark spots, writers of historiographic metafiction rewrite events while adding their own mininarratives which act as "counterhistory." To Michael Foucault (2003, 133), counterhistory refers to "the discourse of those who have no glory, or those who have lost it and who now find themselves, perhaps for a time – but probably for a long time – in darkness and silence."

In this light, as a reflection of unheard voices and unrecorded histories, counterhistory imagines and re-enacts the past to undo the silences. This is to say, postmodern literature intermingles fact and fiction (i.e., faction) to rewrite subjugated and silenced history, implying that "history itself may be a form of fiction" (McHale 1987, 96). For example, Julian Barnes's novel *A History of the World in 10½ Chapters* (1989) retells the biblical tale of Noah's Ark from the point of view of the woodworms, which were not allowed onboard. The woodworm that hides in the body of the ark narrates the first chapter and questions the wisdom of appointing Noah as God's representative. Another example, Tim O'Brien's *The Things They Carried* (1990) relies on fiction to rehistoricize the Vietnam War as a historical event. O'Brien interweaves history and fiction throughout the novel to convey his own experience of fighting in the Vietnam War. Historiographic metafiction contends that both history and fiction are human constructs, and "as such they are already interpretations – that is distanced from brute reality or experience unmediated by time or by act of transcribing" (Hutcheon 1986, 307). For its part, historiographic metafiction denaturalizes "notions of historical documents as representations of the past and of the way such archival traces of historical events are used within historiographic and fictive representations" (Hutcheon 2002, 48). In postmodernity, fake things can be offered as real, and real things as fake, and, accordingly, reality is no longer real, but hyperreal. Thus, postmodernity is also defined by a shift into "hyperreality" in which simulations replace the real (Baudrillard 1993, 342–343). Based on this assumption, there tends to be no direct access to the sense of the real which has been simulated.

Alongside historiographic metafiction and simulation, magical realism combines realistic events with impossible or unrealistic ones. It is characterized by blending, for example, daily life happenings with dreams to unveil the magic within reality. To expose the magic behind real events, magical realism collides and integrates contradictory codes, including natural and supernatural, fictional and nonfictional, realism and fantasy, magical and rational, story and history, to create an atmosphere of mixedness. Stephen Slemon (1995, 409) concurs that

> [i]n the language of narration in a magic realist text, a battle between two oppositional systems takes place, each working toward the creation of a different kind of fictional world from the other. Since the ground rules of these two worlds are incompatible, neither one can fully come into being, and each remains suspended.

In this climate, both codes remain dependent on each other, and "neither of the two codes can establish its supremacy" (Kluwick 2011, 17). Moreover, the combination of the dissimilar codes might create unharmonious, uncanny, and unknown worlds for readers.

In addition, postmodern hybridity uses "double-coding" as well as "palimpsest" techniques to enhance hybridity. In architecture, "double coding" is used to describe the architects' attempts to establish links between the present and the past through blending new techniques with old patterns in a construction (Ghasemi 2016, 87). For instance, they fit new buildings into old structures; thus, a building may look ancient, but upon entering it, one finds it totally new and advanced. As a postmodern technique utilized also in literature, double-coding links the present to the past through revisiting and recontextualizing previous texts and their old themes and appropriating them for present conditions. In palimpsest, the original text of, for example, an old manuscript made of papyrus, is partially erased or scraped, and this makes room for a new text to be superimposed and grafted over the layers of the original one which results in the creation of a hybrid text. Thus, the palimpsest offers multi-layered texts which include both the old and the new views. Through employing palimpsest technique, postmodern writers fill in the parts which have been effaced from the historical records, and in their hybrid works, two vectors simultaneously operate: the vector of "similarity and oldness" and the vector of "difference and newness" (Hall 1990, 223), which work together to represent a double view of history. Double-coding and palimpsest techniques also replenish the exhausted history and story, providing readers with alternative perspectives to the recycled history (Ghasemi 2019, 80).

The combination of the two vectors challenges the 'author'ity of authors who cannot claim sole authorship and originality of their recycled works. Viewed in this light, postmodern literature generates the death of centres, "from the 'death of god' to the 'death of the author'" (Hassan 1986, 505). In fact, the death of the author brings about the birth of readers, who are invited to contribute to texts' construction. As a result of the readers' contributions, postmodern literature becomes participatory and hybrid. Postmodern writers engage their readers in the writing process and decodification and invite them to decipher the encrypted texts and/ or fill in the gaps that exist in their writings. This can be seen as a transition from passive readers to active agents who can function as co-authors. Naturally, the readers' contributions may differ from one another, simply because each reader, affected by their ethnicity, gender, and class as well as their religious, political, and cultural orientations, approaches the works differently.

The above-mentioned features are some of the hallmarks of hybridity in postmodern literature which are traced and analyzed in Cliff's *No Telephone to Heaven*, Parks's *The Death of the Last Black Man in the Whole Entire World*, and Rushdie's *The Satanic Verses*. The employment of these techniques represents several periods, places, and peoples at once in a splintered and nonlinear style, disrupts boundaries between dominant and marginal discourses, and questions the veracity of outworn metanarratives. As we discuss, Cliff, Parks, and Rushdie employ hybrid aesthetics to problematize hegemonic narratives and bring together discrete and hence bounded histories, identities, cultures, and languages in their works.

Textual Analysis 1: Hybrid Identities and Bricolage in Michelle Cliff's *No Telephone to Heaven*

Michelle Cliff (1990, 246) introduces herself "as a writer of Afro-Caribbean (Indian, African, and white) experience and heritage" who "attempts to draw together everything [she is] and [has] been" in "a liberated and synthesized version." As a bildungsroman with a multiple of narrative fragments mostly based on Cliff's autobiography and Jamaica's history, her novel *No Telephone to Heaven* weaves together different personal and national mininarratives. The novel begins with a guerilla group in khaki uniforms riding on an open-backed truck in the Jamaican countryside fighting for Jamaica's independence ending, in a circular plot, with their mission accomplished, and in-between it moves back and forth through transnational journeys of the protagonist to the United States, the United Kingdom, and France. As Frederick Buell (1994, 102) observes: "The hybrid form of the novel – it is one-third North American immigrant literature, one-third British bildungsroman, and one-third nativist lyric of attempted return to roots – mirrors a hybrid Jamaica set in a hybrid and hybridizing world."

Like the hybrid form of the novel, Clare Savage, the main biracial light-skinned young Jamaican character, manifests hybridity: "She is white. Black. Female. Lover. Beloved. Daughter. Traveler. Friend. Scholar. Terrorist. Farmer" (Cliff 1987, 91). The novel further introduces Clare in the following way: "There are many bits and pieces to her, for she is composed of fragments" (Cliff 1987, 87). This introduction manifests Clare's postmodern subjectivity and multifarious dimensions and shows how she is perceived by different parties, including her family, friend, and foe. Clare, "whose fragmented diasporic identity seems the quintessence of hybrid '*post*-marked' subjectivity" (Moynagh 1999, 116; emphasis original), embraces a multitude of identities as black and white, lover and beloved, Jamaican, and American, a heterosexual and homosexual, a teacher and fighter. Clare's hybrid identity is not located in a single pole of binary oppositions, but it constantly oscillates between a proliferation of different poles.

Her hybrid identity further manifests itself in her name, "Clare Savage," which represents biraciality. For instance, as a biblical and English name, "Clare" is juxtaposed with "Savage," combining Western and non-Western, civilized and uncivilized sentiments. As a negative racial indicator, "Savage" signifies barbarism and "wildness that has been bleached from her skin" (Cliff 1990, 265), and the whole name together, as Cliff (1990, 264) notes, offers the image of a "crossroad character," who consists of multiple and contradictory components and fragmented identities in one single body. Owing to these contradictory traits, Clare is also called "white chocolate" and "white cockroach" in the novel (Cliff 1987, 85). She is described as white outside and black inside. The opposite is applied to white Americans in the novel: "WHITE PEOPLE CAN BE BLACK-HEARTED" (Cliff 1987, 81; capital letters in original), meaning that white Americans might be of black nature. In this regard, Roberto Strongman (2007, 100) writes that "[a]llegorically, [Clare's] name and the names of most of the characters speak to the racial characteristics attributed to them. To call a Jamaican family 'the Savages' is an obvious reference to the primitivization of colonized peoples." By the same token, Kaisa Ilmonen (2012, 53) sees Clare's skin-color as the embodiment of "the colonial hierarchies" that "becomes a site of both hybridity and creolization in the novel therefore appearing as a political signifier." Through naming her characters as such, Cliff indicates how English language and culture have affected Jamaicans' identities during its long-term colonial period (1655–1962) and how the Jamaicans have been perceived by the colonists.

Also the novel's texture resonates with Clare's fragmented and hybrid identity and name. The three successive paragraphs below clearly represent the fragmented and hybrid texture of the novel:

For Kitty [Clare's mother] and her other daughter, Jennie [Clare's sister], there were two rooms at an auntie's in Mountain view Gardens. Kitty got her job back. She was prepared to wait out her husband's stubbornness. *Absence makes the heart grow fonder*, she ended one letter. Could so easily turn to *Out of sight, out of mind*. […]

The truck lurches. She grabs the hand of the comrade at her left. The material under the tarp shifts and rolls. Still the truck climbs. The sun has come out – hot. And the khaki is stuck to her back, and trickles of moisture collect under her breasts. When the truck steadies she lifts her breasts and blots the wet spaces with the khaki.

Boy took Clare to a high school. The principal, brass ornament indicating she was Mrs. Taylor, a woman with a flushed face and thin body, timepiece dangling on a chain around her neck, greeted the two of them, asked them to be seated.

(Cliff 1987, 97; emphasis original)

In the first paragraph, Clare describes the living condition of her mother and sister in Jamaica, while in the second paragraph, she shows her inconvenient state on the truck after their operation in Jamaica, while the last one portrays the moments when Boy Savage along with his daughter visit a school in the United States to enrol her. The three successive paragraphs occur in three different settings, and this hybrid texture of juxtaposing time and space recurs throughout the novel. In fact, Clare's frequent mental and physical oscillation between multiple locations distorts the narration linearity and provides the ground for spatiotemporality, wherein the timeline between past, present, and future is blurred, and different occurrences at different locations are represented as simultaneous happenings. Cliff's use of multi-perspective or ever-shifting settings, occurring in different cultural, historical, and geographical landscapes and periods, indicates that identities are fluid and polylithic, and they are not confined to one single era and area.

Likewise, the texture of Clare's narration, combining history, autobiography, and fiction, further highlights her own fragmented hybrid identity. In parallel with her own personal experience, the protagonist evokes Jamaicans' collective memories of oppression, tribulation, and triumph alongside their stereotypes, archetypes, and myths and provides readers with alternative images of Jamaica. The presence of all these pieces of canvas stitched together creates a patchwork, representing the hybrid texture of Jamaican communities. To show this hybrid society, Boy Savage refers to the 128 Aristotelian racial categories in the Spanish colonies they had to memorize on a course of the history of Jamaica: among them were "mulatto, offspring of African and white; sambo, offspring of African and mulatto; quadroon, offspring of mulatto and white; mestee, offspring of quadroon and white" (Cliff 1987, 56). The long list shows both the diversity of multiracial identities and also the colonial practice of control through categorizaton.

Since the novel frequently moves from one time and location to another, it reflects linguistic and cultural hybridity, too. For instance, to show cultural hybridity in the United States, Cliff represents a shop that is run by a woman originally from Puerto Rico. The creole woman speaks Spanish along with English. Upon entering the shop, Clare's mother Kitty starts the conversation as follows:

> "I am newly arrived. I am a Jamaican."
> "*De Jamaica?*" The shopkeeper gave the name of the island the Spanish pronunciation.
> "*Si, de Jamaica.*"
> "*Bueno.* What can I do for you?"
>
> *(Cliff 1987, 79; italics original)*

The use of Spanish alongside English shows the interaction of superordinate and subordinate discourses, transforming English to "Hinglish" as Cliff (1987, 17) names it. Linguistic bricolage manifests itself when Cliff juxtaposes formal English, as the dominant language, with some of its accents. For instance, as Clare narrates,

> [w]hen he was eight, Christopher's grandmother died. What she thought was a touch of dropsy was in fact something else, and her belly swell up and she gone. Him grandmother dead when him eight but him stay on in de shack.
>
> *(Cliff 1987, 40)*

In this excerpt, the narrator mixes standard and vernacular languages. The first sentence is formal, while the second one is a combination of formal and informal languages. The last sentence, however, turns into vernacular English. The three sentences manifest a quick transition from English to Hinglish. In addition to the linguistic bricolage, the novel frequently combines direct and indirect speech so that different voices are mingled, complicating the storyline. This can be seen in a phone conversation between Paul and Christopher's girlfriend:

He reached the girl. She told him that Christopher had not been with her that night and that if Mas' Paul see him, him to tell de bwai she damn vex'. Is jus' who him t'ink him is? Fockin' Shaft? Paul hung up the phone and went out onto the verandah. At that instant he saw Christopher strolling up the driveway. Paul ran to meet him in a sudden, as he had run to meet him when they were boys.

(Cliff 1987, 29)

As the passage shows, Cliff employs a vernacular dialect that resonates with the rhythms of Jamaican English. Her use of different forms of language, formal and vernacular, juxtaposed via linguistic bricolage, not only raises polyvocality but also enhances indeterminacy.

It is worth noting that besides employing vernacular language, there is also a three-page glossary at the end of the book, defining the less-familiar terms. The glossary creates metatextuality and paratextuality. References to the glossary disrupt the linearity of reading, because readers are held in motion and oscillation between the main text and the meta- and paratexts, which is in tune with Clare's constant moves from country to country. Hutcheon (1986, 304) calls these types of notes "extra-textual references" that refer to the world outside the text. Through references to the glossary, the borderline between the main and supplementary texts, or rather the central and marginal texts, is blurred – a postmodern hybrid attempt to highlight textually marginalized notes.

In addition to the use of meta- and paratextuality, *No Telephone to Heaven* includes numerous intertextualities. For example, the book opens with an excerpt from Derek Walcott's poem "Laventille" (1970) (Cliff 1987, i). The excerpt directs the readers' attention to an open wound which has not healed yet, and deep amnesia adds insult to that injury. Jennifer J. Smith (2009, 147) notes that "Cliff's novel attempts to memorialize histories that have been forgotten under the amnesia induced by colonial rule." Cliff benefits from the potential of historiography and fiction alike in demarginalizing unheard voices and discourses which have been passed into oblivion. In addition to an excerpt from Walcott's poem, the novel hosts numerous other intertexts. Nine chapters out of eleven begin with excerpts from other literary works. Inside the chapters, the text also employs intertexts, including George Orwell's *Coming Up for Air* (1939), Thomas Mann's *Death in Venice* (1912), and C.L.R. James's *The Black Jacobins* (1938), to name a few. The most notable one, however, is the reference to Charlotte Brontë's *Jane Eyre* (1847):

She picked up the book beside her. *Jane Eyre.* Used, bought recently in a bookshop in Camden Passage, shabby nineteenth-century binding, pages bearing vague stains, fingered, smoothed. She opened the book to the place she left it when the taxicab pulled up.

"My daughter, flee temptation."

"Mother, I will," Jane responded, as the moon turned to woman.

The fiction had tricked her. Drawn her in so that she became Jane.

Yes. The parallels were there. Was she not heroic Jane? Betrayed. Left to wander. Solitary. Motherless. Yes, and with no relations to speak of except an uncle across the water. She occupied her mind.

Comforted for a time, she came to. Then, with a sharpness, reprimanded herself. No, she told herself. No, she could not be Jane. Small and pale. English. No, she paused. No, my girl, try Bertha. Wild-maned Bertha. [...] Yes, Bertha was closer to the mark. Captive. Ragôut. Mixture. Confused. Jamaican. Caliban. Carib. Cannibal. Cimarron. All Bertha. All Clare.

(Cliff 1987, 115–116; italics original)

As the passage shows, Clare draws a comparison between herself and Jane. First, she highlights her resemblances with Jane as a betrayed, lonely, and motherless figure, but soon she detects her racial differences with Jane as a small pale English girl. Then, she identifies herself with Bertha, who is also a mixture and a confused Jamaican girl. Through the employment of intertextuality, the text manifests that it is not 100% original, but that it consists of, or is built upon, other texts. From one perspective, this is a remake of the old, a rereading of the exhausted texts. From another perspective, references to other authors make *No Telephone to Heaven* multi-voiced with the voices of literary antecedents. In a similar vein, the wide range of intertexts in the novel recalls the idea of "cultural mulattos," dubbed by Trey Ellis. As Ellis (1989, 235) notes:

> Just as a genetic mulatto is a black person of mixed parents who can often get along fine with his white grandparents, a cultural mulatto, educated by a multiracial mix of cultures, can also navigate easily in the white world.

Thus, Cliff recontextualizes old literary sources to challenge and reform the old monolithic trend of representing the Jamaicans.

By the same token, the novel navigates in the historical sources of Jamaica. The novel employs the palimpsest technique to bring to surface submerged hi/stories of the Jamaicans and add them to the erased or scraped areas. Cliff uses incidents from history – or rather herstory – to fill in the gaps that exist in the history of the Jamaicans. From this standpoint, the indigenous mininarratives challenge the genuinity and authenticity of the master narratives. This is seen in Clare's interrogation before being admitted as a member of the guerrilla group. The interrogator asks Clare about her profession:

> What history do you bring to your students?
>> The history of their ... our homeland.
>> How have you found this history?
>> I have educated myself since my return. Spoken with the old people ... leafed through the archives downtown ... spent time at the university library ... one thing leads to another. I have studied the conch knife excavated at the Arawak site in White Marl ... the shards of hand-thrown pots ... the petroglyphs hidden in the bush ... listened to the stories about Nanny and taken them to heart. I have seen the flock of white birds fly out at sunset from Nanny-town ... duppies, the old people say.
>> Duppies?
>> Ghosts; the spirits of Maroons.
>> What else ... what other sources?
>> Stories of Anansi ... Oshun ... Shango ... I have walked the cane ... poked through the ruins ... rusted machines marked Glasgow ... standing as they were left. I have swam underwater off the cays.
>> History can be found underwater.
>> Yes – some history is only underwater.
>
> *(Cliff 1987, 193)*

The dialogue shows that Clare does not confine herself to the written history. Rather, she consults a variety of sources, written and oral, and searches for hidden, untold, immersed, or effaced histories. Through exploring different narratives, listening to different voices, leafing through the archives, and adding her own living and reading experience, Clare aims "to restore matrilineal histories that have been effaced by colonial and neocolonial discourses" (Smith 2009, 141). In other words, recycling Jamaican history enables the author to establish some links between the past and present, old and new views of history, and to renew the history of her homeland, which is in line with the double-coding technique. The revision of history shows that she does not accept the institutionalized discourses as they are. Instead, she searches different layers of history and blends them with her own findings. In this context, Cliff adds her own personal and family mininarratives, the ones received from her own research, and words of her peoples' mouth to the blank spaces of the official histories, making them more inclusive. Fiona R. Barnes (1992, 30) writes that "the hybridization and multiplication of narrative forms undermine any attempts at totalization or containment by Western critics." This is to "otherize" rather than "authorize" history through rewriting Jamaican's mininarratives into history. Adding the obscured marginalized mininarratives to the existing history provides readers with a multiplicity of perspectives which are not available in colonial history.

Textual Analysis 2: Intertextuality and Spatiotemporality in Suzan-Lori Parks's *The Death of Last Black Man in the Whole Entire World*

In her play, *The Death of the Last Black Man in the Whole Entire World*, African American playwright Suzan-Lori Parks engages with postmodernism to historicize African American history and call into question a number of prevailing metanarratives and stereotypes imposed on African Americans. Parks promotes the development of a political agenda to incorporate African Americans' mininarratives within the context of dominant discourses and proffer alternative perspectives to reshape African Americans' identities.

Like Cliff's *No Telephone to Heaven*, Parks's play is set in a world where time and place are fragmentary and slide away from the norms of logic. Although the time of the play is given as "The Present," the play moves backward and forward in time in a non-horizontal and nonlinear way, creating time distortion. The time distortion is perceived, for instance, in the words of one of the figures, named Queen-Then-Pharaoh Hatshepsut: "Yesterday tuhday next summer tuhmorrow just uh moment ugoh in 1317 dieded thuh last black man in thuh whole entire world. [...] He falls 23 floors to his death" (Parks 1995, 111). As Jennifer Larson (2012, 21) writes, "Black Woman's yesterday, today, and 'long time uhgoh' coexist, but in a jumbled and fragmented state." Yet in another case, another figure, Lots of Grease and Lots of Pork, says: "In the *future* when they *came* along I *meeting* them" (Parks 1995, 104; emphases added). Here, tense incongruity is used to blend and blur the timeline between the past, the present, and the future. Owing to temporal hybridity, "memories converge, condense, conflict, and define relationships between past, present, and future" (Malkin 1999, 23), creating a sense of omnitemporality or, in Anne Ubersfeld's (1999, 135) terms, "non-time." The non-time is also represented through such innovative wordplays as "diediduh," which consists of "die," "died," "did," and "duh" (do), implying: Do or Die (Ghasemi 2016, 58). According to Deborah Geis (2008, 58), "the Black Man speaks of living in both the past and the present at the same time, though his way of putting it is amusingly confusing." A part of the confusion arises from the hybridity of tenses, since the reconfiguration of the past emerges in the present, and the reconfiguration of the present manifests itself in the past. Viewed in this light, Parks's play is suspended between the past and the present, between here and there, and between what was and what is. Consequently, the mixture of tenses enhances indeterminacies in the play. For example, Old Man River Jordan's word-play – "Do in dip diddly did-did thuh drop? Drop do it be dripted?" (Parks 1995, 116) – renders past and present tenses unidentifiable, and the alliterative use of the consonant "d" as well as the indeterminate use of "Do" and "Did" as past and present tense identifiers magnify the sense of omnitemporality.

The mixing of tenses draws simultaneously upon a repertoire of history in miniature, tracing African Americans' histories from their imagined roots in the biblical curse of Ham and pharaonic Egypt to the time before Columbus and the Middle Passage to enslavement and subjugation, continuing up until the Civil Rights Movement and the assassinations of two of its leaders. To mix and match patches of history from different times and locations, Parks employs collage–montage technique. Like pieces of torn photographs, the technique offers portraits of African Americans and displays different and, in cases, contrasting images. These devices evoke the effects of fragmentation, heterogeneity, multiplicity, and plurality. Thus, like *No Telephone to Heaven*, *The Death of the Last Black Man in the Whole Entire World* looks like a dramatized mosaic built out of the juxtaposition of a number of glimmering and dimmed images, derived from the elements of history, ethnicity, and politics that blend and clash, manifesting polyvocalism in a discontinuous way. In this light, Cliff's novel and Parks's play are "a lot like standing in an appliance store trying to watch three or four television shows at once" (McDowell, Hoistetler, and Bellis 2002, 12), or a "giant screen," in Baudrillard's (2001, 55) terms, which represents miscellaneous periods, places, and peoples at once.

The multiscreen also displays numerous intertexts that are used in the play. The intertextuality starts with the title of the play and the name of the main figure, Black Man With Watermelon. The Black Man resonates with titles of previous African American literary works, amongst them Richard Wright's *Native Son* (1940) and *Black Boy* (1945), and the nameless character who reached maturity, for example, in Ralph Ellison's *Invisible Man* (1952). Ellison's anonymous mature man reappears in Parks's play, still unidentified but bearing the collective memories and identities of earlier African Americans, to act as the last contestant in this relay race. Additionally, *The Death of the Last Black Man in the Whole Entire World* resonates to a great extent in tone and in the use of repetition and revision with the speech delivered by Invisible Man at his friend Tod Clifton's funeral ceremony. When Clifton is ruthlessly shot dead by the police for no logical reason, he is determined to

make it known that the meaning of his death was greater than the inci-
dent or the object that caused it. Both as a means of avenging him and
of preventing other such deaths ... yes, and of attracting lost members
back into the ranks.

(Ellison 1952, 338)

As the first step, he decides to "use his funeral to put his integrity together
again" (Ellison 1952, 338). In her play, Parks promotes a political agenda
through holding another commemoration ceremony for Clifton and other
anonymous and/or "lost members" of the African American community.
It is worth noting that Parks simulates multiple violent deaths of Black Man
With Watermelon. He is hunted, hanged, jettisoned, drowned, falling from
23 floors, lynched, and electrocuted in the play. However, he always returns
right after his death. The simulation of different types of recurring deaths
of the black figure and his reappearance furnishes the play with a sense of
magical realism (Ghasemi 2016, 55).

Black Man With Watermelon's name resonates with *Watermelon Man*, a
1970 American movie directed by Melvin Van Peebles. It tells the story of
a bigoted white insurance employee who wakes up one morning and finds
that he has turned into a "negro" (Berra 2010, 43). Moreover, Black Man
With Watermelon's name reverberates with Boy Willie and Lymon, the
black characters in August Wilson's play *The Piano Lesson*, who sell watermelon in white neighbourhoods. However, in Parks's play, Black Man With
Watermelon repeatedly insists that the watermelon is not his: "This does
not belong tuh me. Somebody planted this on me. On me in my hands"
(Parks 1995, 105). In another instance he asks: "melon mines? –. Dont
look like me [...]. Was we green and stripedly when we first comed out?"
(Parks 1995, 107). This indicates Black Man With Watermelon's endeavors
to question stereotypical representations of African Americans, perpetuated
by popular culture. Here Black Man With Watermelon should not be seen
as an individual but a representative of his race. According to Henry Louis
Gates, Jr. (1989, 242), "[i]t is clear that black writers read and critique other
black texts as an act of rhetorical self-definition." Gates, Jr.'s (1988, xxi)
theory of "signification" "functions as a metaphor for formal revision, or
intertextuality, within the Afro-American literary tradition." Based on this,
postmodern authors like Cliff and Parks reuse motifs from previous works
but appropriate them for their own objectives.

The intertextual dimension is also detected in the constructed natures
and generic names of almost all figures in the play. It is worth noting that
Parks employs eleven stereotypical, biblical, historical, media, and intertextual figures from different locations and times, each representing a group.
Here is an example of figure juxtaposition in the play:

Queen-Then-Pharaoh Hatshepsut: An I am Sheba she be me. Youll mutter thuh words and part thuh waves and come uhlong come uhlong.

And Bigger And Bigger And Bigger: I would like tuh be fit in back in thuh storybook from which I camed [...]. I'm grown too big for thuh words that's me [...].

Prunes and Prisms: Prunes and Prisms, Prunes and Prisms, Prunes and Prisms: 14.

Before Columbus: Before Columbus directs thuh traffic: left right left right.

(Parks 1995, 116)

Queen-Then-Pharaoh Hatshepsut alludes to the woman pharaoh ruling in ancient Egypt for about twenty years and achieving remarkable triumphs. Through the employment of this historical figure, Parks opens readers' eyes to the rich civilization of people of African descent. Another figure, And Bigger And Bigger And Bigger, is drawn from the image of Bigger Thomas in Richard Wright's *Native Son* (Geis 2008, 69). The transfer of this character to Parks's play shows that "characters in black metafiction move gracefully from one world to the other, taking advantage of the juxtaposition of the imaginary and the real worlds" (Jablon 1997, 56). This shows that hybridity is part and parcel of black metafiction, which represents itself in intertextuality and self-referentiality, creating a multitude of voices and discourses. As his objection – "I would like tuh be fit in back in thuh storybook from which I camed. [...] I am grown too big for thuh words that's me" (Parks 1995, 115–116) – shows, he does neither like the name he was given nor the way his story has been recounted. Thus, like Black Man With Watermelon, he struggles to rebut his negative portrayals. The name of another character, Prunes and Prisms, is drawn from a phrase spoken aloud in order to form the lips into a pretty pursed shape, as per the instructions by Mrs. General to Amy, that is, Little Dorrit in Charles Dickens's *Little Dorrit* (1857) (Geis 2008, 70). Mrs. General advises Amy: "The word Papa [...] gives a pretty form to the lips. Papa, potatoes, poultry, *prunes, and prism* are all very good words for the lips: especially *prunes and prism*, [...] *prunes and prism, prunes and prism*" (Dickens 1868, 503; emphases added). Furthermore, Prunes and Prisms alludes to Chapter 13, "Nausicaa," in James Joyce's *Ulysses* (1922): "And the dark one with the mop head and the nigger mouth. I knew she could whistle. Mouth made for that. [...] Say *prunes and prisms* forty times every morning, *cure for fat lips*" (Joyce 1993, 354; emphases added). Like Cliff, Parks satirizes the racist stereotypes about African Americans in an ironic way and coerces readers to see the construction of negative images.

As a counterhistory play, *The Death of the Last Black Man in the Whole Entire World* represents marginal parts of histories of African Americans that are not found in American historical narratives. For example, the inter-textual figure Before Columbus, who signifies the pre-Columbian conditions before the European discovery and colonization of "the New World," desubjugates some of the marginal mininarratives of African American histories. His/her name resonates with the title of Ivan Van Sertima's (1976, 35) book, *They Came Before Columbus: The African Presence in Ancient America*, in which he claims that a group of Africans during the Mandingo dynasty had already travelled from Mali to North America in the early fourteenth century, before the voyages of Columbus. Thus, as Geis (2008, 66) writes: "Before Columbus's name challenges the traditional credit that Columbus gets for having 'discovered' America." Generally speaking, Parks's play brings forth figures that "are absent in normative historical narratives" (Johung 2006, 44), and their presence challenges the veracity of widely accepted historical records. The employment of these figures indicates that Parks does not take the represented history and culture of African Americans as a total and disinterested entity, and accordingly she detotalizes and hybridizes it. In short, through reenacting "the debris of history" (hooks 1992, 172) and its deviant moments, Parks destructures the authenticity of professional historiography via incorporating challenging perspectives and mininarratives in one single text.

Textual Analysis 3: Historiographic Metafiction and Magical Realism in Salman Rushdie's *The Satanic Verses*

As a hybridized postmodernist novel, Salman Rushdie's *The Satanic Verses* is a pastiche, which patches together numerous paradigms, literary texts, languages, religions, histories, and temporalities. In *Imaginary Homelands*, Rushdie (1991, 394) writes that *The Satanic Verses* "celebrates hybridity, impurity, intermingling, the transformation that comes out of new and unexpected combinations of human beings, cultures, ideas, politics, movies, songs. It rejoices in mongrelization and fears the absolutism of the pure." Likewise, Pnina Werbner (2001, 147) believes that "*The Satanic Verses* was a book about hybridity written in a hybrid mode that challenged both pure theories of religion (Islamic fundamentalism) and pure theories of the nation (racism or cultural racism)." As Joanne P. Sharp (1994, 67) notes, Rushdie reconfigures and mixes several discourses in his book, "discourses of the colonizer and colonized, the secular and the religious, the political and the 'apolitical', the high cultural and the vernacular, the global and the local." To do so, Rushdie constructs a narrative that includes magical realism, satire, intertextuality, and historiographic metafiction to challenge the closure of religions as well as racial biases and to pluralize views on dominant ideologies.

Sharp (1994, 65) introduces *The Satanic Verses* as "a postmodern magical realist novel written from a boundary site, a hybrid identity, by an author, born in India and writing in Britain." Like its writer, the novel contains inextricable elements from both the Eastern and Western worlds, and it "communicate[s] experiences from disparate worlds" (Sanga 2001, 15). Thus, in addition to contemporary Britain, *The Satanic Verses* takes place in some other settings: India of the past, the contemporary Indian village, Titlipur, and the seventh-century Jahilia, Rushdie's name for Mecca, during the period of darkness before Mohammed's prophethood. Thus, Rushdie's oeuvre creates an in-between position wherein the characters can simultaneously move between the binary of the East and West, while they include and represent multitudes from both worlds. While the novel brings together different worlds, it challenges them with its counter-discourses. Accordingly, the novel, which shows the coexistence of different eras and areas, devils and angels, cultures and languages side by side, offers hybrid prism-like visions.

Even though the two protagonists – Gibreel Farishta (the archangel Gabriel) and Saladin Chamcha (the archangel Satan) – generate a feeling that they are binary polarities, they act as hybrid figures that include both angelic and demonic features. To show their hybrid identities, Rushdie (1988, 5; 92) combines "Gibreelsaladin Farishtachamcha," and to show that these characters are neither blessed nor damned, he writes "salvation-damnation" as one word, which signifies the collapse of binarism, metaphorically merging demonic and angelic characters to show that nothing is 100% good or evil. The merger is further illustrated on a number of occasions in the text by the narrative voice: "For are they not opposites, these two, each man the other's shadow?" (Rushdie 1988, 427). In this light, the protagonists who are "intrinsically part of each other" become "each other's dialogic other" (Beville 2009, 134). Joel Kuortti (1997, 192) believes that

> [t]he double protagonists Saladin Chamcha and Gibreel Farishta act out several polarities but the themes of good and evil, true and false, continuous and discontinuous are treated in a way which does not allow any easy preferences for ethical judgement.

In this light, "each man carries traits of the other within him as well: Gibreel is said to have always encompassed a devilish side, and Saladin will be shown to have angelic qualities" (Pervez 2004, 157). Thus, they, who oscillate between heavenly angelic positions to earthly manly positions, have plural and hybrid identities.

In one scene, Rekha, a married businesswoman who has an affair with Gibreel, invites him to her penthouse in the absence of her husband. After drinking together, she teases Gibreel that

> surely gods should not partake of alcohol, and he answered with a line he had once read in an interview with the Aga Khan, O, you know, this champagne is only for outward show, the moment it touches my lips it turns to water.
>
> *(Rushdie 1988, 26)*

Rekha's remarks and Gibreel's responses call angels into question. When God is dead, His angels are left without support and have "to search for a new principle" (Barthelme 1981, 137). In this climate, old values and beliefs are decolonized. To further question angels, in another case, Gibreel shouts: "I am Gibreel," "in a voice that shook every building on the riverbank," but then, "[h]e ista ista istepped right in fafa front of the wee-wee vehicle" and is "badly bruised, with many grazes on his arms and face" (Rushdie 1988, 336–337). These assertions juxtapose and expose both Gibreel's supernatural power and his vulnerability. The juxtaposition of these two states also happens when Gibreel decides to change London into a tropical city, which also hosts the Eastern climate and culture, with his own angelic capability:

> Gibreel enumerated the benefits of the proposed metamorphosis of London into a tropical city: increased moral definition, institution of a national siesta, development of vivid and expansive patterns of behaviour among the populace, higher-quality popular music, new birds in the trees (macaws, peacocks, cockatoos), new trees under the birds (coco-palms, tamarind, banyans with hanging beards). Improved street-life, outrageously coloured flowers (magenta, vermilion, neon-green), spider-monkeys in the oaks. A new mass market for domestic air-conditioning units, ceiling fans, anti-mosquito coils and sprays [...]. Religious fervour, political ferment, renewal of interest in the intellegentsia. No more British reserve; hot-water bottles to be banished forever, replaced in the foetid nights by the making of slow and odorous love [...]. Spicier foods; the use of water as well as paper in English toilets [...]. Standing upon the horizon, spreading his arms to fill the sky, Gibreel cried: "Let it be."
>
> *(Rushdie 1988, 354–355)*

However, at that moment, "Gibreel Farishta open[s] his eyes to find himself collapsed, once again" (Rushdie 1988, 356). Here again, the subversive potential of magical realism is portrayed with Gibreel's superhuman and human features when an angel, who aims to tropicalize London, faints.

As a magical realist text, the novel contains a plethora of natural and supernatural elements as two contradictory codes. As Ursula Kluwick (2011, 18) writes, "Rushdie's magic realism does not allow for such a hierarchy between the two codes, but rather complicates any stable conception of their relationship." Kluwick (2011, 181) further discusses that the tension between the two codes points to the potential of hybridity, and the two codes, constantly contradicting each other, draw our attention to the coexistence of a multiplicity of realities, truths, and worldviews. The combination of magic and realist elements is perceived when Ayesha, who suffers from epilepsy, introduces herself as Gibreel's spokesperson and claims that she has the ability to divide the Arabian Sea for Haj pilgrims on their way to Mecca. Later, the corpses of the pilgrims signify that Ayesha has failed to redeem her supernatural promise. Ayesha's fiasco provides the ground for Mimi Mamoulian, a highly skilled Jewish actress, to question Ayesha's supernatural power when she asks: "Why the waters parted for you and the other guy but closed over the rest? Don't tell me you were worthier? People don't buy that nowadays" (Rushdie 1988, 259). From another perspective, this episode satirizes the history of Moses's and the Israelites' crossing the Red Sea as recounted in the Book of Exodus. Rushdie uses mimicry and mockery to question fundamentalist religious beliefs and historical narratives. To this end, he draws upon historical sources on the history of religions, and at the same time he contests the validity of those histories with satire and hybrid techniques. The veracity of hegemonic and monolithic narratives when questioned with counter-hegemonic narratives brings about polyphony and indeterminacy.

Like in Cliff's novel and Parks's play, in *The Satanic Verses*, polyphony and indeterminacy are created also by the use of linguistic bricolage. As an example, the juxtaposition of Arabic terms transcribed into English based on their Dari pronunciation throughout the novel shatters the unity of English language as the dominant one in the novel. The expressions such as "*Kan ma kan/Fi Qadim azzaman*. [...] It was so, it was not" (Rushdie 1988, 143; italics original), and "she [...] cursed him for a useless *lafanga* and *haramzada* and *salah*" (Rushdie 1988, 27; emphases added) use Arabic terms, which complicate reading and comprehension for those who are not acquainted with Arabic language and culture (see Brians 1996). Sometimes English terms are juxtaposed alongside their Dari or Arabic equivalents: "Viva! Zindabad!" (Rushdie 1988, 399) or "allahgod" (Rushdie 1988, 92). The use of several languages in parallel signifies "heteroglossia," which can represent immigrant communities of mixed languages, in this case, South Asian Muslim communities in the UK. Moreover, the language diversity is not confined to English, Dari, and Arabic, but also French is used: "After all, 'les acteurs ne sont pas des gens', as the great ham Frederick had explained in *Les Enfants du Paradis*" (Rushdie 1988, 34). In such a heteroglossia, the high-prestige language sits next to the language of low prestige. Mikhail Bakhtin (1981, 342) refers to these language varieties as authoritative and periphery discourses. The former is used by those holding positions of authority in the society, whereas the latter is used by those who are "denied all privilege, backed up by no authority at all, and is frequently not even acknowledged in society (not by public opinion, nor by scholarly norms, nor by criticism), not even in the legal code." Rushdie (1990, 7) confirms that the novel offers a space wherein "different languages, values and narratives quarrel" and challenge the establishment of any lingual and cultural privilege. Moreover, the adoption of heteroglossia is a dissident attempt to portray the diverse and polyphonic Britain. To further exhibit linguistic plurality, Rushdie combines several words together to make hybrid words. As an example, in "if the summer weekenders grew brazen, – *getoutofitsillyoldmoo, itsthesoddingbeach*" (Rushdie 1988, 134; emphases added), one hybrid word is created out of several words. This technique of word hybridity shows that words are not fixed entities, and like societies and identities, they are liable to transformation.

In addition to combining high and low languages and cultures, Rushdie, just like Cliff and Parks, uses numerous intertexts. As he expresses in a lecture at the University of Toronto, "the act of authorial creation does not happen in a vacuum, is not the product of an inspired moment of original genius, but depends upon, indeed springs from, innumerable preceding acts of authorial (and artistic) creation effected by other writers, storytellers, artists and intellectuals" (qtd. in Teverson 2007, 55). Maria Beville (2009, 129) believes that "*The Satanic Verses* might be better understood […] as a celebration of genres, of intertextuality, hybridity and the dissolution of fact and reality." In this novel, Rushdie simultaneously installs and subverts, uses and abuses, asserts and denies the conventions of both history and fiction (Hutcheon 1989, 5). In this light, the novel self-consciously uses pastiche to draw upon a wide range of Eastern and Western cultural references, extending from Aeschylus to Isaac Asimov, the Mahābhārata to Madonna, the Rig-Veda to Bollywood films (Warnes 2009, 97). To bring all these pieces together, Rushdie employs parody "as the paradoxical postmodern way of coming to terms with the past" (Hutcheon 1989, 14). As Hutcheon (1989, 11–12) writes,

> Rushdie […] employ[s] parody not only to restore history and memory in the face of the distortions of the 'history of forgetting' […] but also, at the same time, to put into question the authority of any act of writing by locating the discourses of both history and fiction within an

ever-expanding intertextual network that mocks any notion of either single origin or simple causality.

With its critical power and subversive potential, parody provides the ground for Rushdie to revisit the past while pinpointing contradictions and dismantling radicalism and fundamentalism.

Conclusion

As discussed, Cliff, Parks, and Rushdie respond to the paradigm shift of postmodern hybridity to open up space within their literary works to host multitudes of views, values, languages, cultures, histories, and (counter) narratives. The three writers create multi-textured characters and/or figures who are made of different languages, cultures, histories, and temporalities, and their works blend several realistic and fictional pieces. They look like mosaics with numerous fragments from different times and locations, histories and stories, traditions and modernities, religions and ideologies. The authors embed diachrony and synchrony, continuity and discontinuity to simultaneously include several paradigms in their nonlinear and multitemporal works to promote the politics of difference and tolerance.

Cliff's and Rushdie's novels and Parks's play echo each other in some ways. For instance, they approach conventional and professional historiography by impugning totality, objectivity, certainty, and essentialism. Thus, through using historiographic metafiction, they rehistoricize history via fiction writing and balancing mininarratives with the existing history, which creates a dynamic view of history and provides readers with new significations. In this climate, these hybrid postmodern texts, as kaleidoscopic and prism-like inclusive textures, recycle elements of history, religion, legend, and other discourses. Additionally, they use the potential of postmodern hybridity to eschew totalizing and homogenizing trends, deconstruct essentialist categories, and reconstitute identities through questioning, reforming, and even subverting hegemonic discourses, values, beliefs, and visions. As a vantage point in their postmodern works, they introduce new or different perspectives which challenge the former ones and subvert the homogenizing closure of dominant discourses. In this climate, they use multivocality and polytheism as the hallmarks of postmodern hybridity to shatter absolutism, fundamentalism, and essentialism.

These literary works also contest and blur the essentialist categories of high and low cultures and languages by using linguistic bricolage which promotes language fluidity and plurality. Moreover, to enhance hybridity, the texts make use of extra-textuality in the forms of intertextuality, paratextuality, and metatextuality to replay and recontextualize the past forms of representation, transform old themes, and appropriate them to the contemporary life conditions. They also incorporate techniques such as parody, double-coding, and palimpsest to establish relationships with other texts and undermine notions of fixity, unification, and assimilation.

Further Reading

Hassan, Ihab. 1986. "Pluralism in Postmodern Perspective." *Critical Inquiry*, vol. 2, no. 3, pp. 503–520.

Hutcheon, Linda. 1986. "Postmodern Paratextuality and History." *Texte – Revue de Critique et de Théorie Littéraire*, vol. 5, no. 6, pp. 301–312.

Natoli, Joseph, and Linda Hutcheon, eds. 1993. *A Postmodern Reader*. Albany: State University of New York Press.

O'Donnell, Patrick, and Robert Con Davis, eds. 1989. *Intertextuality and Contemporary American Fiction*. Baltimore: Johns Hopkins University Press.

Warnes, Christopher. 2009. *Magical Realism and the Postcolonial Novel*. London: Palgrave Macmillan.

Further Exercises

Salman Rushdie, Quichotte *(2019)*

Salman Rushdie's novel *Quichotte* follows Bombay-born Ismail Ismile, who works as a travelling salesman for a pharmaceutical company in the United States. The 70-year-old Ismail, whose name is pronounced "Smile" by American customers, is unmarried and childless. After a stroke, he spends his time watching TV which results in developing an infatuation for Salma R, a former Bollywood actress, serving as a host for a talk show in New York. He begins sending Salma love letters, signing them with the pseudonym "Quichotte," hoping to win the celebrity's heart. Quichotte spots a shooting star and makes wishes, which sound impossible, but to his great surprise, they come true. For instance, he wishes for a son, and without any relationship with any woman, he, whom the imaginary father names Sancho, comes into existence. The following passage shows Quichotte's firm belief in the occurrence of anything in the Age of Anything-Can-Happen. What specific indications and techniques of postmodern hybridity are presented in the text? How does the use of intertextual as well as magic realist elements make Rushdie's text a hybrid postmodern one?

It was the Age of Anything-Can-Happen, he reminded himself. He had heard many people say that on TV and on the outré video clips floating in cyberspace, which added a further, new-technology depth to his addiction. There were no rules any more. And in the Age of Anything-Can-Happen, well, anything could happen. Old friends could become new enemies and traditional enemies could be your new besties or even lovers. It was no longer possible to predict the weather, or the likelihood of war, or the outcome of elections. A woman might fall in love with a piglet, or a man start living with an owl. A beauty might fall asleep and, when kissed, wake up speaking a different language and in that new language reveal a completely altered character. A flood might drown your city. A tornado might carry your house to a faraway land where, upon landing, it would squash a witch. Criminals could become kings and kings be unmasked as criminals. A man might discover that the woman he lived with was his father's illegitimate child. A whole nation might jump off a cliff like swarming lemmings. Men who played presidents on TV could become presidents. The water might run out. A woman might bear a baby who was found to be a revenant god. Words could lose their meanings and acquire new ones. The world might end, as at least one prominent scientist entrepreneur had begun repeatedly to predict. An evil scent would hang over the ending. And a TV star might miraculously return the love of a foolish old coot, giving him an unlikely romantic triumph, which would redeem a long, small life, bestowing upon it, at the last, the radiance of majesty.

(Rushdie 2019, 7–8)

Karen Tei Yamashita, Through the Arc of the Rain Forest *(1990)*

Through the Arc of the Rain Forest, written by the Japanese American author Karen Tei Yamashita, is primarily set in Brazil. However, the novel includes characters coming from different nationalities and locations, including Japan, Brazil, and the United States. The novel also transgresses defined literary genres. Part fairy tale, part urban nightmare, part soap opera, it incorporates humour and satire, magic and reality to address themes of globalization, transnationalism, immigration, capitalism, and the environmental crisis. Consequently, the book is simultaneously entertaining and depressing. Narrated from the standpoint of an extraterrestrial plastic ball, the novel details the temporary rise and subsequent challenges of a Brazilian local community after the discovery of the Matacão, an impenetrable and resilient black recyclable substance, which can be transformed into commercial products. In what ways does the Matacão plastic manifest elements of postmodern hybridity?

Matacão plastic was so true to reality that, even upon touch and a lot of palpating examination, one could not tell the difference. At the plastics convention, two tiger lilies, one natural and the other made from Matacão plastic, were exhibited for public examination. Few, if any of the examiners could tell the difference between the real and the fake [...]. Matacão plastic managed to recreate the natural glow, moisture, freshness – the very sensation of life [...]. [It] would infiltrate every crevice of modern life – plants, facial and physical remakes and appendages, shoes, clothing, jewelry, toys, cars, every sort of machine from electro-domestic to high-tech, buildings, furniture – in short, the myriad of commercial products with which the civilized world adorns itself [...]. Matacão plastic would even be used to create artificial food (sushi samples, etc.). A few people had mistakenly eaten artificial food samples with no bodily discomfort or detriment.

(*Yamashita 1990, 142–143*)

Suzan-Lori Parks, Fucking A (2001)

Suzan-Lori Parks's play *Fucking A* has intertextual connections with Nathaniel Hawthorne's 1850 novel *The Scarlet Letter*. Living in a small town in a small country in the middle of nowhere, as the play informs, Hester Smith works as an illegal abortionist, branded with the letter "A." She works hard and regularly pays money to Freedom Fund Lady to free her son Boy, who has been imprisoned for the last twenty years since his childhood for stealing a piece of meat from the Rich Family. Later, Boy escapes from the prison and resorts to his mother. He who finds himself surrounded by three Hunters – who track down and catch runaway prisoners with their dogs and torture and mutilate them mercilessly – begs his mother to kill him before Hunters capture him. Hester, who desperately slits her own son's throat, is enraged over the death of her son and is bent on revenge against the Mayor's wife, the First Lady. The following passage depicts the moment that Hester along with her companies and accomplices, Canary Mary and Butcher, kidnaps the First Lady and transfers her to Hester's office to perform an abortion on her. What postmodern technique(s) has the playwright used in the passage to create hybridity?

> Butcher: I help you———
> Hester: Ive got her. Canary, keep Butcher company.
> Canary: Whats this stuff here?
> Hester: Just some garbage.
> Canary: Theyre letters you wrote to Boy. Says so right here.
> Hester
> Canary

First Lady: I snitched. I snitched.

Canary: *Jamah, Hester, jamah?*

Hester: *Doht.*

Canary: *Jamah?*

Butcher: No fair you two Talking in front of me. *Uh, noonka Talking-mehnavee.* No fair.

Hester: A friend of his brought them by. *Le traja Scrapeahdepth woah-ya, C-Mary.*

(Parks 2001, 211; original spelling)

References

Bakhtin, Mikhail. 1981. *The Dialogic Imagination: Four Essays*, edited by Michael Holquist. Translated by Caryl Emerson and Michael Holquist. Austin: University of Texas Press.

Barnes, Fiona R. 1992. "Resisting Cultural Cannibalism: Oppositional Narratives in Michelle Cliff's *No Telephone to Heaven*." *Journal of the Midwest Modern Language Association*, vol. 25, no. 1, pp. 23–31. https://doi.org/10.2307/1315071

Bartheleme, Donald. 1981. *Sixty Stories*. New York: G.P. Putnam's Sons.

Baudrillard, Jean. 1993 [originally published 1981]. "The Precession of Simulacra." Translated by Sheila Faria Glaser. In *A Postmodern Reader*, edited by Joseph Natoli and Linda Hutcheon, 342–375. Albany: State University of New York Press.

Baudrillard, Jean. 2001 [originally published 1999]. *Impossible Exchange*. Translated by Chris Taylor. London: Verso.

Berra, John, ed. 2010. *Directory of World Cinema: American Independent*. Chicago: University of Chicago Press.

Beville, Maria. 2009. *Gothic-postmodernism: Voicing the Terrors of Postmodernity*. Amsterdam: Brill.

Brians, Paul. 1996. "Notes for Salman Rushdie: *The Satanic Verses*." The Website of Prof. Paul Brians. Online. https://brians.wsu.edu/2017/02/08/notes-for-the-satanic-verses/

Buell, Frederick. 1994. *National Culture and the New Global System*. London: Johns Hopkins University Press.

Cliff, Michelle. 1987. *No Telephone to Heaven*. New York: Plume/Penguin.

Cliff, Michelle. 1990. "Clare Savage as Crossroads Character." In *Caribbean Women Writers: Essays from the First International Conference*, edited by Selwyn R. Cudjoe, 263–268. Wellesley: Calaloux Publications.

Dickens, Charles. 1868 [originally published 1857]. *Little Dorrit*. New York: Books, Inc.

Dwivedi, O.P. 2008. "Linguistic Experiments in Rushdie's *Midnight's Children*." *Transnational Literature*, vol. 1, no. 1, pp. 1–6. https://core.ac.uk/download/pdf/14931412.pdf

Eco, Umberto. 1984 [originally published 1983]. *Postscript to The Name of the Rose*. Translated by William Weaver. San Diego: Harcourt Brace Jovanovich.

Ellis, Trey. 1989. "The New Black Aesthetic." *Callaloo*, vol. 12, no. 1, pp. 233–243. https://doi.org/10.2307/2931157

Ellison, Ralph. 1952. *Invisible Man*. New York: Random House.

Foucault, Michel. 2003. *Society Must Be Defended*. Lectures at the Collège de France, vol. 3, edited by Mauro Bertani and Alessandro Fontana. Translated by David Macey. New York: Picador.

Gates, Jr., Henry Louis. 1988. *The Signifying Monkey: A Theory of African-American Literary Criticism*. Oxford: Oxford University Press.

Gates, Jr., Henry Louis. 1989. *Figures in Black: Words, Signs, and the "Racial" Self*. Oxford: Oxford University Press.

Geis, Deborah R. 2008. *Suzan-Lori Parks*. Ann Arbor: University of Michigan Press.

Ghasemi, Mehdi. 2014. "Revisiting History in Hayden White's Philosophy." *SAGE Open*, vol. 4, no. 3, pp. 1–7. https://doi.org/10.1177/215824401454

Ghasemi, Mehdi. 2016. *Quest/ion of Identities in African American Feminist Postmodern Drama: A Study of Selected Plays by Suzan-Lori Parks*. Turku: University of Turku. https://urn.fi/URN:ISBN:978-951-29-6496-3

Ghasemi, Mehdi. 2019. "Replenishing and Recycling an Exhausted Hi|story in Lydia R. Diamond's *Voyeurs de Venus*." *Journal of Literary Studies*, vol. 35, no. 3, pp. 80–93. https://doi.org/10.1080/02564718.2019.1657284

Hall, Stuart. 1990. "Cultural Identity and Diaspora." In *Identity: Community, Culture, Difference*, edited by Jonathan Rutherford, 222–237. London: Lawrence and Wishart.

Hassan, Ihab. 1986. "Pluralism in Postmodern Perspective." *Critical Inquiry*, vol. 2, no. 3, pp. 503–520. https://doi.org/10.1086/448348

Hassan, Ihab. 1993 [originally published 1982]. "Toward a Concept of Postmodernism." In *A Postmodern Reader*, edited by Joseph Natoli and Linda Hutcheon, 273–287. Albany: State University of New York Press.

hooks, bell. 1992. *Black Looks: Race and Representation*. Boston: South End Press.

Hutcheon, Linda. 1986. "Postmodern Paratextuality and History." *Texte – Revue de Critique et de Théorie Littéraire*, vol. 5, no. 6, pp. 301–312. https://tspace.library.utoronto.ca/bitstream/1807/9477/1/TSpace0031.pdf

Hutcheon, Linda. 1989. "Historiographic Metafiction: Parody and the Intertextuality of History." In *Intertextuality and Contemporary American Fiction*, edited by Patrick O'Donnell and Robert Con Davis, 3–31. Baltimore: Johns Hopkins University Press.

Hutcheon, Linda. 1995. *A Poetics of Postmodernism: History, Theory, Fiction*. London: Routledge.

Hutcheon, Linda. 2002. *The Politics of Postmodernism*. New York: Routledge.

Ilmonen, Kaisa. 2012. *Caribbean Journeys: Intersections of Female Identity in the Novels of Michelle Cliff*. Turku: Uniprint. https://urn.fi/URN:ISBN:978-951-29-4942-

Jablon, Madelyn. 1997. *Black Metafiction: Self-Consciousness in African American Literature*. Iowa City: University of Iowa Press.

Jameson, Fredric. 1981. *The Political Unconscious: Narrative as a Socially Symbolic Act*. Ithaca: Cornell University Press.

Johung, Jennifer. 2006. "Figuring the 'Spells'/ Spelling the Figures: Suzan-Lori Parks's 'Scene of Love.'" *Theatre Journal*, vol. 58, no. 1, pp. 39–52. https://www.jstor.org/stable/25069778

Joyce, James. 1993 [originally published 1922]. *Ulysses*. Oxford: Oxford University Press.

Kluwick, Ursula. 2011. *Exploring Magic Realism in Salman Rushdie's Fiction*. London: Routledge.

Kuortti, Joel. 1997. "Dreams, Intercultural Identification and Salman Rushdie's *The Satanic Verses*." *Contemporary South Asia*, vol. 6, no. 2, pp. 191–200. https://doi.org/10.1080/09584939708719813

Kuortti, Joel, and Jopi Nyman. 2007. "Introduction: Hybridity Today." In *Reconstructing Hybridity: Post-Colonial Studies in Transition*, edited by Joel Kuortti and Jopi Nyman, 1–18. Amsterdam: Rodopi.

Larson, Jennifer. 2012. *Understanding Suzan-Lori Parks*. Columbia: University of South Carolina Press.

Lévi-Strauss, Claude. 1996 [originally published 1962]. *The Savage Mind*. Translated by George Weidenfield and Nicolson Ltd. Oxford: Oxford University Press.

Lyotard, Jean-François. 1984 [originally published 1979]. *The Postmodern Condition: A Report on Knowledge*. Translated by Geoffrey Bennington and Brian Massumi. Minneapolis: University of Minnesota Press.

Malkin, Jeanette R. 1999. *Memory-Theater and Postmodern Drama*. Ann Arbor: University of Michigan Press.

McDowell, Josh D., Bob Hostetler, and David H. Bellis. 2002. *Beyond Belief to Convictions*. Wheaton: Tyndale House.

McHale, Brian. 1987. *Postmodernist Fiction*. New York: Routledge.

Moynagh, Maureen. 1999. "The Ethical Turn in Postcolonial Theory and Narrative: Michelle Cliff's *No Telephone to Heaven*." *ARIEL*, vol. 30, no. 4, pp. 109–133. https://journalhosting.ucalgary.ca/index.php/ariel/article/view/34337

Natoli, Joseph, and Linda Hutcheon, eds. 1993. *A Postmodern Reader*. Albany: State University of New York Press.

O'Donnell, Patrick, and Robert Con Davis, eds. 1989. *Intertextuality and Contemporary American Fiction*. Baltimore: Johns Hopkins University Press.

Parks, Suzan-Lori. 1995. "The Death of the Last Black Man in the Whole Entire World." In *The America Play and Other Works*, by Suzan-Lori Parks, 99–131. New York: Theatre Communications Group.

Parks, Suzan-Lori. 2001. "Fucking A." In *The Red Letter Plays*, by Suzan-Lori Parks, 113–225. New York: Theatre Communications Group.

Pervez, Summer. 2004. "Hybridity Is Heresy: Homi Bhabha and *The Satanic Verses*." *South Asian Review*, vol. 25, no. 2, pp. 153–164. https://doi.org/10.1080/02759527.2004.11932351

Pettersson, Lin. 2013. "The Private Rooms and Public Haunts." In *Twenty-first Century Fiction: What Happens Now*, edited by Sian Adiseshiah and Rupert Hildyard, 97–114. London: Palgrave Macmillan.

Puri, Shalini. 2004. *The Caribbean Postcolonial: Social Equality, Post-nationalism, and Cultural Hybridity*. New York: Palgrave Macmillan.

Rushdie, Salman. 1988. *The Satanic Verses.* London: Vintage, and New York: Viking.

Rushdie, Salman. 1990. "Is Nothing Sacred?" *Granta*, no. 31, pp. 97–110. https:// granta.com/is-nothing-sacred/

Rushdie, Salman. 1991. *Imaginary Homelands: Essays and Criticism, 1981–1991.* London: Granta.

Rushdie, Salman. 2019. *Quichotte.* New York: Penguin Random House.

Sanga, Jaina C. 2001. *Salman Rushdie's Postcolonial Metaphors: Migration, Translation, Hybridity, Blasphemy, and Globalization.* Westport: Greenwood.

Schmidt, Kerstin. 2005. *The Theater of Transformation: Postmodernism in American Drama.* New York: Rodopi.

Sharp, Joanne P. 1994. "A Topology of 'Post' Nationality: (Re)mapping Identity in *The Satanic Verses.*" *Ecumene*, vol. 1, no. 1, pp. 65–76. https://doi.org/10.1177 /14744740940010

Slemon, Stephen. 1995. "Magic Realism as Postcolonial Discourse." In *Magical Realism: Theory, History, Community*, edited by Lois Parkinson Zamora and Wendy B. Faris, 407–426. Durham: Duke University Press.

Smith, Jennifer J. 2009. "Birthed and Buried: Matrilineal History in Michelle Cliff's *No Telephone to Heaven.*" *Meridians*, vol. 9, no. 1, pp. 141–162. https:// doi.org/10.2979/MER.2008.9.1.141

Strongman, Roberto. 2007. "Postmodern Developments in Michelle Cliff's *No Telephone to Heaven* and Esmeralda Santiago's *When I Was Puerto Rican.*" *Journal of Caribbean Literatures*, vol. 4, no. 3, pp. 97–104. https://www.jstor .org/stable/40986214

Teverson, Andrew. 2007. *Salman Rushdie.* New York: Manchester University Press.

Ubersfeld, Anne. 1999. *Reading Theatre.* Toronto: University of Toronto Press.

Van Sertima, Ivan. 1976. *They Came before Columbus: The African Presence in Ancient America.* New York: Random House.

Warnes, Christopher. 2009. *Magical Realism and the Postcolonial Novel.* London: Palgrave Macmillan.

Werbner, Pnina. 2001. "The Limits of Cultural Hybridity: On Ritual Monsters, Poetic Licence and Contested Postcolonial Purifications." *The Journal of the Royal Anthropological Institute*, vol. 7, no. 1, pp. 133–152. https://www.jstor .org/stable/2660840

Yamashita, Karen Tei. 1990. *Through the Arc of the Rain Forest.* Minneapolis: Coffee House Press.

Young, Robert J.C. 1995. *Colonial Desire: Hybridity in Theory, Culture and Race.* London: Routledge.

CODA

Critique of Hybridity – Whither Hybridity?

Mehdi Ghasemi

Introduction

Despite the fact that hybridity is considered a major trend of our world today, some groups, movements, and scholars remain critical of hybridity and its underlying supporting mechanisms. Critiques of hybridity are common, and demands to abandon or limit the operation of hybridity have been presented in almost all areas and fields. The anti-hybridity proponents see hybridity as an inauthentic mode that erodes boundary, unity, originality, and purity. Thus, they eschew any collisions between distinct genes and genres, ideologies and discourses, as well as ethnicities and cultures, generating problematic outcomes from the standpoints of holistic homogeneous models. In other words, since hybridity has the potential to problematize the totality of monologic discourses, systems, and ideologies, the opponents of hybridity shy away from the varieties and ranges of hybridity. To offer comprehensive views on hybridity, in this chapter, we study a number of grounds that support boundedness to maintain anti-hybrid discourses. It is our contention that the study of backlashes against hybridity in different fields and principles further deepens our understanding of the phenomenon itself.

DOI: 10.4324/9781003269670-6

Anti-hybridity and Monogenesis

In "The Problems with Hybrids," Fred W. Allendorf et al. (2001, 613) claim that "[h]ybridization has contributed to the extinction of many species through direct and indirect means." In their studies, these scientists (Allendorf et al. 2001, 613) have found that hybridization is "problematic for rare species that come into contact with other species." They believe that producing new species via mixing one plant with another does not necessarily develop plant species. Rather, the breeders might endanger the original species. They have found that the protection of hybrids not only fails to recover a list of endangered species but also jeopardizes the continued existence of plant taxa. As a result of hybridity, hybrid plants cannot reproduce naturally. Likewise, the genetic recombination in some crossbreed animals such as mules – a cross between a horse and a donkey – causes malfunctions in their chromosomes and makes them infertile. Based on this, they see hybridity as a subversion that de-naturalizes the natural breeds. Accordingly, Allendorf et al. (2001, 614) conclude that "hybrids should not receive protection under the ESA [the US Endangered Species Act]."

The opponents of hybridity also emphasize that the positionality of varied components, coming from different loci and genes, might not match neatly and lead instead to asymmetricity and abnormality. Like in plant and animal taxa, hybridity in the combination of humans with animals brings about dysplasia, an abnormal growth disorder in the development of cells and/or organs. Dysplasia is perceived in, for example, Gabriel García Márquez's short story "A Very Old Man with Enormous Wings." The story portrays "a very old man, lying face down in the mud, who, in spite of his tremendous efforts, couldn't get up, impeded by his enormous wings" (García Márquez 1972, 105). The story reads that "[h]is huge buzzard wings" make people take distance from him, and thus, he looks like "a lonely castaway" (García Márquez 1972, 107). Eventually, he is "locked [...] up with the hens in the wire chicken coop" and a curious crowd comes from faraway to visit the captive freak like "a circus animal" (García Márquez 1972, 111). As García Márquez shows, the addition of two overgrown wings to a man becomes a burden on him and negatively affects the manimal's normal activities.

With the development of natural sciences in the nineteenth century with a focus on the human species, debates recurred between monogenesists – who held that all humankind belongs to the same species – and polygenesists – who firmly believed that different skin colours signify different species. The position of the latter, backed up by the pseudo-scientific racism, paved the way for the introduction of race hierarchies and accordingly the implementation of strict codes against interracial union. The pseudo-scientific racism, used to justify white supremacy, also resulted in the promotion of racist and colonialist discourses. As Christopher Richard Baker (2007, 14) notes: "Within colonialist discourse, therefore, hybridity is seen as a potentially dangerous condition that needs to be carefully managed. Strong warnings were issued on the dangers of weakening genetic purity and cultural identity through the persistence of ethnic assimilation," because, as Haim Hazan (2015, 16) sees, "as an aberration," hybrids are even "worse than the inferior races, a weak and diseased mutation which should be a concern for racial purity."

To shield racial purity and superiority, alongside pseudo-scientific racism, the Jim Crow laws legalized racial segregation throughout the Southern States of the United States during the nineteenth century. The laws forbade African Americans from living in white neighbourhoods and segregated schools, hospitals, restrooms, telephone booths, and even cemeteries of white and black Americans. The implementation of the Jim Crow laws resulted in the formation of ruthless organizations such as the Ku Klux Klan that vandalized African Americans. To minimize contacts between black and white Americans, the KKK mobs lynched thousands of African American men and women under various, and in cases senseless, pretexts. Lisa M. Anderson (1997, 6) discusses one of the main pretexts for black men's lynching: "Tales of black men raping white women resulted in lynch mobs who, in their murderous frenzy, would kill the first black they could find." Suzan-Lori Parks's anti-lynching play *The Death of the Last Black Man in the Whole Entire World* draws upon lynching and its aftereffects in the lives of African Americans. In the play, the main figure, Black Man With Watermelon, appears with a rope around his neck, attached to a tree branch. He informs that he has escaped lynching in the eleventh hour. His wife, Black Woman With Fried Drumstick, gives an account of this frequent dreadful event as follows:

> They comed for you and tooked you. That was yesterday. Today you sit in your chair where you sat yesterday and thuh day afore yesterday. [...] Thuh chair was portable. They take it from county tuh county. Only got one. [...] Put thuh Chair in thuh middle of thuh City. Outdoors. In thuh square.

> *(Parks 1995, 107)*

In Panel III, Black Man With Watermelon also recounts the scene of his lynching where a large group of people had thronged his platform on a rainy day, "pullin out their umbrellas," and then: "Sky flew open and thuh light went ZAP. Tree bowed over till thuh branch said BROKE" (Parks 1995, 119). Parks protests against the unjust laws that justify the murder of the blacks without trial and right of appeal. It is worth noting that the act of lynching is also represented in Michelle Cliff's *No Telephone to Heaven*. While Boy Savage presents America to his family as "the greatest country in the world," his wife, Kitty, repeats the words written on a small sign on a window of an abandoned office of National Association for the Advancement of Colored People (NAACP): "A MAN WAS LYNCHED YESTERDAY" (Cliff 1987, 54). Later, they face another signpost in a motel, reading "YOU ARE IN KLAN COUNTRY" (Cliff 1987, 58). The signs show that the legacy of the Jim Crow and KKK is still felt today in some ways in the United States, and a major part of mixed-race people are likely subject to racial discrimination.

As the outcome of hybridity, any shades of mixed raceness bring into play identity crisis and have lasting effects on the lives of multiracial people. This is what Alfred negotiates in Gish Jen's *Mona in the Promised Land*, when he says: "White is white, man. Everything else is black. Half and half is black" (Jen 1997, 155). The statement shows that hybridity, regardless of its degree, brings about impurity, and people with one white and one black parent are categorized as black. Thus, "mixed-race," "half-caste," "biracial," "mulatto," and so on, all demonstrate blackness in hegemonic bipolar thinking. Langston Hughes's poem "Cross" is an emblematic example in this context. The mulatto speaker, who is the result of exogamy, identifies himself as an outcast or stigma because of his hybrid progeny in a world wherein purity counts. Viewed in this light, hybridity stands as the "source of pollution and danger" (Hazan 2015, 31). As an alleged degenerate and unnatural offspring, the mulatto is a hybrid, impure being who finds himself in a cross-like status as neither a white nor a black person. Here, as a master signifier, "whiteness" brings about domination, while other colours signify submission. The fruit of this interracial marriage wishes to deracinate himself and get rid of his racial characteristics which make him unwelcome to this world.

Like the speaker in "Cross," Alem suffers from mixed raceness in Benjamin Zephaniah's *Refugee Boy*. Alem's father is Ethiopian, while his mother is Eritrean. With both countries at war, the whole family is admitted in neither Ethiopia nor Eritrea. In Ethiopia, "[t]he soldier raised his rifle and pointed it at Alem's father. 'You are a traitor'" (Zephaniah 2001, 10), and in Eritrea, "[t]he soldier raised his rifle and pointed it at Alem's mother. 'You are a traitor'" (Zephaniah 2001, 11). In both locations, they "pointed the rifle at Alem's forehead. 'And he is a *mongrel*'" (Zephaniah 2001, 12; emphasis added). As Robert Young (1995, 18; emphasis added) writes, "miscegenation produces a *mongrel* group that makes up a 'raceless chaos,' merely a corruption of the originals, degenerate and degraded, threatening to subvert the vigor and virtue of the pure race with which they come into contact." Based on this rhetoric, hybridity is associated with racial degeneration, and privileged ethnic groups show contempt for inter-marriage in order to maintain their pre-existing power equation, warning against social and racial mixing with foreigners. As the result of miscegenation and mixed raceness, Alem is unwanted and unwelcome in both places, where sensitivity for racial purity stays at a high level. According to Amar Acheraïou (2011, 79),

> [t]he fear that mixed-race offspring engendered in the colonial authorities led to policies which often condemned these children to cultural, social, and political marginalization [...]. They faced a wide range of socio-economic and political obstacles that led to poverty and often to pauperization.

Acheraïou (2011, 79) adds that "the duplex, unique identity of mixed-blood offspring is subject to a double denial: it is tacitly or explicitly rejected by both sites of identification." In this climate, hybrid offsprings fail to reconcile their contradictory identities. Moreover, the status of their mental duality negatively affects their social, political, cultural, and economic conditions.

Anti-hybridity and Aversion

Like people of mixed race, some minority and/or hyphenated subgroups are not embraced by majorities, and they are affected by their failure in integrating into their dominant societies. Their non-belongingness prevents them from mentally settling down and improve their socio-political, cultural, and economic conditions. As Gloria Anzaldúa (1987, 63) depicts in her *Borderlands/La Frontera*,

> Chicanos and other people of color suffer economically for not acculturating. This voluntary (yet forced) alienation makes for psychological conflict, a kind of dual identity – we don't identify with the Anglo-American cultural values and we don't totally identify with the Mexican cultural values. We are a synergy of two cultures with various degrees of Mexicanness or Angloness.

For such people, standing on a double edge creates double consciousness. However, as Anzaldúa (2011, 85) clarifies, it is not always the nativists' resistance to otherness that causes non-belongingness for newcomers, since "[m]any women and men of color do not want to have any dealings with white people." Thus, the nativists' contestation around their ethnic biases on one side and some newcomers' refusal to integrate into the new environment on the other side result in the construction of ghettoization which signifies anti-hybridity. In this light, those who have "a stable commitment to one's class and nation" (Ahmad 1995, 14) minimize the synthesis between majorities and minorities.

The spatial exclusion of the minorities in, for example, shantytowns, fractures the supposedly unified national space and creates undesirable forms of class encapsulation. The centre–periphery dichotomy, which divides socio-economically lower and upper classes, fosters the society's socio-spatial fragmentation. In Cliff's *No Telephone to Heaven*, Christopher and his grandmother live "in a lickle shack in a shantytown near the Esso refinery on the outskirt of Kingston" (Cliff 1987, 31). As Cliff (1987, 32) specifies, in that shantytown, residents had made houses "with cardboard or newspaper [...]. Structures made from lengths of corrugated paper, sheets of corrugated metal." The emergence and development of such poor residencies shows the failure of both parties, those who reside within and without, to cross these malformed boundaries. In *Mona in the Promised Land*, Jen singles out another form of ghettoization – the Chinatown in New York – as a typical embodiment of boundaries between the European natives and the indigenous population. As Edwin J. McAllister (2007, 145) writes, the Chinese were figured as invaders importing "diseases and drugs to wipe out whatever Anglos the armies [did] not kill first, leaving the entire continent under Chinese control." Such anti-immigrant propaganda galvanized public opinion against Chinese immigration and resulted in the passage of Chinese Exclusion Act in 1882, prohibiting immigrants from China. In parallel, such labels, placed upon Chinese immigrants, distanced them from the mainstream society and affected their lives in the United States. As David Palumbo-Liu (1999, 65) notes, "the exclusion and deportation of countless Asians, and the proliferation of anti-miscegenation laws [...] based on a violent aversion to the idea of hybridity" are parts of the "disturbing history" of hybridity in the United States. The formation of Chinatowns signifies the violent aversion to hybridity and "demonstrates the way in which racial thinking determines architectural planning" (Rembold and Carrier 2011, 371). From one perspective, these towns within towns are "form[s] of lingual, ethnic, cultural, political and commercial segregation, which cut off their residents from the mainstream society, limited their connections and prospects and postponed their integration" (Ghasemi 2020, 262). From another perspective, the tendency for grouping is to enhance intergroup interaction and "bounded collectivity with a sense of solidarity, corporate identity, and capacity for concerted action" (Brubaker 2004, 12). A common ethnicity, language, culture, and economic status are the factors that oblige marginal groups to stay together in ghettos and shantytowns.

Anti-hybridity and Ethnocentrism

As another group who wish to minimize the synthesis between majorities and minorities, nationalists strive to maintain their national identities. It is their contention that "humanity is divided into distinct groups, and that it is the interest of these groups to govern themselves" (Lawrence 2014, 1). Based on this abstract ideology, nationalists disfavour hybridity, problematizing their nationalist tendencies, and oppose "globalization – so often celebrated for enabling the free circulation of peoples, goods and ideas" (Parry 2004, 11). However, they favour the globalization of nationalistic doctrines. Moreover, discourses of nationalism and ethnocentrism, formed based on the ethnic superiority and exclusivism, withstand immigration, simply because the arrival of immigrants challenges the "boundary that marks the nation's selfhood" (Bhabha 1992, 148). Thus, in nationalists' opinions, globalization and immigration admit cultural, social, political, and lingual impurity into the heart of homogeneous societies. In this climate, they see hybridity as degeneration to ethnocentrism, which causes de- and re-territorialization. Benita Parry (2004, 10) sees nationalism as an ideology and practice of denigrating hybridity, which develops forms of contestations within societies. Thus, groups who wish to preserve their essentialist, nationalist textures, read the dialectics of hybridity as a threat to their locality, homogeneity, and ethnicity. They see hybridity within their borders as a transgressive and subversive process that challenges their culture, alters their existing social order, and denaturalizes their hegemonic identity.

To maintain their fundamentalist identity, cultural essentialism, and ethnic absolutism, nationalists long for strict border control. In *Borderlands/La Frontera*, Anzaldúa draws upon some of the challenges of border crossing. As Anzaldúa (1987, 3–4) informs:

> Do not enter, trespassers will be raped, maimed, strangled, gassed, shot. The only 'legitimate' inhabitants are those in power, the whites and those who align themselves with whites. Tension grips the inhabitants of the borderlands like a virus. Ambivalence and unrest reside there and death is no stranger.

Thus, border crossing and adopting cosmopolitan ethics are so demanding that numerous immigrants, who are seen as misfits in the eyes of natives, lose their motivation and regret their decision. Consequently, to confront hybridity, nationalist, first and foremost, struggle to control their territorial borders as the first contact zones, since free movement imperils their localism, ethnic absolutism and nationalism. With regard to strangers who manage to pass filters, nationalists clutch to ethnic boundaries to keep the melting pot so cold wherein nothing melts. According to Sara Ahmed (2000, 36), "[t]he stranger is figured as the violent monster whose elimination would mean safety […]. Such a figuration allows the home to be imagined as a safe haven." In this anti-hybridity climate, "the ultimate violent strangers […] figured as immigrants" (Ahmed 2000, 36), whose "behaviour seems unpredictable and beyond control" (Merry 1981, 125), are not welcome, and different preventive measures, including aversion, distancing, and discrimination, are used to drive them away. As a result of such pressures, in Leila Aboulela's (1999, 157) *The Translator*, Sammar returns to her homeland Sudan, and in her letter to Sammar, Yasmin, who still resides in Scotland, writes: "You are doing the right thing, Sammar, staying with your family, not coming back […] we too would like to leave Britain." Thus, crossing borders does not guarantee that immigrants have entered the circle, and their endeavours to become integrated are usually of no avail, simply because they have to cross stronger borders than the geographical one, including racial, cultural, linguistic, and ideological, which can impede the newcomers' integration and belongingness.

Through disconnection, these borders segment peoples even within the physical border of a nation. In *Harare North*, Brian Chikwava demonstrates how an undocumented African immigrant contributes to his own non-hybridity state through his nationalist mindset, lack of language skills, unfamiliarity with the English culture, and insistence to maintain and publicly demonstrate his customs. Before long, the unnamed protagonist detects a sense of being unwanted in people's eyes. In one case, he sees that some customers in a café change their seats to avoid sitting next to him. As he narrates,

> I pick my suitcase, lift it onto my head and go to Elser Cafe where I buy myself cup of tea. When the waitress bring it, the tea is too hot, so me I start to fan it with Shingi's hat. One woman carrying she baby come to sit at the table near me, but suddenly move to another table because our eyes have clash.
>
> *(Chikwava 2009, 225)*

Under such pressures, he also feels frustrated, voicing his concern because they "make me feel like I don't belong to earth" (Chikwava 2009, 122).

As a result of racial, cultural, religious, and other differences, encounters between natives and alien peoples cause anxiety and tension for both parties. In *No Telephone to Heaven*, Cliff (1987, 137) demonstrates the violent march by the National Front in London while marchers furiously shout "KAFFIRS! NIGGERS! WOGS! PAKIS! GET OUT!" carrying also a banner which reads "KEEP BRITAIN WHITE." Yet in another example,

Aboulela's *The Translator* depicts cases when Scottish citizens lash out at immigrants in public places. In the novel, during the Persian Gulf War, "a man shout[s] at [Sammar] in King Street," calling her "*Saddam Hussein*" (Aboulela 1999, 99; italics original). In such a hostile climate, hybridity, as a result of crossing of geographical, cultural, and racial borders, affects the national, cultural, and individual identities of all parties involved in the exchange process. However, not all immigrants have the same experience and ethos in their new environments, and those who have similar appearances and cultures or immigrate from countries seen as higher in the eyes of natives are better embraced. Clara Eisinger (2013, 4) writes that "so-called 'black' immigrants to Great Britain face challenges the like of which many of their white counterparts could not imagine."

Moreover, while one is neglected in one setting, even in their homelands, owing to their identifications, they might have a different status in another era and area. As an example, Jen's *Mona in the Promised Land* shows that after moving from China to Scarshill, an affluent and predominantly Jewish suburb near New York City, Mona and her elder sister Callie, who have converted to Judaism, find it "a liberal place, not like their old town, where [… locals] used to throw crab-apple mash at Callie and Mona, and tell them it would make their eyes stick shut" (Jen 1997, 6). As a Chinese American with Jewish background, Mona leads a prosperous life: "Mona is a Jewish now, and it's made a big difference in her life" (Jen 1997, 137). Thus, while anti-Semitism, hostility towards and prejudice against Jews, is at its zenith in one setting, Judaism might be considered as a privilege in another setting. This is to say that classifications and orientations are not fixed and absolute, and they recalibrate themselves at different loci.

In parallel with the increasing transnational flows, the idea of nation-states is growing stronger nowadays. Those who prefer to control and safeguard nation-states disavow any intermingling with other nations. As nation-states "are criss-crossed and undermined by transnational actors with varying prospects of power, orientations, identities and networks" (Beck 2000, 11), nationalists claim that border-crossing processes of globalization threaten the maintenance and purity of national values and traditions. Against such a backdrop, some nationalist political parties over-emphasize the retention of their national ties, threaten their fellow citizens of the consequences of their open borders or membership, for example, in the EU and Schengen Agreement and urge them to exit from such unions and agreements. As Arthur Schlesinger (1991, 102) writes, "the cult of ethnicity exaggerates differences, intensifies resentments and antagonisms, drives ever deeper the lawful wedges between races and nationalities. The endgame is self-pity and self-ghettoization." Brexit, the withdrawal of the United Kingdom from the EU, is a recent example of self-pity and self-ghettoization, wherein some British nationalist political parties ignited the fear of their country being swamped by immigrants. Likewise, in some other European countries, right-wing political parties are becoming stronger under the promises of preventing immigration, safeguarding their alleged homogeneity, and revitalizing national identity. These groups wish to spatially bound and territorialize identity and culture. In France, Marine Le Pen's anti-immigrant and xenophobic rhetoric echoes fears and anxieties over foreign cultures affecting French values. Such politicians' objectives are to bold out the impossibility of immigrants' integration in their host societies and to reiterate that they never become one of 'us.' Neil Lazarus (2011, 22) terms this trend as a pitfall of national consciousness and notes that "[t]his way of putting things has the effect of homogenizing 'Europe.'" Unlike ethnocentrism, post-ethnicity "pushes for communities of wide scope, recognizes the constructed character of ethno-racial groups, and accepts the formation of new groups as a part of the normal life of a democratic society" (Hollinger 1995, 116). According to David Hollinger (1995, 3), post-ethnic hybridity "promotes solidarities of wide scope that incorporate people with different racial and ethnic backgrounds." Hence, in deconstructing the boundaries of ethnicity, post-ethnicity offers a backlash against ethnicity as a sole determining identity, calling into question the prevailing Eurocentric xenophobic rhetoric.

Anti-hybridity and Religious/Cultural Convictions

In line with racial, political, and national tendencies, religious convictions impede hybridity between and within peoples. For example, in Aboulela's (1999, 100–101; italics original) *The Translator*, after Rae, an agnostic Scottish Islamic scholar, has an interview with radio about Islam, he receives hate mail on the department's answering machine:

> *You wog bastard, may I remind you that England is a Christian country, and it would be a good thing if you and all the rest odious wog bastards were to go back to the land of Allah. Since you bastards came to England this country has become the asshole of the West.*

Faëza Guène's *Kiffe Kiffe Tomorrow* portrays the difficulties of a Moroccan Muslim woman in France. Because of her different religion, Doria's Muslim mother faces challenges in her workplace that affect even her life. As Doria reveals, her challenges are doubled during Ramadan when she fasts. She has to hide her religious commitment from her co-workers and boss, lest they are totally pissed (Guène 2006, 2). To her different religious beliefs, we should add her racial difference, which worsens her condition:

Everyone calls her 'Fatma' at the hotel. They [...] keep a close eye on her to make sure she doesn't steal anything from the rooms. Of course, Mom's name isn't Fatma, it's Yasmina. It must really give Monsieur Winner [her supervisor] a charge to call all the Arabs 'Fatma.'

(Guène 2006, 2)

In this condition, negative portrayals and stereotypes are barriers that ostracize such peoples from mainstream societies. Guène and Aboulela manifest the Western–Islamic polarity as "Islam has on many occasions been described as an Other, even The Other, of Europe" (Kuortti 1997, 191). As Joel Kuortti (1997, 191) writes: "One of the main problems is that neither Europe (or the West) nor Islam can be taken as a single entity against which to mirror the Other." Then, Kuortti (1997, 191) sceptically asks that "could there be paths for true contact?" The question shows how complicated it would be for the clash between these cultures and ideologies to give place to a dialogue. As Hazan (2015, 19) notes, "hybridity is about a space of negotiation of discourse and interactivity of subjects," while "non-hybridity is a social impasse where discourses cannot be negotiated and any dialogue is halted."

To eschew hybridity with followers of other religions and faiths, religions sometimes prohibit interfaith marriage. They require conversion as a precondition, or rather a substitute, for interfaith marriage. In this case, converts might lose their family ties and inheritance. In *The Translator*, Rae narrates the story of his Uncle David, who goes to Egypt during World War II and falls in love with an Egyptian Muslim girl. To marry her, he converts to Islam and changes his name. Then, Rae discloses that, upon hearing the news, his grandmother and mother stopped answering his uncle's letters, "or maybe sent him nasty letters, in return, so he stopped writing" (Aboulela 1999, 17–18). Rae's grandmother keeps saying that David has been missed "until she believed it and everyone else in the family came to believe it too" (Aboulela 1999, 18). Later in the story, also Rae converts to Islam, moves to Khartoum, and marries Sammar, a Sudanese Muslim woman. The novel shows that, despite Sammar's great affection for Rae, she refuses to start any serious relationship with Rae before Rae's conversion to Islam. As Sammar declares, "unless you become a Muslim we will not be able to get married" (Aboulela 1999, 89). As her friend Yasmin advises: "If I were you, I'd avoid him like the plague till then. Go home and maybe you'll meet someone normal, someone Sudanese like yourself. Mixed couples just don't look right, they irritate everyone" (Aboulela 1999, 93). This shows how religions can issue special regulations for their followers' contact with others. As the narrator says, "Sammar felt separate from him, exiled while he was in his homeland, fasting while he was eating turkey and drinking wine. They lived in worlds divided by simple facts – religion" (Aboulela 1999, 34). Like firm believers and nationalists, aristocracy attempts to conserve their blue blood pure, while stern philologists hold a grudge against linguistic hybridity to keep language genuine (Nederveen Pieterse 2001, 226). In this light, they denounce hybridity since it challenges the originality, privilege, and hegemonic positions of their faith, social status, or rigid linguistic convictions.

Anti-hybridity sentiments are not confined to ethnic, nationalistic, religious, or linguistic certainties. Other cultural differences can cause gaps between people, too. In Rushdie's (1988, 39) *The Satanic Verses*, when Saladin plans to leave India for England, his mother gives him some advice: "'Don't go dirty like those English,' she warned him. 'They wipe their bee tee ems with paper only. Also, they go into each other's dirty bathwater.'" The advice shows how differences in canons, cultures, and customs can create poles between peoples and cause misunderstanding and distance between members of different cultures. To this long list of factors hindering anti-hybridity, Hazan (2015, 58) adds ageism and autism and discusses how they bring about "disengagement" and "disintegration" between people. As Hazan (2015, 54) writes: "Age itself becomes an outcast [and is] kept as far away as possible," whereas autism is expelled from communities as unwanted categories. In *Kiffe Kiffe Tomorrow*, Guène draws upon ageism and shows how Doria as a school student expresses her dissatisfaction with the school programme, sending her regularly to visit an elder lady, Madame Burland. She says:

> It's Monday and, like every Monday, I've been over at Madame Burlaud's. Madame Burlaud's old, she's ugly and she stinks of RID anti-lice shampoo. She's harmless, but sometimes she worries me. Today, she took a whole bunch of weird pictures out of her bottom drawer, these huge stains that looked like dried vomit. She asked me what they made me think of. I told her and she stared at me with her bugged-out eyes, shaking her head like those little toy dogs in the backs of cars.
>
> *(Guène 2006, 1)*

As the excerpts show, age causes distance and widens gaps between generations, and since both young and old people have different interests, hobbies, and physical abilities, they understand each other less, and thus, they cannot find ways for joint activities.

It seems that the opponents of hybridity wish to see things unchanged. To shield purity, they base their analyses on traditional values which shy away from hybridity and oppose models of combining diverse cultures. Those who employ a critique of hybridity emphasize the significance of authenticity and originality and believe that hybridity de-essentializes canons and traditions. Those who rebut hybridity see it as a threat which disrupts order, harmony, and unity and poses a fracture to the structures of categories they wish to preserve. They also understand hybridity as something that undermines stability of ethnic categorization. Thus, as a threat to cultural, racial, and lingual homogeneity as well as ethnic absolutism and privilege, those who advocate critique of hybridity resist delocalization and nomadic forces. In their views, the dialectics of hybridity intervene and disrupt cultural, ethnic, and ideological essentialism.

Post-hybridity

Debates over hybridity and anti-hybridity often lead to polarization. To show such polarization, Hazan (2015, 32) asks: "What is the source of this infinite new tolerance for hybridization, accompanied by zero tolerance for non-hybridity?" Hazan's question shows that one should not see hybridity as essentially good and anti-hybridity as intrinsically evil, or vice versa. Rather, the discussions of hybridity and anti-hybridity could coexist in plural and multiple manners to open a new path, so-called "post-hybridity." Post-hybridity, constituting a dual inclusive and discursive competence, sees both the hybridity-centeredness or the anti-hybridity orientation as pitfalls, ending up reproducing another essentialism. As Chich-Yu Shih and Josuke Ikeda (2016, 460) note: "Post-hybridity warns against the loss of critical and analytical usefulness of hybridity." In such circumstances, post-hybridity guards us against essentializing either hybridity or anti-hybridity.

As a double-edged tool, the discourses of post-hybridity both contest binarism and open up discursive spaces for polylithic modules. These modules coexist within the same paradigm, which impact upon and redefine each other. In post-hybridity, the discourses of hybridity and anti-hybridity are seen as products of two vectors, making sense together in a diagram. Instead of taking an either/or direction, post-hybridity endorses a both/and policy, because "any categorical rejection or enthusiastic endorsement of either binarism or hybridity discourse may be misleading as well as dogmatic" (Acheraïou 2011, 158). In this light, post-hybridity forms a third hybrid space for non-essentialist configurations of new hybridities in the twenty-first century.

Further Reading

Acheraïou, Amar. 2011. *Questioning Hybridity, Postcolonialism and Globalization*. New York: Palgrave Macmillan.

Hazan, Haim. 2015. *Against Hybridity: Social Impasses in a Globalizing World.* Cambridge: Polity Press.

Lawrence, Paul. 2014. *Nationalism: History and Theory.* New York: Routledge.

Nederveen Pieterse, Jan. 2001. "Hybridity, So What? The Anti-Hybridity Backlash and the Riddles of Recognition." *Theory, Culture, and Society,* vol. 18, no. 2, pp. 219–245. https://doi.org/10.1177/026327640101800211

Shih, Chich-Yu, and Josuke Ikeda. 2016. "International Relations of Post-Hybridity: Dangers and Potentials in Non-Synthetic Cycles." *Globalizations,* vol. 13, no. 4, pp. 454–468. https://doi.org/10.1080/14747731.2016 .1143729

Further Exercises

Lauri Lemberg, St. Croix Avenue *(1992)*

The novel *St. Croix Avenue,* by the Finnish American author Lauri Lemberg, portrays the life and times of a Finnish family, Saara and Topias Mönkkönen, who move to the United States at the turn of the twentieth century. They buy a farm near Duluth, Minnesota, but right after Topias loses his life in an accident on the farm, Saara sells the farm in desperation and buys a restaurant on St. Croix Avenue, a Finntown in the central district of Duluth. Despite her difficult financial circumstances, she sends her daughter, Johanna Serafiina, to high school, which was difficult for many Finnish immigrants at the time. After graduation, Johanna Serafiina, who changes her name to Gloria, finds a job in an American law firm. Unfortunately, she is raped and impregnated while drunk by James, the youngest shareholder of the firm. When helpless Gloria unexpectedly enters James's residence to inform him of her pregnancy, she finds out about his furtive relationship with his new secretary. She furiously throws a heavy cup at James, and when he ducks to avoid it, he loses his balance and hits his head on the fireplace, resulting in his death. The following passages depict the trial held to decide over Gloria's homicide charge. What are the specific indications of anti-hybridity presented both in the court and in the arguments between the Finnish American witnesses?

The Jury, like the spectators, held various opinions. Because of the paucity of testimony and the sensational nature of the case, they were influenced more by feelings than by cold, rational analysis. Several of them had ingrained prejudices against European immigrants and their descendants. They were uncivilized rabble who had come to snatch the bread out of the mouths of American workers because of low wages they would work for and their low standard of living. Some agreed with the prosecutor that nothing good could come from St. Croix Avenue.

Others, who themselves were descendants of recent immigrants, looked at the matter more from the defendant's point of view.

(Lemberg 1992, 315)

"Those skull-faced buzzards won't stop throwing around their prison sentences until we bang our fist on the table and tell them a new order has arrived," huffed Pikku-Joona angrily [...]. "I agree that Judge Monson looks at immigrants with a jaundiced eye and that we aren't particularly well thought of among the *toiskieliset* [foreign language speakers], but we have to bear some of the blame for that. After all, we live in the worst part of town, in our own ghetto like Jews in Germany, we drink and we fight, we don't learn English, we don't apply for citizenship, and we don't try to get into unions. We need to clean off our own doorstep and show, by our work and our achievements, that Finns are ambitious, honest, and altogether proper people. In brief we must raise ourselves to American levels of working conditions, housing and social life."

(Lemberg 1992, 317–318)

V.S. Naipaul, The Enigma of Arrival *(1988)*

The Enigma of Arrival is one of the most celebrated novels by V.S. Naipaul, the Trinidadian Nobel Prize winner in 2001. The semi-autobiographical novel follows an anonymous young Trinidadian of Indian background, immigrating to Wiltshire, England, where he settles in a small cottage and lives as a writer. The novel captures his observations of his new home, neighbours, and countryside and shows how his reflections on the new location and residents change over time. Naipaul's narration illustrates the narrator's growing understanding of his new environment and the intricate relations of the surrounding people with him. By reflecting, for example, on his neighbour Jack, the narrator comes to see how much a home reflects its owner. Please read the following excerpt from the novel and think about the impediments that the narrator sees on the way of his incorporation into the social structure of the host society.

That idea of ruin and dereliction, of out-of-placeness, was something I felt about myself, attached to myself: a man from another hemisphere, another background, coming to rest in middle life in the cottage of a half-neglected estate, an estate full of reminders of its Edwardian past, with few connections with the present. An oddity among the estates and big houses of the valley, and I a further oddity in its grounds. I felt unanchored and strange. Everything I saw in those early days, as I took my surroundings in, everything I saw on my daily walk, beside the windbreak or along the wide grassy way, made that feeling more acute. I felt that my presence in that old valley was part of something like an upheaval, a change in the course of the history of the country [...]. I had thought that because of my insecure past – peasant India, colonial Trinidad, my own family circumstances, the colonial smallness that didn't consort with the grandeur of my ambition, my uprooting of myself for a writing career, my coming to England with so little, and the very little I still had to fall back on – I had thought that because of this I had been given an especially tender or raw sense of an unaccommodating world [...]. My tramps about London were ignorant and joyless. I had expected the great city to leap out at me and possess me; I had longed so much to be in it. And soon, within a week or less, I was very lonely. If I had been less lonely, if I had had the equivalent of my shipboard life, I might have felt differently about London and the boardinghouse. But I was solitary [...]. I had come to London as to a place I knew very well. I found a city that was strange and unknown—in its style of houses, and even in the names of its districts; as strange as my boardinghouse.

(Naipaul 1988, 19)

Paula Ivaska Robbins, Below Rollstone Hill (2000)

Below Rollstone Hill by Finnish American writer Paula Ivaska Robbins is a historical novel. The novel narrates the life of Helmi and her husband August before and after immigrating to the United States. Despite August's professional skills, he fails to find any appropriate job in their adopted home, and they must squeeze themselves into a tiny flat wherein Aunt Lempi Salo – Helmi's favourite sister – and her family also reside in "Finntown" in Fitchburg, Massachusetts. August begs his wife to return to Finland despite their hardships there, but his wife strongly resists. Following Aunt Lempi's suggestion, Helmi buys an old house and converts it to a boarding house, but August, who always thinks of men as breadwinners, sees this as shaming himself. He finally resorts to alcohol, commits acts of mindless vandalism, and fights with people while drunk, and consequently, he is occasionally arrested and jailed by the police. He, then, becomes a cause of shame for the whole family and eventually dies due to a liver problem. The passages below are narrated by Aino, August and Helmi's youngest daughter. What do Helmi's conversation with her sister and Aino's comments reveal about anti-hybridity sentiments?

> Yankees wouldn't rent to immigrants, most of Finns were clustered together in one small section of the north-west part of the city [...].
> "Finntown" was a long narrow silver beginning where Main Street ended

at the Upper Common. At one time the area must have been a ravine with a little brook carving its way down to the river. The brook was long gone; its flow must have followed what is now Elm Street [...]. The argument that I had overheard the previous night was continued, in more polite tones, over coffee and bread at my aunt's kitchen table the next morning. "What are we going to do, Lempi?" queried my pale and exhausted mother. "We've been here taking advantage of your hospitability now for two weeks. August has spent every day since we arrived looking for work, and he has still hasn't been able to find a job that will support us".

(Robbins 2000, 7)

Despite many attempts, Father was never able to find a job in the mills. Although he had held highly skilled positions in the Finlayson cotton mill in Tampere and had been a foreman supervising many men, the factories in Fitchburg were uninterested. Father's few words in broken English were not enough to convince them.

(Robbins 2000, 16)

References

Aboulela, Leila. 1999. *The Translator*. Edinburgh: Polygon.

Acheraïou, Amar. 2011. *Questioning Hybridity, Postcolonialism and Globalization*. New York: Palgrave Macmillan.

Ahmad, Aijaz. 1995. "The Politics of Literary Postcoloniality." *Race & Class*, vol. 36, no. 3, pp. 1–20. https://doi.org/10.1177/03063968950360

Ahmed, Sara. 2000. *Strange Encounters: Embodied Others in Post-coloniality*. New York: Routledge.

Allendorf, Fred W., Robb Leary, Paul Spruell, and John K. Wenburg. 2001. "The Problems with Hybrids: Setting Conservation Guidelines." *Trends in Ecology & Evolution*, vol. 16, pp. 613–622. https://doi.org/10.1016/S0169-5347(01)02290-X

Anderson, Lisa M. 1997. *Mammies no More: The Changing Image of Black Women on Stage and Screen*. Boston: Rowman and Littlefield.

Anzaldúa, Gloria. 1987. *Borderlands/La Frontera: The New Mestiza*. San Francisco: Spinsters/Aunt Lute.

Baker, Christopher Richard. 2007. *The Hybrid Church in the City: Third Space Thinking*. New York: Routledge.

Beck, Ulrich. 2000 [originally published 1997]. *What Is Globalization?* Translated by Patrick Camiller. Cambridge: Polity Press.

Bhabha, Homi K. 1992. "The World and the Home." *Social Text*, no. 31/32, pp. 141–153. https://doi.org/10.2307/466222

Brubaker, Rogers. 2004. *Ethnicity without Groups*. Cambridge: Harvard University Press.

Chikwava, Brian. 2009. *Harare North*. London: Jonathan Cape.

Cliff, Michelle. 1987. *No Telephone to Heaven*. New York: Penguin.

Eisinger, Clara. 2013. "To Be Born Is to Die: A Critical Overview of *The Satanic Verses* and Global Modernism." In *Beyond Postmodernism: Onto the Postcontemporary*, edited by Christopher A. Brooks, 1–17. Newcastle: Cambridge Scholars Publishing.

García Márquez, Gabriel. 1972 [originally published 1968]. "A Very Old Man with Enormous Wings" ("Un señor muy viejo con unas alas enormes"). Translated by Gregory Rabassa. In *Leaf Storm and Other Stories*, by Gabriel García Márquez, 105–112. New York: Harper.

Ghasemi, Mehdi. 2020. "A Study of Double Consciousness in Lauri Lemberg's *St. Croix Avenue* and Paula Ivaska Robbins' *Below Rollstone Hill*." *Immigrants & Minorities*, vol. 38, no. 3, pp. 254–278. https://doi.org/10.1080/02619288.2021.1916475

Guène, Faïza. 2006 [originally published 2004]. *Kiffe Kiffe Tomorrow*. Translated by Sarah Adams. London: Chatto & Windus/Orlando: Harcourt.

Hazan, Haim. 2015. *Against Hybridity: Social Impasses in a Globalizing World*. Cambridge: Polity Press.

Hollinger, David A. 1995. *Post-Ethnic America: Beyond Multiculturalism*. New York: Harper Collins.

Hughes, Langston. 1994 [originally published 1926]. "Cross." In *The Collected Poems of Langston Hughes*, edited and annotated by Arnold Rampersad and David Ernest Roessel, 58–59. New York: Knopf.

Jen, Gish. 1997. *Mona in the Promised Land*. New York: Vintage.

Kuortti, Joel. 1997. "Dreams, Intercultural Identification and *The Satanic Verses*." *Contemporary South Asia*, vol. 6, no. 2, pp. 191–200. https://doi.org/10.1080/09584939708719813

Lawrence, Paul. 2014. *Nationalism: History and Theory*. New York: Routledge.

Lazarus, Neil. 2011. "What Postcolonial Theory Doesn't Say." *Race & Class*, vol. 53, no. 1, pp. 3–27. https://doi.org/10.1177/0306396811406778

Lemberg, Lauri. 1992. *St. Croix Avenue*. Translated by Miriam Leino Eldridge. Superior: Tyomies Society.

McAllister, Edwin J. 2007. "Smallpox, Opium, and Invasion." In *Complicating Constructions: Race, Ethnicity and Hybridity in American Texts*, edited by David S. Goldstein and Andrey B. Thacker, 143–156. Seattle: University of Washington Press.

Merry, Sally E. 1981. *Urban Danger: Life in a Neighborhood of Strangers*. Philadelphia: Temple University Press.

Naipaul, V.S. 1988 [originally published 1987]. *The Enigma of Arrival*. New York: Vintage Books.

Nederveen Pieterse, Jan. 2001. "Hybridity, so What? The Anti-Hybridity Backlash and the Riddles of Recognition." *Theory, Culture, and Society*, vol. 18, no. 2, pp. 219–245. https://doi.org/10.1177/026327640101800211

Palumbo-Liu, David. 1999. *Asian/American: Historical Crossings of a Racial Frontier*. Stanford: Stanford University Press.

Parks, Suzan-Lori. 1995. "The Death of the Last Black Man in the Whole Entire World." In *The America Play and Other Works*, by Suzan-Lori Parks, 99–131. New York: Theatre Communications Group.

Parry, Benita. 2004. *Postcolonial Studies: A Materialist Critique.* New York: Routledge.

Rembold, Elfie, and Peter Carrier. 2011. "Space and Identity: Constructions of National Identities in an Age of Globalisation." *National Identities,* vol. 13, no. 4, pp. 361–377. https://doi.org/10.1080/14608944.2011.629425

Robbins, Paula Ivaska. 2000. *Below Rollstone Hill: Growing up in the Finnish Quarter of Fitchburg, Massachusetts.* St. Cloud: North Star Press of St. Cloud.

Rushdie, Salman. 1988. *The Satanic Verses.* London: Vintage.

Schlesinger, Arthur M., Jr. 1991. *The Disuniting of America: Reflections on a Multicultural Society.* New York: W.W. Norton.

Shih, Chich-Yu, and Josuke Ikeda. 2016. "International Relations of Post-Hybridity: Dangers and Potentials in Non-Synthetic Cycles." *Globalizations,* vol. 13, no. 4, pp. 454–468. https://doi.org/10.1080/14747731.2016.1143729

Young, Robert. 1995. *Colonial Desire: Hybridity in Theory, Culture and Race.* London: Routledge.

Zephaniah, Benjamin. 2001. *Refugee Boy.* London: Bloomsbury Publishing.

GLOSSARY OF TERMS

Acculturation A term often used in migration studies to describe a migrant's process of coming to terms with and adapting to the culture and society of the host country. In contrast to full assimilation into the host society's way of life and values, acculturation indicates a degree of freedom and leaves space for constructing mixed cultures that combine elements from both the migrant's past and their current culture.

Ambivalence Ambivalence reflects one's simultaneous and contradictory attitudes such as attraction and repulsion, love and hatred towards the same person, animal, or object. The mixture of feelings, which negatively affects attitude strength, makes the subject experience indecisiveness. Eugen Bleuler first introduced "ambivalence" in 1910 and applied the term to a psychological sense as a major symptom of schizophrenia. In the view of Homi K. Bhabha, the concept describes a similar contradictory interrelation between the colonized and the colonizer.

Border-crossing This term is widely used in situations in which someone crosses geopolitical, state, linguistic, cultural, species, ethnic, or other borders into a space characterized by a sense of newness and unfamiliarity. While concrete geopolitical border-crossings are often regulated and prohibited, cultural border-crossings may involve an encounter with difference and lead to a transformation of previous identity. As a result of the potential in the idea of border-crossing, it may generate hybridity as expressed in music, literature, and the arts, both thematically and formally.

Bricolage Bricolage is a word of French origin, meaning the construction or creation of an artefact from diverse elements. In literature, bricolage combines heterogeneous materials from several contexts, juxtaposing them in a new context. Intertextuality and linguistic bricolage are two main forms of bricolage in literary texts. In linguistic bricolage, for example, different terms and phrases, coming from different languages, are grafted in a text which shatters the unity of language.

Code-switching An originally linguistic term that has described language-contact situations where the participant moves from using one language or dialect to another. Such code-switches characterize language use in contact settings and borderlands, and a good example is the use of English and Spanish in the United States as represented in ChicanX literature. More recently, such occasions are understood to indicate that the language user is able to use the linguistic and cultural resources of more than one language and in so doing places themself in two or more languages and cultures, revealing the hybridity of their identity.

Contact zone Introduced by Mary Louise Pratt, the term "contact zone" refers to spaces where disparate cultures, languages, and perspectives contact, communicate, and clash with each other. The contact zone provides the ground for the co-presence and interaction of peoples from different cultural, racial, and linguistic backgrounds. The term is used in the studies on (post)colonialism, multiculturalism, multilingualism, and borders. It draws upon asymmetrical power equations between different groups, for example, colonizer and colonized, native and tourist, and so on.

Cosmopolitanism The concept suggests a view where all human beings belong to a global community uninhibited by politics or nationalism. While the traditional definition often prioritized privileged individuals who understood themselves as "citizens of the world" – such as allegedly free-moving intellectuals or writers – the current usage of the term reflects changes generated by globalization and increased mobility since it recognizes everyday cosmopolitanisms associated by labour and student mobilities that involve increased encounters with others in spaces beyond one's original home.

Creolization Creolization refers to the process of blending elements of different cultures together, which leads to the formation of new cultures and identities. Creolization was first used by linguists to show how contact languages could turn into creole languages, but later, the term entered other fields of studies. The cultural transformations, which manifest themselves in food, music, religion, language, etc., take place as a result of the intersection of diasporas, converging in a new location to which they have not previously belonged.

Cyborg The term is originally associated with robots and other "cybernetic organisms" that combine the human or the animal with machines, often represented in speculative and science fiction. Exemplifying a border-crossing between the human and non-human, the concept plays a key role in the work of the theorist Donna Haraway and her critique of fixed identities. Following Haraway, the concept has been renewed in posthumanist thinking, describing how human–non-human hybrids, such as horses and their riders, function together as whole regardless of species boundaries.

Diaspora The word "diaspora," meaning "to scatter about," was first used to address the dispersion of Greeks in the Hellenic world, and later, the exile of Jews after the Babylonian captivity. The term is used today in reference to people who have been separated from their homelands because of colonialism, slavery, trade, and labour immigrations. A major example is the involuntary displacement of Africans during the transatlantic slave trade.

Double consciousness Introduced by W.E.B. Du Bois, double consciousness was originally used to address the negative effects of white supremacy and systematic racism on the lives of African Americans in American society. The notion unveils a sense of inward twoness, bringing about internal conflicts for African Americans and situating them between being African and American. The notion can be applied to other subordinate or minority groups, who frequently oscillate between two opposing worlds, cultures, ideals, and ideologies in oppressive societies.

Globalization Globalization refers to the free flow of information, technologies, products, services, capital, labour, investments, and cultures across (national) borders. As a process of worldwide interaction among nations, companies, and governments, globalization refers to the interdependence of the world's economies, politics, and cultures, brought about by cross-border trade, integration, and transaction. Mobility of capital and work force, internationalization, and cooperation between people characterize the cumulative and commutative phenomenon of globalization.

Heteroglossia The term "heteroglossia," coined by Mikhail Bakhtin, describes a diversity of voices, styles of writing, and points of view within a literary work as represented in language. The coexistence of multiple voices, discourses, and dialects in a single narrative signifies the intersectional stratification of education, ethnicity, culture, class, and gender and can sound contrasting in some cases. However, the contrasts between language elements and representations are part of the meaning creation process in a literary work.

Historiographic metafiction Historiographic metafiction, as the term name indicates, is a literary genre that embeds elements of history and fiction. Through mixing elements of history and story, it rethinks and reworks historical content, challenges monologic discourses of history, and includes repressed or absent subgroups' narratives in the textures of history. To illuminate existing blank spots in history, writers of historiographic metafiction make use of its potential to rewrite history through fictional means.

Inter-, meta-, and paratextuality Intertextuality, defined as a text within a text, is an implicit or explicit reference to other texts. The device, which manifests itself in the form of allusion, quotation, referencing, etc., provides the ground for, for instance, comparing the present conditions with the past or touch upon the roots of ideologies. "Metatext," then, is defined as a text about another text in which one text describes, or makes critical commentaries, on another text, while "paratext" refers to materials in a book/text that provide a frame for the main text, such as forewords, indexes, blurbs, endorsements, and glossaries.

Liminality A term widely used in anthropology to indicate an individual's ambiguous position between different stages in their life, such as a rite of passage. Owing to the insecurity attached to such a position and an expected transformation, the concept has been utilized, for example, in Homi K. Bhabha's theory of hybridity where in-betweenness plays a key role. For Bhabha, hybrid identity is constructed in the liminal space between cultures where identity is recast in unexpected ways.

Magical realism Magical realism is a narrative strategy, characterized by blending realistic events with impossible or unrealistic ones. It can combine, for example, events of daily life with dreams to unveil the magic within reality. Hence, in magical realism, a story is still grounded in reality, but magical, fantastical elements refashion that 'reality.' To expose the magic within real events, magical realism collides and integrates contradictory codes – fictional and nonfictional, natural and supernatural, magical and rational, story and history – to create an atmosphere of hybridity.

Miscegenation The word "miscegenation" is derived from a combination of the Latin terms "miscere" ("to mix") and "genus" ("race"). It means mixing people of different ethnic backgrounds who engender racial hybridity. The term is often used in relation to interracial marriage, regarded as a threat to racial purity. The term is also associated especially with historical laws against the marriage of white Americans with black slaves.

Passing The term "passing" has been used primarily in the United States to describe black or coloured persons who attempt to assimilate themselves into the white dominant society. 'Racial passing' occurs when members of groups regarded as inferior in the eyes of the dominant society endeavour to uplift themselves by adhering to conventional cultural codes of dress, accent, or manners, in order to avoid discrimination and to be accepted by members of their dominant societies. Higher education and taking distance from local or ethnic communities also assist them with racial uplifting.

Spatiotemporality Spatiotemporality refers to conditions that have both spatial and temporal qualities. In the context of hybridity, spatiotemporality deconstructs the concepts of place and time as linear and singular. Time is not understood as a linear movement, because it intermingles past, present, and future, which results in omnitemporality and time distortion. Place also becomes a dislodged and multiperspectival space with multiple variables. Thus, time and place are fluid and defy the principles of normative logic.

Third Space The term "Third Space," which is attributed to Homi K. Bhabha, refers to a metaphorical or physical space that lies between the positions of dominant subjects and the subaltern others. Thus, the third space creates an environment for interaction and integration of ruling and subjugated groups. Within postcolonial theory of identity and community, Third Space is used to characterize hybridity and hybrid cultural identity that emerge from converging elements of different cultures in a liminal or an in-between space.

Transculturation Coined by Cuban anthropologist Fernando Ortiz, transculturation describes the process of mixing cultures. Transculturation does not simply mean losing one's culture (deculturation) nor assuming another culture (acculturation). Rather, it signifies the merging of several different cultures to produce a new hybrid culture. Unlike ethnocentrism, transculturation or ethnoconvergence is involved in the continuous reformation of cultures and is marked by the influx of hybrid cultural elements.

Transnationalism A term used to describe a way of thinking based on the view that nations and national cultures are not closed systems but they are always embedded in networks that cross state and other borders. In transnationalism, people, ideas, and objects move across borders uninhibited and the resultant transnational cultures can be understood more fully by taking into account the whole process. For instance, the study of ethnic US literatures gains more depth when one takes into account the national and linguistic identity of the group in question and reads such texts in the contexts of the literary and cultural history of their places of origin as well as that of the United States.

INDEX

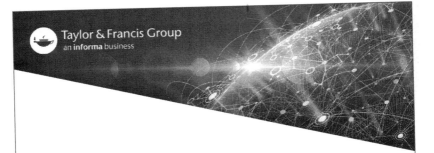